Loner

Loner

Paul Rodgers

HODDER AND STOUGHTON
LONDON SYDNEY AUCKLAND TORONTO

The Lure of the Sea by D. H. Clarke, quoted on
page 9, is published by Adlard Coles Ltd.

British Library Cataloguing in Publication Data
Rodgers, Paul
  Loner.
  1. Spirit of Pentax *(Ship)*
  2. Voyages around the world – 1951 –
  I. Title
  910.4'1   G440.s/

ISBN 0-340-27840-4

To a long-legged green–eyed goddess from the Emerald Isles. Who made it possible.

To Jack Hue, the adventure's best friend, too.

And to John Fewster who saved Captain Fantastic from certain destruction.

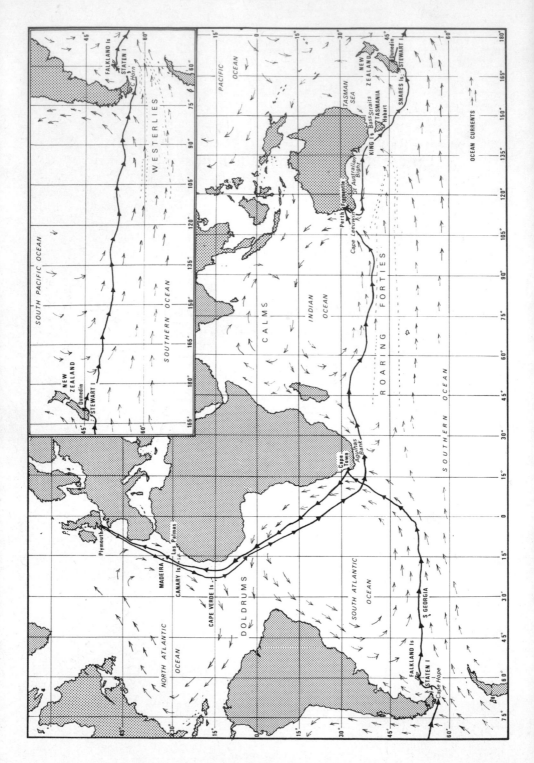

Spirit of Pentax

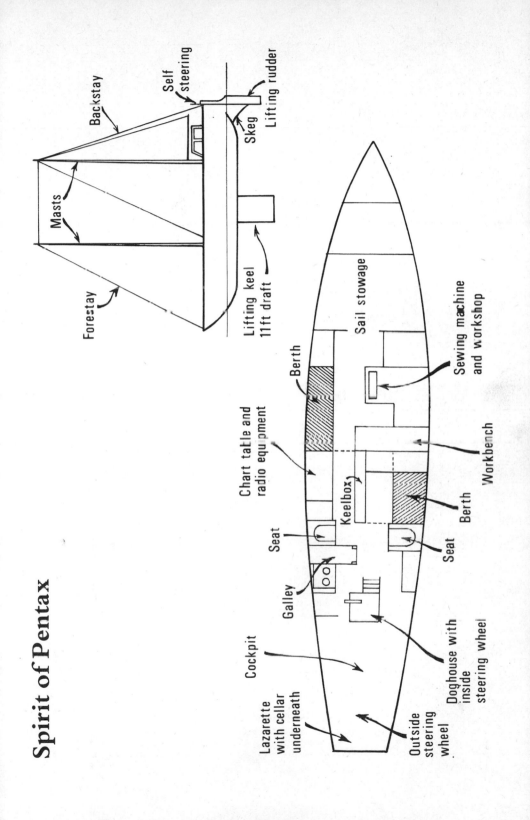

Backstay

Self steering

Masts

Lifting rudder

Skeg

Forestay

Lifting keel 11ft draft

Berth

Chart table and radio equipment

Sail stowage

Sewing machine and workshop

Keelbox

Workbench

Seat

Berth

Galley

Seat

Cockpit

Doghouse with inside steering wheel

Lazarette with cellar underneath

Outside steering wheel

To the genuine loner, illness or accident to self is the greatest hazard, and there have been some cases of death. There are always greater risks in going it alone, rather than sharing your experiences with others, yet I feel sure that those who really want to be alone can face even old age and the final blanking off of life with equanimity. Perhaps they have found something at sea which is denied to land-bound rat-racers; perhaps they are not really lonely at all? So the final analysis of whether you are a natural single-hander is really just that one question: could you face dying alone?

from *The Lure of the Sea* by D. H. Clarke

Illustrations

1

Man and machine become one. I feel what the schooner feels, I react to changes in her normal pattern as quickly as I would wipe spray stinging my eyes. She is the muscle, I am the brain dictating direction and progress. If it is possible for man to feel such emotion, I am in love with the boat. This deep affection is returned, if it is possible for woven steel and wood to have feeling. You may doubt it, but I do not. I have seen too much, suffered too much. I have been at sea for ever, it seems.

I think I do not have that warmth for the ocean, but I cannot be sure. I use these boundless wastes as one might use a past lover on a lonely night; it's perhaps a sort of dependence. In return the sea serves me; she will always be available to one who shares her intimacy. But this lover is armed and without a doubt will kill me if my guard is down. That is not the sea's emotion, that is her compulsion.

My subconscious is linked to the element, just as I experience the boat's motion as my own. I know from below when fog is about to destroy vision, when a storm is abating, in fact when the barometric pressure is increasing, presaging improving conditions and hope, or dropping to bring seas stampeding and despair. The one-to-one with my world is more than precious to me and I cherish it. It is God-given. Scientists will say such things do not exist, are not possible in this modern age. But science and time are a long way from the Southern Ocean. Here the earliest instincts emerge, all based on survival. I think I must always have been here.

I couldn't sleep and that is a warning. Out into the cold of the galley, matches to the cooker and soon the kettle is steaming. Looking around the horizon. The ocean is flat and breathing quietly, very black. Not many clouds to dull the starlight and the deck bright and I can even see the winch handle in the pocket on the foremast. Four knots. White streaks from the hull.

Calm before the storm, I think, and later wish I hadn't. Tapping the barometer, it falls ominously. It will be all right, just normal daily variation. But the consoling doesn't reach the inner me. I hate foul weather and if this is to be a full gale it will be the boat's first real test on this voyage and, much more frighteningly, it will also be mine. Drink your tea and stop worrying. Of course the boat will be all right. Hadn't the designer said so, hadn't it been in bad weather before on a race to Australia?

Yes, but this is winter and this part of the Southern Ocean below South Africa has a dreadful reputation with early sail mariners. More milk into the tea please. Milk soothes nerves. It is cold. Thank God for polar wear. This scratching inside, I wish the tea would reach it and stop it. Relax, relax, be philosophical; if it's a gale, it's a gale. She's a big boat, you'll be all right.

But the unease isn't so easily calmed. Back into the sleeping bag, but the great void doesn't come. It never does when you need it, when you want it to help time pass so you know if it is to be a gale. This berth is so uncomfortable. Try the other side but that bruises soon as well. In the darkness behind my closed lids, the face of Carol appears. Carol pouting, arms tight around me. Carol walking away on Waterloo Station.

Two hours have passed. Out into the cold, torch on the barometer. No change, hooray. Tapping it and the finger slips four millibars. Bloody Judas. But it could be daily variation, couldn't it? Sometimes it happens and, after all, this is such a weird part of the world all sorts of extraordinary things can happen. Go back to bed, go to sleep. I would if I could. Should I start reducing the sail area now? It will be much easier before the wind gets up and the sea copies it. Go back to bed. What are you worried for, it'll be all right.

But I am worried. The scratching at stomach walls. I always know when bad weather is coming, I don't need a barometer. Back to bed and I imagine Carol saying, Of course there's no one else, I do love you, and then walking away at Waterloo. Forget that, and forget the sea. It's half an hour, get up, inspect the barometer. Stupid, what's the point; it can't change much in half an hour. That's the point, if it hasn't changed it is reassuring. You'll probably be able to sleep then. It might even have started to rise.

That's enough to get me up, getting the torch. No change; thank God, no change. Tap-tap and it falls two points. What a damned instrument. The thing's broken, got to be. The air pressure couldn't sink that quickly. Why didn't we buy a new one? It was one of the priorities on the list; I said right at the start that I had to have a proper barometer. I've never had one on any voyage and I'm sick of being continually terrified by these living-room devices, vying for space with ceramic ducks in flight. Hot milk for the stomach, a bar of chocolate. Back to the sleeping bag. It will be all right. Trust the boat.

"Please, God," I shout. A lone howl in the huge Southern Ocean. "Please, God, let me sleep."

He grants it, but in bad grace. Three hours of occasional unconsciousness and dreams that make me worry. The noise. Rising wind, uneven rhythm from the hull. We're off course. Oilskins on, self-steering gear adjusted, reefing down a big chunk of mainsail. The wind's freezing and the cloth spites back at fingertips and wet nails. Reefing a line through the eyes to secure the sail, but now the wind gauge says thirty knots. So take down all the mainsail, and tie it off. The sea is waking up, flinging cold water at us. Get stuffed, sea; an old reminder I can do without.

Breakfast, watching the dawn showing low clouds, barometer dropping. Down seven millibars more. Good charge from the wind generator now. Playing the eight-track stereo, but the ears strain towards the elements, listening to the hull, then the music is without an audience when I am out on deck, reluctantly downing sails. Up heavy weather staysail. Cursing the foremast winches, which I hate. They have never worked properly. On a swaying, bucking deck they want to kill me. I loathe them and they know it, but they know they won't beat me. I've told them.

Down below to stamp feet warm and make some lunch. It's womb-like below now and I like it. Turning up the stereo, singing to Roxy Music. It's harder to hear the wind then as it peaks at fifty knots. The self-steering gear struggles with the course, the log reading ten knots, then twelve and back to ten. The front must be near. In the doghouse watching out. Eyes to the sails, the sea, the water now crashing along the decks. One hour. Four hours. It's getting dark again; fifty-eight knots of wind. Barometer still dropping. I turn the stereo off. I don't want that now. I need to concentrate on what's happening. Or is it just mesmerism? God, I wish the front would get here. The pressure can't drop much more, it's already below a thousand millibars. The wind speed is incredible. We surge forward, forcing phosphorescent white walls from the bow to amidships. Go, boat, go. Fourteen knots, twelve and ten. Fourteen again.

Down below to light the cooker. And the boat crashes to port, grabbing the handrail, pushing away from the flaming meths. Over to sixty degrees and she springs up, sails thrashing at the masts. My God, we've been thrown upwind. The sea has heaved the boat on to her side and with the self-steering out of control, she's gone head to

15

wind. Now we see how huge the waves are. Don't look. Struggle with the wheel. Self-steering gear broken, tearing the control lines loose, I begin to steer. Back on course slowly, away from treacherous breakers. And on course she goes again, the log swinging up to fourteen knots. I press the button on the auto-pilot and the lights blink. Down staysail, down number two yankee, up storm jib. Hurry. The winches jam, the angle of heel trying to pitch me overboard, halyards snatching. It takes three-quarters of an hour, torn fingers, skin white and sea-soaked. I'll improve that time one day. She's just such a big bitch for me sometimes. In the doghouse, door closed to keep out the rain and any chance of a rogue sea climbing over the stern. Auto-pilot off, and me steering again.

Now normal storm tactics. Point the boat straight down the waves and hear the bottom try to edge towards the wind; so she doesn't bury herself in the trough and topple forward. But she hates it, and struggles to sheer off to right, or slew to port.

Come on, boat, behave. Mine is the only safe route. But she forces herself from the course, and the jib crashes from one side to the other, threatening to fracture the halyard. Don't do that; come on, girl, you can do it. Clouds lower, a dash below and the barometer is even further down, grabbing the doghouse wheel but the jib crashes across with a Concorde boom.

Mind wandering. Carol, why did you do it? What the hell am I doing here? We could have been married, a mortgage, babies, a warm bed, never alone. I hate sleeping on my own. An hour has gone, more; the wind edges higher. The light is going. Got to sleep, got to get an hour or so. If things get worse, if the sea gets higher, got to have a clear head. The fatigue slows everything. Crazy thinking; ha-ha, how could conditions get worse?

Press the button and the auto-pilot takes over, but the course is bad for him and the motor screeches port, starboard, a rush back to port, adjusting again. It will have to do. Too exhausted to change the heading even a fraction. Downstairs, grabbing for handholds, on to the bunk in wet oilskins and boots. I want to lie on my back but there is not enough space at the foot of the bunk for boots upright; my back is hard against the hull. Try to sleep, please let's go straight to the void. The noise, God, the noise is overbearing. Screaming rigging, thundering breakers along the hull, the boat dropping from a wave; the auto-pilot screeching like a starved child. Water in the bilges washing, splashing from side to side with the rolls, reminding of what will take me.

Slipping off to the half-world where voices murmur at me that

16

I'll never make it, that if this boat turns over she won't come back up.

The dreaded Southern Ocean front arrives.

The wind suddenly higher, the schooner pressed on her side, auto-pilot complaining. The barometer jumps four millibars. A winter front. Adjusting the course, gybing the jib over, hypnotised by the waves. The wind has jumped through ninety degrees. The sea pushed up to extraordinary heights from the north west is now being attacked from the south west. The lulls don't drop below sixty knots. There's nothing I can do. Go back to bed, watching the light returning through tired eyes. God, dawn in the Southern Ocean. What am I doing here?

I feel the noise before I hear it. A great thundering express train bearing down on us. I don't see it, I've never seen a rogue wave, but I know what it is and I know it will take us. The roaring of surf, closer and closer, everything in slow motion now. Thousands of tons of energy gone mad, hitting the starboard quarter, the boat pushed up, up . . . then the crashing, smashing so close. It's the hull. God, the hull, the hull's going, heart trying to escape from within. I can't breathe. Waiting for tons of freezing water to fill the boat. No, it's not the hull, it's the lockers emptying. I'm pressed against the keel housing. We're over! My God, we're over! And she's being pushed through the water, the mast's stuck down into the sea. It's black here, got to push myself off, got to get to the doghouse, I can't die here. But the gravity is too monstrous; I'm just pressed flat against the side. We can't take this, the boat cannot survive now. Will it hurt to die?

Light, it's getting lighter. The boat is coming up. The gravity's off. Pushing out into the galley, tools, bolts, gear falling back to the other side of the boat. The lockers are empty, contents catapulted. That was the noise. Into the doghouse. The masts are there, rigging's intact. But, my God. The sea, look at the bloody sea. It's white. Pure, boiling, furious destroying white wherever you look. Oh, my God, it's a hurricane. No, it's worse. The boat shaking herself defiantly. You have to do it now, girl. Only your strength, your spirit can save us. Halyards over the side, wind-vane broken, cockpit filled, and the screaming, deafening wind. And the smell, a sweet choking stench that fills the doghouse and forces vomiting. The batteries? Saltwater in the batteries could make chlorine gas. No, the batteries are clear of the lake inside that carries clothes and plastic boxes and anything that will float from hull to hull. I can't stand the smell, pushing the door open, against the freezing, stabbing wind that staves cheeks in, pressing against the eyes, flattening the nostrils. I can't breathe there, door slamming. Got to stop the smell. Oh God, it's me. The smell is from me. Is it fear of death, this stench from my skin? The schooner goes over again. Hold on, hold on, and upright again. The jib must come down. I have to get the jib down. But how can I get along the deck without falling into the white mass? But there's no choice. Leave the jib up and we'll die soon; take it down, get it down any way at all and we might postpone the inevitable.

Help me, God. Help me. I can't do it myself and I don't want to die.

Our Father which art in Heaven, Hallowed be thy name. Hallowed be thy Kingdom . . . Hallowed . . . No, I can't remember it. But, help me, God.

A lifeline wire runs the length of the boat on either side, usually I hang on to the one upwind, the higher side. But now the schooner is rolling badly and sinking both sides into the waves. Go on, hang on, you pays your money and takes your choice. Climbing up out of the cockpit and starting slowly beside the doghouse roof. The night is dark but we are in a bright glare from phosphorescence boiling round the boat and clinging to rigging. The wind screams at the shrouds, pushing the oilskins tight to me. Can't look upwind, it's too strong. How long would it take to actually skin the skull, like peeling a tomato for Bolognese? Bits at a time. Happy to have the beard growing protectively. Now the dash between the masts. Holding the lifelines and moving forward, between breaking crests. It's hard to keep a foothold. At the foremast and the jib crashes across, boom! and the mast shudders. Get it down, get it down before it takes the forestay. Untie the halyard at the mast, free it from the self-tailer; we're leaning at fifty degrees, water over boots. Then she swings back; go, and the jib starts to sag and slams in the wind. Forward to pull the sail down by the luff, but the halyard jams, so back to the mast to free it. Wait till she goes back to starboard, rush to the forestay. Spitting saltwater, jib's almost down, but the halyard catches again. A life on the ocean wave, a life on the ocean wave, dum-de-dum-de-dum, it's all a really good rave. Sing you scared little fellow, then you won't be quite so scared. To the mast, the wind catches the jib, pushes in, whipping, snatching upwards. Watch the sheets. They've gone mad too, striking out at rigging, trying to reach the man. Grab the sail again. Pull, damn you, pull. Get it down before the mast crumbles around us. Damn, damn, the halyard end is over the side and we have to pull against the press of water rushing. But it's coming, it's coming. Thank you, God. Grabbing a tie from the weather rail, stiff in the

wind. The noise, the overpowering screaming noise. Cold where it
hits the skin, but I'm hot, scorching inside the oilskins. Unhank the
jib. Crawl with it to the forehatch, bracing against waves that come
over, trying to join me inside the clothes. Thrusting the jib down
the hatch, untying the sheets last. She's different without sail. A
miracle. It's all changed. The motion isn't violent any more.

My God, that's incredible, forcing my way back to the cockpit.
Halyards hanging over the side. To hell with the halyards. Do all
that tomorrow or whenever; try to survive. The schooner now
slipping through the water, not jarring. Bobbing, sliding, like a
bottle thrown from a trawler. We're just a bit of flotsam now. The
sea doesn't care any more. It doesn't want to destroy us now, we're
a part of the ocean. Back to the doghouse wheel, steering down the
waves. Yet we don't go fast enough to make pitchpoling a worry. A
wave thunders along and bulldozes into the hull, but that's the first
for ages. I feel safe. Just keep steering. As long as the bilgewater
doesn't increase. It is deep, but not a danger yet. She's off course,
look out, and gradually she comes back. If she would steer herself, I
could get some strength back.

The Southern Cross and pointer stars like Rigil Centaurus occasionally show the size of the huge shower masses moving across
our track. Now it's dawn, and daylight, and I see the incredible
height of these clouds; vast like the sea, they make our unimport-
ance in the whole way of things so apparent. The sea clerical-grey,
then slowly blue and dark-grey. Long fat fingers of white; roaring,
crushing scratches of washday white; then at the fringes, greenstone
teal. Frightening, shocking, yet very beautiful. My beard is wet,
look instinctively for the leak, but the flow is from my eyes. Tired,
straining, nearly blinded by the sun when it comes through. Just
keep steering. I see a plastic container in the bilgewater and dash
down for it. Written on it is: "Mrs A's little treats". Inside are some
bars of Godiva chocolate and a Mars. Stuff the food down and it
helps. Good old Gerry Adamson. The wind now lulls to thirty
knots, though the peaks are still well over sixty. It's got to be
getting better. Keep steering, and stop rubbing your eyes. You'll
look 110 by the time this is over. The direction is much more
automatic. I hate steering inside, but I wouldn't survive long out
there. Oh, to be an albatross. I could almost touch two mighty
wandering birds as they pass right over the cockpit. See that one,
what a character, and oh so vain! Looking at himself, head cocking
over to the right, checking the feathers are in place, like a youth
slicking blow-waves at the disco loo. And then mesmerised by his
own perfect gliding, up, up on the wind eddies and then soaring

round and down. Absolute minimum of effort, hardly a muscle flexed, he just uses the wind. Just like we do. I'm laughing. It's a strange sound. Don't hear it much on this boat. Not sure why. I'm pleased with how things are going. Here we are a couple of hundred miles off the Cape of Storms, as the old sail mariners knew it. Cape of Good Hope as we say. They were terrified of it and I am, too, but we're progressing; we're getting past and we seem to have survived her first fury. Hurricane force. Christ, I've been out there working on the decks in winds of God knows what force. I've seen the sea driven absolutely flat and white in the gusts and we've survived it. Knocked down, but not knocked out. I'm starving. That's got to be a good sign.

It's dark. The wind peaks at fifty-eight knots now, fifty-five, damn, off the clock again. But it's definitely coming down. The barometer's climbed fourteen millibars. Sound of laughter again. If that happened in the North Atlantic we'd call it the end of the world.

We've survived the first big storm and we've learned plenty. There will be a lot of work to be done when conditions are better. But now I'm exhausted. I've got to sleep. The wind is peaking at fifty-eight knots. I tie the wheel with some rope, the boat comes side-on to the sea and lies there. Waves unhampered going round the world come thundering and hissing, yet pass under us. It is magic, it's a miracle. There they are towering above, smashing onward, but when they get to us the swell lifts the boat and the waves go underneath. I can't believe it, yet it's happening. A few smash heavily, but most are not interested any more.

I throw some bucketfuls of water out of the bilges and take some of the stores off the floor. I'm able to use a hand pump to help, but the main bilge pump won't work. I'm quite philosophical about gear that's failed after sixty days at sea. Tomorrow I'll mend the self-steering. But now, close the eyes. Go to the void. My first sleep for, God, it must be three days. After an hour I wake. The ship's okay. So I take off oilskins and boots – it feels so good – and get into the sleeping bag. Stale sweat and body smelling awful, but it's not important any more. For three or four seconds I'm aware of being extraordinarily relaxed in that bruising, cramped bed. Then I slide into a very deep sleep, a long, long way from another living human.

2

I'd been working on the graveyard shift on the *Daily Mirror*, reading Vito Dumas, the first man to pass the Horn on his own from west to east, the way I wanted to go. Old sailing ships, he said, favoured June for the passage round Cape Horn. June, winter. *Winter*? I was suddenly awake and excited in that big empty office, waiting to spice up the last edition. This was the final piece in the jigsaw of how to do a double circumnavigation of the world.

No matter how many times I studied the charts, winter always got in the way. In the Southern Ocean, I had read, that season was all icebergs, colossal seas and winds. Too much for a yacht, they said. But was it? A sailing ship is much less manoeuvrable, it's big and clumsy in many ways which a sailing yacht isn't. Here was a possibility. Before the end of Vito's book I had resolved to attempt the double.

Dumas is an Argentinian, so I wrote to their embassy and asked if they had any advice to offer on passing the Horn in winter. They produced a record of storms in Drake's Passage and warned that it was "very tempestuous" at all times of the year, but I didn't care. Someone with deepwater experience had said the Horn was passable in the winter. That was all I needed.

I decided to plan for six years ahead. I would leave on my voyage after the *Observer* Single-handed Trans-Atlantic Race (OSTAR) in 1980 which would give me the best ocean experience I could get. I would do the Azores Race single-handed the year before that and the Round Britain Race, too, because that would take me to 60°N, to Muckle Flugga in the Shetlands. They call it the Cape Horn of the north.

I planned what knowledge I would need. Navigation, of course, but much more than dead reckoning and piloting. I would need to be able to measure the sun with a sextant. Or satellite navigation? No, sextant. The way the real sailors did it. And I'd have to be able to recognise stars and work them through tables. Oceanography, marine biology, meteorology. I'd have to be able to repair wire shrouds, be a sailmaker, an ocean racer and my own psychologist, dentist and doctor. As much of each subject as I could digest in the time. Most difficult of all, I'd have to learn to be my own best friend. That's a vital need in humans, I had found, whether it's a workmate, wife, or jailer. We all need someone to confide in, to talk to, and I would have no one. Well, I'd have a girl friend back home and I would lean very heavily on her psychologically. I knew that would have to be the case, but I still needed to crop a lot of the self-criticism from within. And I'd study to be a radio amateur so I could keep friends and relations from worrying too much. I would have to be strong and fit. I revised that point. Fitness would be much more important than strength. It would take a while, but I'd give up smoking and all drinking except occasional beers or wine with food. There was one other thing I would need, of course. A boat.

I had learned the rudiments of sailing in the early 1970s and found I enjoyed being alone at sea in a sailing dinghy. A ten-foot yellow boat called *Opus*, who tipped me over, smashed against rocks, and scared me. A good initiation. I carried Sir Francis Chichester's books around with me like bibles.

A friend on the *Mirror*, Frank Pynn, invited me to crew a Twister for him. We were to meet in Le Havre. I was sick in the ferry all the way across the Channel, spent twenty-four hours trying to find Frank's yacht, then was ill all the way back to England in her, except for the last ten miles, which I thought were the greatest. Then for a week we sailed about three hundred miles. I stopped being sick and it was fabulous. Other crewmen didn't arrive, which was ideal. I got the full force of Frank's encouragement and advice and all of the criticism and ex-naval bullying. "Anticipate, always anticipate! Remember what the yacht's going to do and get there first."

Frank had a command during the war, so he was no stranger to correcting crew. I abhor criticism, so I learned fairly quickly. I don't think I've ever helmed since without hearing in my mind Frank's "Anticipate! Anticipate!"

So I progressed from occasional weekend chartering to a thirty-footer of my own. My loyal and sorely tried crew in the early days was Lilian who had excited me the moment I met her large green eyes. She had accepted she would have to share me with the sea, but her patience ran out soon after the second time I stranded us on a Sunday morning sandbank a long way from safety. Lilian was not keen to come sailing after that. I swapped the yacht for an elderly racing machine and started evening classes at the School of Navigation in London. My last winter ashore I also studied amateur radio at night-school twice a week. I jogged every morning and spent at least an hour swimming. I felt fit.

There were many diversions and I left the chosen path often. I became attracted to trimarans and swapped my keelboat in which I won a class prize in the Azores Race in 1979 for a tri. I studied trimaran sailing and became more passionate about that than mono-hull racing. I still much prefer tris, but they are not really the boats for the Southern Ocean. And it was with the tri, *Christian S 2*, after Lilian and I had parted, that I met Carol, who stepped into my life at a very lonely point and made me realise there was much more to existence than ocean racing.

Carol helped me prepare *Christian S 2* for the Trans-Atlantic Race in 1980. We went away together, we sailed together, we were together at the weekends. When I set off in the Trans-Atlantic alone, I realised how much I had relied on her. And between us there was a great feeling. When I had to stop at the Azores for repairs, she phoned to wish me luck and love for the journey onwards. Carol became increasingly important to me.

After the Trans-Atlantic Race, I left my trimaran in America and returned to Britain on a cheap stand by ticket, in order to go straight to the office. It felt strange to be surrounded by people on the underground after spending so long on my own on the vast openness of the North Atlantic. It was so good to be back with Carol, who came to London each weekend. The brutality of that single-handed race slipped quickly away. I wanted to forget the sea for a while, to forget nursing the sinking boat to the Azores and then having to steer all the way to the US when the electrics failed. It had been a bit too traumatic.

One day, soon after I got back, I was called to the phone. "I've found the schooner you're looking for."

It was Angela Green from the *Observer*. She had been in Rhode Island for the end of the Trans-Atlantic Race and knew about my plans to go round the world. I thought she had forgotten her promise to help me find a good racing machine.

"I know you wanted one in metal. This one's wood. But there's a lot of steel in her. I mean, she's very strong and she has just completed a race to Australia and back."

"Oh, that sounds interesting," I said, thinking that it didn't really.

"Come to the Goat in Kensington tonight. I'll have Mike Dunham with me; he's the designer and one of the owners."

Not a chance, Angela. I don't want to talk about boats to anyone.

For a week or two. Why can't we say what we mean? "Sounds great, Angela. See you then."

Both owners arrived with Angela, and soon were describing the fastest, most beautiful thirteen-ton schooner that had ever sailed most of the seven seas. Called *Moondancer* but originally registered as *Seltrust Endeavour*, I could buy her outright, they said, or a half-share. I didn't have the heart to say I was penniless. We agreed to a short jolly that weekend.

Carol was less enthusiastic. She had waited six weeks for me during the Trans-Atlantic and there had been fears that I'd gone missing. Poor Carol. But she said she would come to see this new boat which was moored at Exmouth. It was a long drive but the countryside was so good after the sea and I was happy just being with Carol. We were supposed to find the paragon in a long canal off the River Exe, but only her sister ship, *Sundancer*, was there. *Sundancer* was an anorexic hundred-foot-long schooner with three masts.

"She looks a bit extraordinary," Carol said kindly. I thought she was the most unlikely sailing craft I had ever seen. We caught up with *Moondancer* in Exmouth, and I realised that *Sundancer* was actually the second most unlikely sailing craft I had ever seen.

Moondancer was alongside a wall and because the tide was low we could only see two tall masts and a jungle of rigging until we were standing directly above the hull. It was a shock, like a blind date with a female who appears to be twice the age of your mother. I resented the petrol we had used to get there, the price of the beer in the Goat and that I had given up a whole day of being alone with Carol.

Moondancer was only as wide as a thirty-footer. Yet she was fifty-six feet long: making the length to beam ratio radically extreme. The paint was dull grey and blistering, a dinghy resembling an ancient bath tub destroyed the lines of her deck and the masts and rigging were oversized and seemed to be everywhere. "My God," I said. "The windage."

At least we'd never need to worry about sails. With all that rigging strung about, she wouldn't need any. Carol looked pale. A few of Mike's friends were on board and as soon as we clambered down, he went astern into the strong Exe tide and we were under way. I helped raise a battered genoa and staysail. They were torn, had poor repairs and seemed badly stained. Mike cut the engine and she was sailing. Hardly any sail for the size of boat, yet she was slicing through the water and putting on speed. Amazing, I thought: *Moondancer* scored her first point. I looked at Carol and smiled, but disapproval was returned. I went below and inspected the boat, the dirtiest, untidiest, most cluttered mess I had ever seen afloat. I rescued Carol from a seasick passenger.

"Disregard the untidiness." I tried to encourage. "Watch the speed for such a little amount of canvas. Look at the strength of the hull. There are some touches of genius in this machine, you know." The boat was really just a glorified sailing canoe only nine feet eight inches wide with a twelve-foot movable steel keel which weighed four tons. Schooner-rigged, her two masts were the same height. She was English built, at Exmouth in 1979.

"It's horrible," Carol said. "I want to get off. I'll never go on it again."

And she never did. I think Carol's premonition warned her then that this would be the boat, the one that would break us and take me away. The fact that she called the schooner "it" instead of "she" was proof of her instant hate. But I was inspecting the boat and wasn't paying attention. Carol went up on deck, to sit beside the man now noisily retching, and I remained below. A new woman had entered my life and I was at first repelled. But now she fluttered personality and charm. *Moondancer* was the ugliest, dirtiest young bitch of a boat I had ever met. Yet you couldn't deny her speed. Looking at her hull, the rigging, she was immensely strong. I had been with her just twenty minutes and we were already talking as friends.

"If I look after you, *Moondancer*, will you look after me, if things get too much for a solitary man?"

The answer came from the deep keel, the woodwork, the stale air inside the hull.

We drove to London, with our thoughts and the car stereo. *Moondancer* had coped with the Southern Ocean. She had been in atrocious conditions, yet here she was back and in one piece. What did it matter if she wore the wrong clothes, if her make-up was awful, if she could do with a good bath? Inside there was soul, personality. It was stronger on that boat than I had ever felt before. She really had something. Such a strange shape underneath for a yacht, yet it stopped quarter waves forming, which meant energy better spent.

I turned Sting down and said: "Anyway the price is all wrong. And with twelve feet of draught, how could one man get on with her? You know they had a crew of eight? All the sails are shot. And that rigging, have you ever seen anything like it?"

"I felt sick on the boat and I don't usually. It's just terrible and it's so dirty."

"Yes, but it's how the boat goes that is important. The steering is exceptional off the wind for such a big boat. She's got a lot going for her." Me defending the boat again.

"I hate it. It's ugly."

"Well, anyway, she's out of the question. Costs too much and too much needs doing. After all, I have to leave in June so I can get past the Horn the second time. That's only eight months away, you know."

"If only I could forget for a moment." She sounded as if she were crying but it was too dark to see. "I wish we hadn't gone to see that boat."

"Carol, it's you I love, not the schooner. Not a boat." I felt her looking at me but she didn't say anything, just turned Police up louder. Message in a bottle.

As I planned for the double circumnavigation, I depended on Carol even more and sometimes wondered in quiet moments how I could see the event through if we broke up. I would need to feel her psychologically backing me while I was alone at sea. Fourteen months of enforced celibacy is a long time. Longer still for a young woman to be waiting at home. I wanted to explain, I can't bear to leave you, but I have to get this voyage out of my system – please wait. But I couldn't say it, I made light of it instead, and joked about her being in demand at home once I faced the ocean. It was a sad laugh.

In the Round Britain Race I had met Chris West who appeared knowledgeable about backers, so I went to Brighton to ask him for advice. He had a lot of ideas, and offered to try to arrange spon-sorship.

Chris came with me on a weekend trial run and I was violently ill and couldn't get out of my bunk for about twelve hours. He was seasick, too. The angle of heel was so great and the motion so violent. It was a bad sign, but now time was running out.

Ideally a boat should be designed and built for the voyage, but that would take far too long and would cost a fortune. I wanted a large boat because there was so much equipment to be carried. She would weather severe storms much better, too, and go faster. The only large schooner available was *Moondancer*, and now the owners offered her for charter if I preferred. Then a letter arrived from Pentax, the camera manufacturers, showing interest in the adven-ture. Chris and I went for an interview that lasted barely five minutes. They'd let us know. Chris decided to become honorary project manager and Pentax came back to say they would be sponsors. I concluded a charter agreement for *Moondancer*, for which Pentax was willing to pay, and told Carol how well it was all going. She didn't share the excitement. However, she made the best of it and helped strip *Moondancer* ready for a refit.

Chris and I removed the engine altogether and redesigned the whole interior and deck layout. The boat would now be heated by paraffin; power would come from solar panels and a wind generator.

The project was so ambitious that I depended on other friends, too. Jack Huke is an engineer who has been to sea, looks a real sailing type, bearded and thick-set. He rebuilt and strengthened the rudder, arranged the supply of much equipment, and stood by me to the end. Peter Lambden had helped get my trimaran ready for the Trans-Atlantic and only gave me a forty-sixty chance of making it the first time he saw *Moondancer*. But he took charge of the steering and self-steering and helped with the rigging. Christopher Broadbent designed modifications for a solo journey and became the overseer for employed shipwrights. Carol's mother preserved fourteen months' supply of eggs and near the time of departure was doing an extraordinary amount of work. Lilian returned as a tremendous helper, despite her feelings about the sea. She raised an army of friends to pack food for a year and a half in polythene bags, one of which I would bring to the galley at the beginning of each week to last me for seven days. It was an immense task.

In April, Carol walked away from the project and me. I felt emotionally paralysed. So often I was asked how I thought I would survive the voyage. I tried to be reassuring. Inside I wondered how I would survive the day without Carol.

But the transformation from a racing boat needing a crew of eight to a single-hander was almost complete. Pete Sanders had finished most of the sails and they looked excellent. I was raring to try them out. The self-steering gear was on. The new steering system was installed. It was about the most expensive single item on the boat, but it was the all important one. Her old system had not been tough enough, but the new steering was the strongest in the world, Peter Lambden advised. I was to remember these words, too, often in the following months. She looked terrific in her new colours. White hull with *Spirit of Pentax* in red and black, designed by an artist friend, Bob Abrahams. Below decks she was still in a mess, but that didn't really change until Australia.

Derek Faucett arrived with the electronically driven auto-pilot and decided how it should be installed. Derek has always been a good friend. He is a frustrated single-handed voyager but success in business keeps him from the sea. Solo voyages, Derek advised when we first discussed the circumnavigation, depend on proper

27

self-steering. "You must only look on the auto-pilot as a stand-by. You'll also need really reliable wind-driven mechanical self-steering gear. On the length of this voyage you've got to expect the worst from the electrical side of the boat. Well, you know about saltwater and electrical wiring."

The auto-pilot was installed. I christened it Dead-Eyed Derek and set off for a five-day trial on my own. The English Channel, a motorway of shipping lanes, was not the best place for this, but time dictated the course. It was a sunny day and ships kept well clear. Then we were in the open sea, *Spirit of Pentax* and me. Our first time alone. Fifty-six feet of extraordinary racing machine: a huge canoe, with only a long dagger-type keel to stop her falling right over. And no echo-sounder to tell you if the bottom was coming dangerously close to that great piece of steel.

But she was glorious. Number one yankee, staysail and full main; all fresh tan and magnificently cut. For sail numbers we had the letter P extrovertly on fore and aft sails. She looked a dream. Standing at the wheel right at the end of the boat, looking forward all that way to the bow, the shape of the sails, the quiet wash from the hulls. It was seventh heaven stuff for me. She could have been the *Cutty Sark*. Just five feet seven, ten stone of man conducting this huge beast around the Channel. Mine was the role that thousands would envy, the master of an ocean-going schooner. True, I did not have a crew to carry out my orders, but this is the way I prefer it. I am not a lazy type and don't mind working hard. And I had Derek, the best helmsman in the world, as number one only the touch of a button away. Complete and utter freedom. At least for five days. None of the soul-destroying shore-side work to do, just navigation and seafaring. Whoops of joy along the deck. Dead-Eyed Derek on the helm, me admiring the aerofoil shape of the sails, cutting the freshening breeze. Below to check the charts, make a cup of tea, remove a log impeller fouled by seaweed and get it back in place, waving at a passenger steamer. Isn't life good? Five days, then Plymouth, dinner ashore and many toasts to this fabulous new female in my life.

She steered well, handled nicely, so, if the wind was Force 4 all round the world, it would be an excellent trip. That night I found we had forgotten to instal a compass light, so it was not possible to read the course. But press Derek's button, and he kept us on a perfect magnetic heading. His compass was built in. He didn't need eyes to read it, though he relied on mine, of course, to keep open sea before the bow.

I cooked a meal below on the new paraffin stove, poured a beer and drank to Jack, to Ron and the mates, to everyone who had helped me. And to *Spirit of Pentax,* the most beautiful schooner afloat.

By midnight I got the mechanical self-steering gear to work and put Derek to bed. Stars, clouds, shoosh-shoosh from the hull, a little phosphorescence in the wake, a torch to the compass. Exactly on course. Wind now in the north, our course westward. Go west, young boat, go west. No shipping, clear of land. I turned in, waking every forty minutes to check the horizon and course. Just after dawn the motion was wrong. We were heading south. The self-steering gear had stopped working, its wooden pendulum snapped off at the waterline. Not a good indication in fair weather, I thought, turning Derek out for the morning watch. I didn't realise then how serious the sign was. On Friday, we returned from the Atlantic and through the mist found the Scilly Isles. Late Friday night Eddystone blinked ahead, and right on time I tacked under ghosting genoa into Plymouth Sound, up to Jack, Mike Dunham and Angela Green bobbing in a small runabout, waiting to tow us to the Mayflower marina, for a warm welcome. I thought, If we get a good reception after five days, what'll it be like after the voyage?

Moët and Chandon and Jack beaming satisfaction as if it had been his successful trial run. In a way, of course, it had.

"It was so good to see you sailing in like that," said Angela. "You seemed to handle her so easily. You and the boat have come a long way since the Goat, remember? What do you think of her now?"

"Smashing. Absolutely smashing."

3

"I don't know how you'll be able to stand being alone for so long," said a friend in a Plymouth pub.

"Perhaps that's the point," I replied. "I don't *know* if I can, but I think I'll be able to. Loneliness is worst when you're not doing anything. I expect to be very busy on the boat."

"Well, I don't understand why you want to do it."

"Why do people want to be footballers, or cricketers? I was never any good at ball games. That made me feel pretty inferior at school. I hated others – almost everyone – being better than me at sport. I'm more at home sailing and I don't seem too bad in solo races."

"But twice round the world?"

"Well, like climbers going up Everest on the wrong side. It's only the nature of the challenge; it's not to go twice round as much as it is to go further, I suppose, than anybody else. The mountain down there is never-ending, so by the time you've done a certain number of miles, you are actually doing it again."

"I think mountaineering would be safer for you."

"I can't stand heights."

However nonchalant I may have sounded, I soon began to suffer from an acute nervousness which exploded in my stomach. I'd had it before other solo events. How would I cope on my own? How would I handle such a huge machine in bad weather? What if I broke a bone? Would there be enough food and water? Shouldn't I take some more music, my only link with stability? Bowels out of control, constantly feeling sick, unable to think clearly. And then always that same question over and over again: "How will you cope on your own?" How can I tell, when I've no idea myself?

The nervousness developed into a mental panic. Somehow I must find an excuse for not going. Crossing busy streets; dawdling in front of traffic; hit me, car, and send me to hospital, give me time to think, to forget. Somehow the cars always miss. Up the masts, too, my normal fear of heights is gone. A fall means at least a postponement.

Three days before the start, I became calm and remarkably clear-headed.

At 11 am on Sunday, June 28, all work ceased on the yacht and she was towed from Mayflower marina to the Royal Western Yacht Club. A panic to search for forgotten water-purifying tablets; a last quiet drink in the Navy pub. I gave the barman the last of my money and asked him to treat the others as soon as I had left. To the historic Plymouth steps, interviews, a crowd of well-wishers, a kiss for the earth – my last touch of dear old England – and a motor launch took off for the schooner rolling quietly on the mooring. Last television interviews. Last bear hugs and kisses. On to my new home, photographs, a cannon fired from the yacht club, out through the Sound with the helpers, all off now. Tacking away, the wind so light, tack again; come round, you beauty. We're clearing the Sound, the helpers rushing back to get movie film and stills to London. We're on our own, but it doesn't seem like it, there's no realisation, and no reality. It seems as if we'll be back soon, taking a good hot shower at the yacht club, then the pleasure of other humans tonight.

At the wheel, the boat feels heavy and I am surprised she moves so easily in this light wind. Pity it has to be ahead of us, but the forecast says it will become a following breeze. She likes that best. And by night the wind goes aft, though very light, and the barometer starts to improve. No ships about, so below for an hour's sleep. Going to bed alone for the first time since the trial run. God didn't mean us to sleep lonely. Dead-Eyed Derek making heavy going. Up with the golly wobbler, that huge square sail designed to sit between the two equal masts. All 650 square feet of it. Then an astro sight puts us past Ushant and reaching for the notorious Bay of Biscay, but the weather is kind.

After a day I discover that the staysail winch is broken; the wire from the Aquair, the water-driven alternator which will generate power in non-storm conditions for Derek and for my radios, is too short to reach its plug, and four solid hours of work won't get the self-steering gear to work. But I must have it. Derek can't possibly be my only other helmsman. How could he cope through the tropics when we expect very light winds, and so very little power from the Aquair? Restow gear on board; there is so much, but she's leaning to port and so must get some of the weight on to starboard. Repack film in waterproof containers; found the movie cameras, but where are the Pentaxes? I'm not eating yet. I don't really feel like it as I have been seasick for the past couple of days, but I prepare eggs on toast and it goes down well.

Our course becomes zig-zags, as the only way to keep her going in this light puff is to aim her into it. Then the air stops moving altogether and we roll about, sails slamming, rigging crashing on a perfect mirror in Biscay. Overcast. We are in a high-pressure ridge, and strangely this kind weather follows us to Madeira, the Canaries, the Cape Verde Islands and to the doldrums. At home, many people are praying for fair weather and it stays with me right through the northern hemisphere. A coincidence, of course.

More mistakes appear now. I've left the new saucepans in my flat; I still can't find the cameras; the self-steering still won't go; the state of the spinnaker halyards is frightening. Somehow we have overlooked repairing them and the rope I use for the blooper, my pole-less spinnaker, is too short, adding a new risk to flying this kite. Somehow I have forgotten to replace the kettle. I rescued the one I have from the rubbish during the refit. No whistle, and dents in the side. How long can it last? We ought to go back and get these problems sorted out. Particularly the vane-steering. The batteries are almost flat and now we are among shipping again so I have to weave my way among their tracks, the yacht in blackness. Sorry, Captain, no power for lights. But don't worry, I'll keep out of your way. Measuring the course and distance off for a possible return, I see a large ship's warp floating in the water dead ahead, two inches thick, right on course. I try to swing away, but it's too late and the warp catches around the rudder. Damn, damn that stupid design, so very vulnerable. Pulling in the Aquair rope, it snatches at my fingers, pinching flesh viciously. If I hold on for a second too long it will catch my hand or a finger and burn it off in a tourniquet, while the rope spins on the propeller. Got to get it in before that warp gets tangled. At last, but I'll never do that again without stopping the boat first. Far too risky. When the pain has eased and I can use the fingers again, we heave-to and miraculously the warp drops off the rudder. That was very dangerous, as unexpected weight there could so easily tear the rudder off, and I am left in a mood of despair. "Something so trivial could wreck the project, even at this early stage," I write in the log. A ship, the *Dunavon*, passes close, people waving from the bridge.

Off Spain, the Aquair picks up a fishing line which I carefully unwind and we have two hundred yards of codline plus a plastic buoy in return for one Aquair propeller.

I say, Hi, to Jupiter through the sextant and on a sail change at night spot the month's new moon. These night-sky jewels are soon to become firm friends. The extraordinary hallucinatory phenomenon of strangers seeming to "visit" the yacht, which I had experienced several times on past voyages, happens again. I imagine I can hear them talking.

Log 0900 hours: Mike and a friend "visited" just before dawn. So clear. Mike "talking" about the schooner with just one sail set, but complimenting me on the idea. Feel happier today, thank goodness.

Oddly enough, the happy feeling coincides with a rise in barometric pressure, and I wonder. Humans are not supposed to be sensitive to these changes in the pressure of the atmosphere. One week at sea.

Log 1700 hours: A quiet celebration held on the foredeck where the crew (me) assembled to drink Moët and orange juice to toast the supporters, male and female, who had made it all possible. Headphones were the only apparel.

Another fault appears. The log shows 561 sea miles, yet we have passed through 12° of latitude, which means at least 720 sea miles. I have the first hot meal of the trip, with boil-in-the-bag venison. Good to be eating again. The start of the trade winds and the schooner starts to move at speed, white water now showing from the bow, rushing down her length, making a hollow. But such a shallow trough and even at nine knots, still no distinct quarter wave. Incredible. Almost unheard of. I shout. Her speed increases and slows, increases and lulls, with each of the gusts. Eyes down to the compass and, on the edge of vision, white sweeping either side, acceleration vibrating through the hull, the shoosh of skis, beautiful symmetry of speed, boat under pressure, perfectly in control, man and machine. God, this is what it's all about. At last, she's taking off. Eyes to the instrument panel then to the wind direction indicator atop the foremast and the shape of the sails; ease the blooper, tighten the golly wobbler, ease the main. Shoosh, shoosh, sun dazzling on faultless blue, white tumbling past, like Carol's hair on the pillow. Elton John through the hatch joining the excitement with "the Brown Dirt Cowboy". That's you, schooner, I'm calling you Captain Fantastic. You are the fantastic captain who makes it all happen and I'm the pretender, the brown dirt cowboy, the make believe navigator and brains, the human computer who tries to make it all work, but really only learning as we go along. But it won't be make-believe soon. I'll be a genuine circumnavigator or die in the attempt. Learning about you and of you as we progress. Taught by you. And on the following Sunday's anniversary of two weeks at sea, a measure of Moët on the bows for the new christening of the super schooner, the most fabulous sailing boat of the seven seas, who dodges ships without my help and goes faster than

33

the log can record. To Captain Fantastic, twenty-four hours a day, non-stop. Sipping tea on the starboard seat, watching the staysail and main through the perspex above, the white amidships wave dashing past leeward, reflected in the broken winch chrome. Captain Fantastic, here's to you.

Land-ho! Madeira looms on the horizon as expected, so our navigation must be working out. Up to Ilha de Pôrto Santo and gybing towards Madeira Island as the twilight goes. What a fabulous night, stars, following breeze.

There's Deserta Grande, a big barren island, rushing for the bow fast. It seems very close, but we gybe and run the length of the island. It is very dark by the island's shore. Then we are clear and the wind moves again and we gybe and the Aquair gets fouled and breaks, and catches itself around the self-steering for good measure. I worry about things that go wrong in good weather. What will happen when we reach the Roaring Forties?

> Log 1600 hours: A good sleep, broken by about an hour at the wheel as we went through a doldrum-type cloud. Proof perhaps that these are, after all, the horse latitudes. Thinking – of course, knowing me – of all the things I ought to have said on the VHF last night. I should have reported the good things of the voyage. Lilian and the others put so much effort into the project, I should at least tell them I am grateful. Why do we always think first of the bad things? If I could put fear aside for a little while, I'd have to say that this is a fabulous time and I wouldn't swap with anyone.

I listen in to the amateur net but there is no message for me; there appears to be just one other yacht in these low latitudes. He sounds Australian, called Douglas, but his speed is less than mine so I put his position on the chart and mark him for an extrovert overtaking; I'm a Sunday driver moving up the jams. The sun is hotter and the trade winds become much more established. The stars so bright now, Jupiter and Polaris confirm my navigation. Jupiter should be there in the Southern Ocean with me, but the Pole star will be gone by the equator. I wonder if I'll see him again.

Land-ho! and there's Las Palmas of the Canary Islands in the distance and the wind freshens to a gale. Getting the golly wobbler down is a challenge, as it wraps itself around the forward shrouds. We get pooped by a wave crowding over the stern. A shock to the naked figure at the wheel, brain a long way off. Occasional flying fish and soon they are everywhere, one even lands on deck. But I don't find them attractive, just a navigational aid, a signpost reading, "The tropics welcome safe drivers." They are like the locusts which terrified me when we all lived on a hydro-electric construction camp site in New Zealand as pommy immigrants and the creatures swarmed from underfoot, wings beating the noise of dead bones. I hated them, although I liked cicadas filling the air with their nightly chorus. Working on farms at weekends; driving, riding, milking cows; the start of a passion for the great outdoors, a mongrel called Nuki and the challenge of Catholic Margaret who eventually dropped her tight elastic for me. But I was too young; she called my bluff. I watch fish flying in schools now and wonder what happened to her and all those sunburned kids, after we'd moved on to the next hydro-electric camp site, losing stability again, as surely as if they'd mixed gypsy virus into our polio vaccine. Once when I had gone back for a holiday, I'd seen Jersey cows grazing where five children noisily filled a pine house.

I don't think I'm going mad. But every night Carol seems to be with me. I hang my jacket and waterproof trousers from a hook next to the pigeon-holes. They sway in the rolling motion and when it's dark they become her and someone else. He's tall and slim and she dances in the way I have seen her move so many times. Affection. Affectionate, gentle, warm. The things I miss so much already. Sometimes she is alone and the trousers hanging next to her become a cloud. I do not feel jealous when the other is there. He doesn't count, I'm just pleased she is here.

There're more flying fish for breakfast, six of them, and today I have Henri Strzelecki from Henri-Lloyds "with me". We are talking; it seems they are old conversations between us. We joke about conquests in a chauvinist way and about the voyage so far. I say it was great to see him on the launch that chased me to the Plymouth breakwater to say goodbye and good luck.

Lady Chichester is another "visitor". She seems amused by the state of the boat, but she is encouraging and helpful. Congratulations, she says, on getting fifteen hundred miles. The wind makes sail changes difficult when it strengthens and there is Eddie Ball, saying be careful on that foredeck.

More gear failures and I draw up a list to see if we should go back and get her properly prepared. Now, there is no doubt at all that we have begun too soon.

The wind-vane gear is still not working and I doubt that I will get it going. The transmitters remain dead, the staysail winch is broken, and we are short of headsail sheets, quite apart from those worn-out spinnaker halyards. The lazarette needs a ventilator and a hatch in the cockpit sole leaks. The running poles have not been overhauled and their sheave boxes are breaking out. Water comes into the boat through the cockpit drains, and those mild steel nails rusting through the deck worry me. Now I have discovered that only two torches work. There are no replacement bulbs, very few batteries and none at all to fit the transistor. The Pentax cameras are definitely not on board, including my own Spotmatic which they took away to service.

I list the problems under "for" and "against" turning back. The one favouring a return begins with, "Put boat into proper condition," and reflects my feelings. The last entry is, "My health overall if self-steering fails," and is a fair understatement. For not going back, the list starts with, "Sponsors moan and possibly withdraw?" and that decides me. It isn't their fault that the boat isn't in perfect order. They spent a great deal of money. I feel a tremendous responsibility and loyalty to them, so I continue. After the decision, I write over the list: "Only point in favour of returning is good prudent seafaring sense. But if that's a major part of this project, what are we doing here, anyway?"

A lonely day as we near the Cape Verde Islands. The visibility deteriorates as it does so often in these latitudes. I have been saving a tape recorded by my parents. It is good to hear them, along with my youngest brother Stephen. It is an amusing family talk and I am happier afterwards. How strange that I may see them off Dunedin in a fishing boat, God willing, if I can get word through, when I'm nearing New Zealand. How many months till then?

Log 0425: Gorgeous big full moon. Squall comes near, me up ready, but I think we're free again. Fish flew on board, so I threw it back. Gently. Feeling in better spirits today. Slept well, though I was out each hour to check on the presence of squalls, etc. Three fish and a tadpole-sized one offered for breakfast today. One landed right in the doghouse. It had a parasite growing on a fin and that put me off, so I had muesli instead. Plus bananas, of course. The twenty-eight pounds of bananas all decided to ripen together. It's not easy demolishing twenty-eight pounds of bananas in a week when you're on your own.

My grandmother said of my older brother, Peter, that if there were a piece of chewing gum in the Sahara, he'd find it on his shoe. I thought of that today when a thump against the hull brought me on deck. A lone forty-four-gallon drum sat in our wake. I was taking a break at the time, listening with headphones to Pink Floyd; which gave me a feeling of familiarity, of security in a way, far from the sea. Later I am trimming the sails when the wind comes forward of the beam. I sit wondering under the stars if this is the end of the trade winds and watch an eclipse of the moon. When there are experiences like this, why do people need drugs?

It's the doldrums, all right. The wind disappears and a ship climbs over the horizon and slowly drops over the other side. The sea is very empty here. No birds seen today, but there is a tiny creature like a fly with skates on who shoots around the boat. The rain doesn't strike till after dark. I have the movie camera out the next day, when a pack of killer whales goes into the attack. I cannot see what the prey is, but they turn the sea into foam. God, keep these lethal creatures from me. Dolphins appear and join us, trying to follow the wind which heads us and goes right round, boxing the compass as the sailors used to say. Tremendous downpours now, showing up all the leaks. They seem merely numerous; it's not till much later that they prove to be hazardous.

So many cakes provided by the lady supporters and I have been doing justice to them. Carol's mother includes an encouraging letter with each of hers. Now violent gusts bash at us, sails down, sails up; white clouds of the south-easterly trade winds are here, pushing the schooner over forty-five degrees, which remains our angle of heel across the equator for twelve days. My knees seize, limbs ache with the constant angle and I move about with the speed of a very old man. The pain from the constant bruising and the unnatural leaning is almost beyond bearing, when suddenly we spring upright and are becalmed. The sails slat and threaten to tear down the rigging and the noise is overwhelming. But the feeling is beautiful. I can stretch easily and walk along the deck without caring and my knees flood with a revitalised bloodstream. It's a different world, the air is spray-free; the sea flat. I don't care if we are becalmed for ever. Mariners call it the sub-tropical high-pressure belt. Here is the only place to be in the world. Back there lie the trades, the brutality of forty-five-degree sailing ahead, the Southern Ocean in winter, the unknown horror. No, here in the sunshine and flat sea, clear skies and stars at night, will do me fine.

4

In a few days it will be Lilian's birthday. She was twenty-one when we met, or was it nineteen; anyway, she must be about twenty-seven. No, it's five years since that night; no, that's not right because it has taken six years to get here to the Southern Ocean. Crazy how time shoots past and we don't realise it. Age is so stupid anyway; people count off the years like reading a car speedo, so they can say, Oh, he's a bit past it now, or she's a bit old for him. Meet so-and-so and they say, What's your job, and take a stab at your age and then you're in a compartment in their brain and you're expected to perform accordingly.

Will life begin when I reach the Roaring Forties in a few days' time? I'll certainly find out the hard way if I don't get the self-steering gear, my Anthony Rowley Frog, a-wooing. I took him apart yesterday, bringing all the fittings into the cockpit. It is very difficult working on the transom. The risk of dropping bits into the ocean so great, the chance of falling in myself even better. That's one of the problems with Captain Fantastic; the freeboard is too high. It'd be an awful long way to climb up if I fell off. Only extraordinary luck would ever get me back on board. To die at sea watching her roaring away on her own fills me with dread. There is no way to stop the self-steering if I did go over, so she would keep on sailing, possibly for years. Of course, I have those two pills, wrapped up in waterproof in my right pocket, for just such a nightmare moment.

Frog consists of a water paddle and a wind-vane connected by gears. The wind blows on the vane which turns the paddle in the water and so keeps the boat on course. Now I think that the fitting which holds the water paddle in position has been assembled back to front. I turn it round. It works. Incredible. But to reverse it involves me hanging out over the water. I have two pictures of the gear in the handbook: a photograph showing the gear as it was, a sketch showing the opposite. The sketch is correct, I now know. Perhaps there have been modifications since the photo, or was it taken in a studio to look good and to hell with how it works? This stupidity has cost me hours of work. I put a new connector in, joining the wind-vane to the water paddle, and just as I am about to try it, the tiny puffs stop altogether. No complaints. Without these becalmings I wouldn't have got this far with the gear.

Log Sunday 1600 hours: Sssh! Not a word, but you-know-who has been steering for the last seven minutes – and downwind.
Log 2200 hours: In Frog's hands with ghoster up and light genoa poled out. (If there's a lot of wind suddenly, there will be a complicated sail change, but it is a gorgeous moonlit night.) No comment about the Frog yet. I've worked too damn hard – and been too frustrated by it, too – to speak yet.
Log Monday 0900 hours: Well, Frog's done his first night's steering. Wrong course, but at least it was east. Couldn't understand why, but then found the paddle wasn't fully down. By luck I inspected the old paddle and found a spring was missing. Drop sails, paddle out and off, mistakenly turned blade about and changed bracket on top, but then found that wouldn't help so replaced it. Spring into blade-release and now he's working. (Fingers crossed.) It's downwind and he's dodging from side to side, but the course is there.

The wind returns and is soon hitting twenty eight knots, which upsets the Frog. But it is so good to have him working. He deserves to be more kindly treated now so shall call him Anthony Rowley again, not Frog any more. I stay at the wheel until darkness and then he comes on duty. But his course is wild and exaggerated and will soon add a lot of extra distance to our already extraordinary total. I try elastic round the wind paddle, to make it less sensitive, and make countless adjustments to the rope connecting him on to the wheel.

Log Tuesday 0510 hours: Anthony Rowley heads up into the wind and has trouble correcting the course. I'll look in the daylight. The sky looks like Armageddon.
Log 0900 hours: Anthony Rowley brought us through the night at no cost to electricity, but of course the heading was nothing like Derek's. I fear the paddle may be too long. It sticks out at a frightening, vulnerable angle.
Log 1300 hours: Took spare Anthony Rowley paddle and removed a hundred centimetres from bottom. This makes its length coincide with the plans in the book.
Log 1400 hours: He seems rejuvenated. Paddle holder reversed and the shorter paddle SEEMS to have made a lot of difference. However, I have been so disappointed in the past that I will wait and see. Big swell from south; barometer dropping. I know we'll get it sooner or later . . . But later, please.

39

Log 1800 hours: Waiting for sun (for astro sight) but cloud stops that. I would have liked a good position plotted if we are in for a blow. Anthony Rowley is transformed. Please let it last. Tidy up on deck as the barometer goes down.

I ought to be in a party mood; this is the closest Captain Fantastic has ever been to wind-vane steering. If it continues to work, we can conserve electricity and I will be freed from a lot of the helming. Perhaps we could even use the strip lighting at night for reading? I could spend more time on the navigation, which I enjoy most of all, and would be able to catch up on the maintenance. There is a big and growing list. I cook a pig-sized meal, drink a half-bottle of red wine given me for the voyage by Anne Mason and listen to Pink Floyd, but I still do not feel great. I write in the log that I am homesick for London. Is it just coincidence that the barometer is plunging? Along with my spirits.

Looking out with sleepy brain, my heart suddenly racing before the picture reaches comprehension. Huge cumulus around, heavy black etched in weirdness by the moon. As if we are inside some clouds from hell itself.

Down five millibars in twenty hours, then six more with the wind at thirty-five knots. Anthony Rowley goes on strike and I take over at the doghouse wheel. It is our first cold wind and I am so grateful for Jerry Freeman insisting that I had to have a covered steering position for the voyage, even though the floor's a bit low so I find it hard to see out. We shoot forward, nine, ten knots, touching eleven and back, and eleven again, so effortlessly, while the sea is not particularly rough. You can always keep the staysail and a foresail up, Mike Dunham had said before we left. He's the designer, so I take his word. We roll heavily and a spinnaker pole comes adrift, I dash forward to take it off. Cold water hits me in the face, trying to reach within. The sea hasn't been this temperature since we left the English Channel. Down for a bar of chocolate and a tap on the barometer. Another five and a half millibars in the last six hours. The sea is getting upset now and Captain Fantastic lingers on the tops of waves while following rollers overtake, dumping large, noisy cockpit-loads. But no boat can cope with such a drop in pressure under all the canvas I've got up so I go forward to lower the staysail. Mike's wrong, the boat reacts better under less canvas, although the motion is very unpleasant. Wasn't it just hours ago we had fluffy clouds of the trades and the beautiful clear skies of the sub-tropical high-pressure belt? Now the clouds are solid and scrape the mast-tops aggressively. Derek the auto-pilot takes over and I go

40

below for a breather, boots wet in the bilges. Then it's dark again and Derek is having trouble with the course. Something is wrong but, in an exhausted state, I cannot decide where the fault lies. I go to bed in oilskins, always ready, but the noise is terrible. Derek correcting, always correcting, and I log that he is driving me mad. If anything goes wrong with him, I'm really in trouble. Perhaps he needs more canvas, the wind sounds as if it's down a bit. Up on deck, untie the staysail and hoist it. Wild angle of heel, trying to hold on, crank the broken winch, and keep the halyard end from getting wrapped in the winch handle. Below, boiling hot, now shivering; Derek's not much better, but the block for the staysail is grinding on the deck, amplified through the wood into the hollow of our world below, where it sounds like a tree falling, overpowering the roar of the gale at times. I shall be bonkers soon. At dawn, sitting inside the doghouse, I turn the wheel and it spins freely. Something has broken. My God, this is more than serious. The auto-pilot is connected to the wheel in the doghouse. If the connection rod is broken, the only steering will be from outside in the freezing wind or with Anthony Rowley, who is still virtually untried.

Lilian's birthday. A thousand hours at sea on my own, not a pair of eyes to gaze into; what I'd give for a kiss, a hug. Affection. As vital as oxygen for humans. No wonder you can spot from far off old lags and others denied affection. It does something to the inside, a malignancy beyond any surgeon's skill, yet within the scope of every woman. Lilian's birthday and there's no inside steering, no reliable Derek any more.

Be realistic, for God's sake. Add this little total to the earlier score. Of course the boat is not fit for the Roaring Forties. Be sensible for once and forget your ego. You'll be into vile weather within a week and a half and you can't steer from outside for very long, no matter how excellent Henri's oilskins. What happens when you get tired? Anthony Rowley's only been going a few hours; you can't rely on him, he's too puny. If the wind gets to anything like Fastnet strength, you're a goner. Turn back now, at least while you have the choice. Of course the sponsors won't drop out, of course people won't say you're chicken. You've got to be sensible and then at least you'll be able to sail another day.

Log 1100 hours: Oh, blessed relief. Found the fault which was one of the vulnerable places Jerry Freeman pointed out. I was getting water out of the cellar, under the cockpit, when I found a bolt had sheared in the rod linkage. By great fortune, one of Ron (Pell)'s threaded rods fitted the faulty joint perfectly. We would have looked silly had we been sailing back to blighty. Anthony Rowley is doing the steering and even tacked to order.

Log 2100 hours: What a day. It began with me thinking that I'd be helming for the rest of the voyage. But in fact I've been at the wheel only once today – for about one minute. I'm usually at the helm for several hours at least daily. From a rough sea this morning, it's much more settled with the horizon clear of squalls. There's a big moon out (the one before harvest moon) and just a light breeze. We've been headed off our course, but now we are coming back. Having Anthony Rowley working again has given me a most peculiar feeling of satisfaction. Pintado petrels and albatrosses have been around all day. It seems we are on the sub-tropic convergence. Which means food for ocean life from the upwelling and undersea turmoil. Toasted Lilian's birthday with Barbican alcohol-free beer.

The wind drops away during the night and by dawn we are becalmed, yet surrounded by squall clouds. Life in the Variables; enjoy it while you can. I take advantage of the relative calm of the boat and poach eggs for breakfast; these Goldenlay eggs are great and Gerry Adamson has made such a good job of coating them in Vaseline. There was a picture of Gerry vaselining the eggs in the local paper and a strange voice telephoned her to say: "What big knockers you have." "What did you reply?" I enquired. She said she didn't know what to answer, so hung up. "Nice to be so off-handed about praise," I said. Tea to wash down the eggs and that's the first cuppa for at least a fortnight. The water supply is really being conserved which is good because I'd hate to have to rely on getting rainwater. The paraffin tank for the stove is half empty, so I fill it. We left Plymouth with two hundred gallons; at this rate we will be able to keep the heater burning all the time in the Southern Ocean. By accident my duvet was put on board, so I have been using it to save the sleeping bag for later on. The sun comes out and I put it in the cockpit to air. I change the control lines on the self-steering, lift the floorboards in the galley and navigation area and sponge out bilgewater. I rig a map light on the port side, which seems to be constantly the leeward side, so I can read after the evening meal. The nights are getting much longer the closer we get to the Southern winter.

I would have liked to do this voyage in a trimaran. So much more stable and quicker, but the risk is of being turned over. Unlike monohulls, they do not have a keel to swing them back the right way up. But our movable keel has become slightly twisted at deck level and now I cannot get a restraining bolt through one of the eyes. Only one bolt, instead of two, is holding the keel's four tons of steel in place. Will all twelve feet of it slide out in the event of a capsize? The hydraulic lifting gear should help to keep it in place, but will it? I think of Peter Lamden, his Solzhenitsyn beard waggling, as he gave his doom warning: sixty-forty I wouldn't make it.

So it appears we have a boat slower than a trimaran, much less stable and without the ability of standing up after a knockdown. Here we are sailing into the most troubled ocean in the world with all the drawbacks of a monohull and the major disadvantage of a multihull. This has to be one for the record books.

> Log 0330 hours: On target and going nicely. Moonlit morning with an horizon free of squalls, plenty of cloud, though. She cuts through the water so effortlessly. A joy to be up watching from the bow, where I have been for some time. The brain wouldn't go back to sleep when I returned to bed, so I arose feeling fairly unrefreshed. But glad we're alive and well and now I'm going to do a bit on the exercise bike and then its E for B, scrambled. Cor, it's chilly.

As the Southern winter came near I stopped wearing shorts. Looking for warmer gear I discovered that my woollen gloves had been left behind. I had Henri-Lloyd gloves to wear while on the outside wheel, but nothing for my hands inside the boat. I always have cold hands, so friends say. Warm heart, perhaps, but that's not much use in the Roaring Forties. I made a pair of mittens out of a jersey that was ready for the "laundry". I planned to wash the Helly-Hansen polar wear as I went along, but everything else was to be worn until it fell off. The laundry basket was the briny. As for me, well, I wouldn't be exactly pristine either. So far on the voyage I had not washed and had no plans in that direction. I had often thought washing rather a fad although I showered and shampooed daily on shore. This seemed to be a good opportunity to see if there was any merit in cleanliness. Now, after two months of planned grubbiness, I did not feel as bad as I expected. The smell was not to be recommended, but if I sprayed myself with Jules, I could pass for sweetness itself. Well, it certainly helped disguise the truth. I used disinfectant wipes for places likely to harbour excessive bacteria. I was now able to pinch the stubble of a new beard when thinking. I wanted it to grow well before I hit hail in the Southern Ocean. My scalp and eyebrows seemed to attract dirt, so I sometimes cleaned them with baby lotion. I think I always felt a bit uncomfortable and after two months looked forward to a good bath.

Sir Francis Chichester had been no slow-coach on his circumnavigation; now I was falling behind his time, which surprised me as we had been moving quickly. But he had travelled through this ocean at a different time of the year, when fresher conditions in the northern hemisphere had given him a much better start.

Condensation started to appear in the cabin and clothes were seldom dry. The temperature was dropping almost daily, but I now went through a period where I sweated excessively while sleeping. I would wake up to find the duvet saturated. It never dried out, so it soon became covered in mildew. I had bought the duvet as a do-it-yourself quilt eight years earlier, chokingly filling it with down myself, bathroom door and windows closed. Now a sad ceremony was quietly conducted on the port quarter as I committed it to the deep. I last saw it floating a long way astern. A bit of personal history had gone, with the subtle reminder of what would happen to me should I become less sure-footed.

The next day we sailed into the Roaring Forties. On each of the fifty-three days since leaving Plymouth I'd been terrified of this moment. I logged: I feel very excited and not a little afeared. Not about Captain Fantastic, she'll do it okay. But how will I do?

I change the sight reduction tables over for the 40° of latitude plus and the day's sights confirm we are now thirty miles south of 40°. Clear skies and a barometer that rises and falls, then rises, and stays steady. Albatrosses, skuas and pintados swirl around the yacht and the sky is unbelievably blue. It seems impossible we could have sailed, just me and Captain Fantastic, all this way; to find ourselves on this piece of the world that I have read so much about. Where are the winter storms? A high barometer and clear skies. By dawn the wind is dropping and I ought to be happy, but instead sit watching the sea and Anthony Rowley for a long time. Cold. A great skua passes over and a yellow-nose albatross is studying us. "Tan sails?" he seems to question. "How frightfully bold."

> Log 0500 hours: Began the day with a moon shot and a cheese omelette. I'm getting better at them, but still time to reach perfection. (There are about one million eggs left.) Very cool this morning and the steady 5 discourages loitering on deck.

Most mornings I tried to jog on the spot on deck for five minutes but with a heavy sea I did it behind the wheel. The further we got into the Southern Ocean the more difficult these jogs became. Often exercise was restricted to jamming myself into a corner to stop being flung about.

The wind moved into the north west, preceding a cold front. The clawing feeling inside was there. I unstowed the heavy door for the doghouse and screwed on an eye so that it could be kept closed with a rope. I sealed in the cockpit sole hatch, hoping that would keep out

44

the sea. Angus Primrose, whose boat I had stayed on after my Trans-Atlantic race, was drowned when a hatch came off his boat and she filled with water. I tidied the ropes and topped up the water supply for the kitchen. So far we had only used two gallons. I was pleased.

Log 2100 hours: A reprieve! The barometer remains steady so it can't be a dreaded cold front roaring at us, can it? The wind died away to less than ten knots but now it's back at fifteen to twenty knots. We're lucky enough to have it abaft the beam. A gorgeous dark winter's starry night. Underneath is illuminated phosphorescence.

The water was so fabulously clear that I would stare into it, mesmerised by the rush past me and the hiss of the wake. Anthony Rowley creaking from side to side; he, too, appeared to be hypnotised by the perfect motion as we raced into the blackness. Was anything in the way? Unless it carried a light, you wouldn't know till too late. We couldn't know for certain that land would not suddenly spring up in the middle of the night and destroy us. But I had to believe my navigation was right, and the charts showed clear water ahead.

Two months of loneliness; I hold a party. A large meal is prepared and the stock of small bottles of Moët goes down at a surprising rate. I dance and sing to Supertramp, fortunately there is no audience. We are now ninety miles into the Roaring Forties and soon the chemical change overpowers the clawing inside and I have to tell myself to be very careful when leaning over the side of the boat to relieve some of the wine. I see the water creaming past and it warns me to keep one hand for the ship. One mistake, that's all I need to make, and that will be the end. I tell myself that I will never make that error. The lessons we have to learn in life near death.

The barometer started to plunge. By three days, more than sixty knots of wind was hitting the boat. Then followed the first hurricane – described in chapter one – and Captain Fantastic was thrown over with her keel in the air, thrashing desperately for the stability of water, resembling a harpooned whale in its death throes.

5

Log 1200 hours: Feel sick and wrecked and not at all ambitious. Cape Town is just 240 miles away and very tempting. We are beating and it is a poor heading, but better than watching foaming avalanches.

The wind is down to a gusty thirty knots and the dreadful shriek silenced in the rigging. Splash, splash as the bilgewater crosses and recrosses the floor, trying to reach the batteries. A lonely albatross searching for squid, a long water snake by the main wheel, quite dead now. Pulling in trailing halyards and sheets, I find three are jammed round the rudder. Surging ocean pushing at the ropes, puts massive strain on the rudder pintle. Losing the rudder would be close to the end of everything. Try to free the sheets, thick red and yellow ropes, but they are jammed where the rudder juts down from the skeg. I always loathed that idea and now it is threatening everything. Damn, damn. Clothes off. Jeans and navy jersey on. Can't go in without dark clothes. Sharks see pale human flesh as edibles, they say. It's freezing in the wind, but that makes the water seem warmer as I edge down over the transom and the sharp edges of the self-steering support. Me hanked on with the Britax harness. Okay, in we go.

Christ, it's freezing, water soaking through, me bashed by the surging against the hull. Down, take a breath and dive. Can't get down. Not without colliding with the rudder. The surge of water round the stern is frightening, thumping me into the hull painfully. Up for air. Head rammed against crushed self-steering paddle. Hell, it's beautiful and clear in the water. But the salt stings. Should have used the goggles. No, I can't reach the jammed ropes. I'm not even getting near. Look at that fish by the keel; shining rainbow alive. That's freedom, that really is grace. It is so cold. No, I'll never get there unless I take the harness off. Like hell you do, mate. You'd be swirled right away from the boat. Better to lose the rudder and hold on to life, at least for a while. Death achieves nothing. Yes, yes. I can be a right nag at times. Now I'm bleeding from my forehead. Keep bashing that paddle and it hurts. Blood attracts sharks, so they say. Don't put it to the test, get out. Up on to the rudder top, climbing over the self-steering. That was a good sleep during the night. Thank heavens we're alone in this ocean. Get one of the wooden paddles and try to shift the ropes with that, but it won't reach. Not even when I climb down the transom again. Shuddering with the cold, plongeur's fingers. This is hopeless. But I've got to do something. Cut the bastards off, that's a thought. But then we'll be left with three ropes trailing from both sides of the rudder. But I've got to try something. If the wind starts honking up again we'll lose the rudder. Out with the Sabatier cooking knife; it'll be a long time before that sees a vegetable again. Perhaps a year. A year! How can we continue for a year? I want to speak to someone. Come on, come on, this is no time for tears. Carving through the ropes. Which wrap themselves stubbornly round the rudder. Told you so. You'll have to ask God to help. I can't, I'd feel stupid. Who else can I ask? "God, I need your help." This is crazy. He hasn't got time to watch out for me. Yet, someone has let me survive this far. God is omnipresent, he's everywhere. No, I can't accept that. Well, he might be able to be in a lot of places, but I bet you won't find him in the Southern Ocean. But perhaps he has ambassadors who keep an eye out on his behalf. No. Is it possible? Well, ask and you might find out. In Maori culture there was one master god, Io, and many other gods with special responsibilities. Yes, that seems possible. But how to address my helper? If you don't know a policeman's rank, you call him officer; a bit of flattery here may work, too. Don't be facetious, this is serious.

"God, I can't do it myself. I need help." Shuddering and moving the wheel from lock to lock. Those ropes have to come off the rudder before they wreck it. Leaning over the starboard quarter, turning the wheel and watching. The yellow staysail sheet slips from the rudder and drifts off in the stream. I can't believe it. One of the red ropes now goes. One to go, one to go. Is it me turning the wheel, but I turned it before and nothing happened. Or is it . . .? The third rope goes. The ropes are gone, the rudder's clear. "God, if you did it, thanks very much. I don't know what else to say."

Tea to warm me. Into dry smelly Helly-Hansen polar wear. Out to raise the yankee sails. It takes an hour, but we're doing five knots again. I'll improve this time one day. Then get the mainsail up, bitching that Sir Francis Chichester boasted he could raise his mainsail in a following wind, but he never disclosed his method. So glad to have Dead-Eyed Derek working again. What happened to you, old fellow? The sea is still big, but it is going down and the wind is working its way forward as the depression rushes on eastwards, perhaps never to stop. It's an ill wind that brings no charge, and the batteries are well filled; the wind generator has the voltage up to fifteen.

My route round jutting Africa should keep me well clear of the Agulhas Bank, that shallow water notorious for enormous seas and bad weather. But the current from Antarctica and our lying ahull is pushing us towards it. I need two sextant sights, for a positive fix, to show where we are, but the swell is so big, how can I tell which is sea and which the true horizon? How reliable is the sextant now anyhow? If we get too close to the Agulhas Bank, there will be no sea room to run to when the next cold front arrives, and there *will* be another one, no doubt about that. But when? That is the question. I hope it's a long way off, as the pilot book gives grave warnings of the severity and regularity of these storms. Got to be sure we won't hit a coastline or the Agulhas Bank itself if we are – when we are – forced down to bare poles again. But how else to find out where we are? Then I remember that I have an Aptel radio direction finder on board.

Read the radio signals book, there is one long-range radio beacon off South Africa called George. I take the instrument up on deck and listen. Morse, dah-dah-dit. Letter G. Dah-dah-dit. Letter G again, GG, the identification for the beacon. George, George, I love you. It doesn't show how far off we are but it confirms that way over there is civilisation on a land called South Africa. I've never been there, don't suppose I ever will. Unless we get the navigation wrong in the next storm. I draw a line on the chart. How accurate, I wonder. Really I need more than one beam within range to give a proper fix but at least this shows we need two to three storm-free days to be certain of not being wrecked. Will nature oblige? Unlikely, but it's hard to believe such a ferocious storm could be followed quickly by another. No, we'll be all right. With a bit of luck the wind will hold.

Log 2020 hours: From the torment of the night, we are all but becalmed now. Are we well clear of the Agulhas Bank? Our snatched sun sight says yes. Aptel says GG is 060°. So it is anybody's guess tonight. It's quite nice out. Mild, partly clear sky. Getting cleaned up and ready for the next and praying for sea room for it.

Such a long way to go, me and Captain Fantastic. I am being miserly with the water but, thanks to Barbican beer and wine, I don't have to go thirsty. Now it's colder, I've started using tea or coffee for the first time. I have been logging each time I go to the fresh water. About one cuppa and one coffee a day at present. It has not been used for anything else, my usual racing pattern of the barest minimum. The heater has been used for the first time this week, too, for a total of about nine hours. This Taylor paraffin heater is remarkably economical.

Another day, and the reality of how close we had been to death makes itself felt. I manage to get a meridian sight, which gives the latitude, but that doesn't help. I write in the log: I am suffering the most awful mental anguish – all to do with the storm and thinking that was the end. Now the frustrations of a becalming near the Agulhas. I'm in a cleft stick. I couldn't possibly retire, yet my nerve is unsettled over future prospects if we proceed. The meridian put us at $38° 05'$ S. I can't believe we've been driven this high. Very disappointing.

Now the barometer starts to plunge again. In tune with my spirits.

Celebrate our ninth week at sea today, or is it nine years, I write in the log. The barometer continues to fall – down twelve millibars, and we are in a gale again. The Cape of Storms seems a huge magnet dragging us closer. We are edging past Africa, slowly, but the room needed if this gale develops is becoming more and more restricted. A strong current must be forcing us closer, for the more I try to aim away from danger, the more we are drawn to the Agulhas Bank. I grab a sun sight when a huge black mass comes bearing down. The sea is up again and from the tables I calculate that we've been pushed up 180 miles. It defies reasoning.

The start of the front arrives and the wind comes round till now we are heading hard into the wind, which seems determined to push us towards land, even though it is still a long way off, I hope. I drop the staysail, I raise it. Then it has to come down again. Only a lot of sail can keep us on a course to clear South Africa, but the wind is too strong. The sea is confused and pushes the bow off course. A sight of Venus during dusk helps to confirm how bad the heading is, but the Aptel kindly produces 035° to dear old George, so at least we are getting past the Cape. But how far off? I can stand the peril of storms if there's some fairness about it. This brutality plus the risk of dying on a shore is unfair and too frightening.

The motion below is awful, so dinner has to be an omelette again, which I enjoy, jammed into a corner beside the cooker. The barometer is taking a long time to recover, but it creeps up half a millibar as I go to bed clothed as usual. I go straight to sleep to dream that Carol is walking through Portchester Castle with me. I say how I like timber and stone as decor and we are sitting eating a steak when the schooner comes up into the wind, storm jib flogging with cracks like a bullwhip.

Sleepwarmed body into oilskins, out into the screaming wind. Hank safety harness clip on to the port jackstay, rush through stinging spray and hail to the foremast. Down with the storm jib, and the halyard runs freely. Tie it down. Now she takes the wind on the beam and my jackstay becomes the lee side. Careful mountaineering along the bucking, heeled deck. Unclip in the cockpit and climb over the wheel to get at my self-steering gear. I find his wind-vane has spun round, so reset him as a high wave looms through the blackness more treacherous than the rest. Hold on. Hold on, for God's sake. Roaring fury, feet above the transom and I throw myself on to the backstay, holding on with all my strength. The wave bulldozes through Mr Rowley and the wind generator, rams me at the waist, yanking at my grip, then passes on. Filling the cockpit, bashing the closed doghouse door. Across the roof and along the decks. Anyone for surfing? The water noisy in the cockpit drains, halyards, sheets, over the side; frozen, locked fingers, bleeding nails from the jib, thank God it didn't take me. Bring the ropes in from the briny, spitting saltwater. Always spitting; the air thick with spray. Back to the jib, hauling it up on the winch. God, I hate those winches, so slow, making such a long job of this dangerous stance. Flogging sheets, trying to get me, then it's up. Back along the jackstay, surf racing along the hull. To the door, locking out the screams. It's so peaceful in here. Comparatively.

The chorus is back in the rigging, ghosts with amplifiers, wailing like an old-fashioned police siren. The wind generator spins out three amps. The sea is building, but it'll start dropping soon. These gusts over sixty knots can't last. But, just in case, I am staying in the doghouse to keep a good watch all round. Sun's low again and will soon be gone. Back in Britain it is summer. Carol will be at work, possibly having lunch now, same terrible diet as always, I'll bet. Plastic bread and crisps and hiding what's in her mind. Carol, we had such a good affinity but I never knew what was inside your little head.

We go off course and I feel it before the compass confirms it, this stupid compass which can't show the right direction at all. But always a consistent ten to thirty degrees out. I use it as a course indicator. Zip up my Henri-Lloyd oilskins, push against the wind through frozen and stinging spray to climb over the wheel to Mr Rowley. One of the ropes connecting Mr Rowley to the wheel has broken. Tie him in neutral, then clamber back. Tidying sheets to get them off the cockpit sole, so that water coming in will drain out fast. Back inside the doghouse, the peace of it, and steer myself. Tobogganing down the wave fronts, rolling in the troughs. Barometer's jumped another three millibars, which would mean an increase in wind strength anywhere else, but in this wind, how could we get worse? My reassurances are not heard by the elements and the screams out there increase. More waves break at the tops, then, as if scooped up by an invisible rake, higher and higher goes the pile of water, until the wind catches the summit and despatches it, as a golfer does a ball. More mountains are being raked up with tops exploding white. Waves form over the top of waves and tumble along drunkenly until they all fall into a deeper trough to explode with a roar that exaggerates the strength and weight of water. I hope it is an exaggeration; otherwise how could a man-made construction withstand nature when she is roused?

Early man knew it and took civilisation to places of settled weather. Sometimes harassed by earthquakes, but even that might is puny compared with elements out of control at sea. Politicians and scientists should take sabbaticals in these areas and learn what energy really means.

We struggle in a trough, the wind catches us as the swell lifts our neighbouring acres and we thrust forward. But the panic roaring behind bears our name and screams forward. Hold the wheel tight, don't look back, don't look back! Steering down, down and listening for a change of direction from the roar. No, it's coming our way, stand by. Stand by! It'll catch us on the starboard quarter, perhaps it'll just be an edge of the wave. Shouting now: "Hold on. We're going over. Hold on!" And I'm having to shout to myself, the noise is so great. It's here. Shadow over the doghouse, explosion of water on the hull and up we go. Tighten your belts, it's all systems go. Up, up. That's enough, no more. You'll crack our backbone. We are not over yet, I'm still standing upright, but the contents of the starboard pigeon-holes can't wait and fling themselves at the opposite side of the hull. Crash as the kettle goes. Glass falling heavily. Quarter-bottles of Moët. Roaring above our heads. And we go. I am pressed into the side of the doghouse, turning the wheel down. Keep turning downhill. But the mass forces us right over. Hello, masts, taking a bath? The red tips push at the waves, the storm jib grabs a bulldozer-bladeful. That'll do, that's enough. No further. And the blade takes us on. Water part way along the deck, on the perspex windows, above us. The noise suddenly stops, stylus snatched from the record. Hear smashing below, bottles, tools; there's the hand-held walky-talky that went missing in

Brighton. I should be frightened for my life, but it is too odd to feel anything. I just observe. The water bubbling white. Will we see a fish? "If she turns over, she won't come back up." Again. Well, I can't do anything. I've got the wheel hard over. Come on, girl, come back.

Shower spray from the door surround. How much water to sink her? Fifty-six feet long, nine feet eight inches wide. About six feet of headroom. What's that in cubic feet? Everything multiplies. Still lying on my side, water power jets round the door. Will I fall on my head and drown if I can't move? Don't soak the tape player. Music's all I've got a lot of the time. White, blue, boiling, smashing water, we're being rushed along by a giant road sweeper. Let us up, let us up. Where's the foreman, there's an accident here. Panic seeping into the bloodstream. She'll only take so much of this. The deck'll crush, the masts pop off. Come on, stand up, get up and get out of the sea. I feel the panic, but I'm not scared. It's really quite funny. Strange laughter in the doghouse. We must resemble a submarine with the keel a conning tower. Don't shoot, we surrender. You could be right, Peter, I hope not, but you'd never know. We're alone on another planet, there's no gravity here, so Captain Fantastic won't right herself.

Tins and glasses, cutlery, cups spill back to the starboard. Prematurely. Then she starts to come up. The pressure forcing me into the wood eases, the square box of the speed amplifier comes out of my shoulder muscle where it has been hiding. White light through the perspex and thundering, banging, the fury of the storm back again, angry at losing its victim. Up, up, Captain Fantastic. You beauty, you fabulous boat, you; you've done it. The last of the loose equipment below is still in flight to the starboard. Spares loose from boxes like shrapnel. Ropes over the side, gallons of seawater pouring from the storm jib, the rigging I was so shocked by back at Exmouth has saved us. The huge breaker collapsed now, hopes of its circumnavigation just a saucer of spouting, white foam. We've been forced right round and upwind, but the rudder is now bringing us back. Slowly, slowly, making us so vulnerable to the terrible winter's might stampeding down. But we're given a minute's grace by the brute that tried to crush us. His disintegrating force flattens the giants around. Straighten up, on course, Derek out on watch. Me to down the storm jib. Thick spray, spitting salt out. Can't breathe upwind. Bucket team, action stations. Filling the bucket, up the steps, push the door open. The cockpit's drained. Here's some more. And below to fill again, staggering up, pouring it out, and below. Repeating, repeating. Grab that newly found walky-talky and put it out of the pond. Into the navigation area, pushing the charts back in the holder. Shoving the eight-track as I pass so a tape falls into place. "You are my sunshine, my only sunshine." Thanks, Bryan, Ferry apt. Ferry, very, get it? God, you don't improve; but we've made it, we're alive still. Back to the doghouse to watch out. The sea is mighty and the barometer is up three more millibars. Under the Henri-Lloyds I am soaking, but it is not from the sea. Sweat is pouring. "If you could see me as I can see you, for just an hour."

Dusk. It's getting dark. That's good. Let it hide the fear away, I don't want to see the fury out there. But it would be terrible to die in the dark. It would be terrible to die at sea. It would be useless to die, anyway. I don't want to die, whatever awaits us. I don't want to die, I *won't* die.

A light. There, on the starboard beam. Gone, behind the mighty swell. Can't be. Must be exploding phosphorescence. No, can't see it now. If she had filled with water, would she go straight down? Would I be able to push the door open and get out; would I be tangled in the ropes as I tried to surface? Captain Fantastic pendu-luming softly down to Davy Jones, me trailing obediently above on a leash of red genoa sheet. Fresh knife-cut to get its end from the rudder. There it is again. The light. It can't be. Yes, it is. It's a bloody ship. Heart thumping. My God, he couldn't be thinking of rescuing us in this bloody hurricane. Christ, we'll be destroyed. Out to the cockpit, climbing on to the deck, holding the boom. Spray blind-ing, but I've got to see. We rise on the swell. Nothing. Is it imagination? Spitting, coughing saltwater. There. My God, one, two ships. How far off? One mile, no, less. What, two swells away. How wide are the swells. They must be less than a quarter of a mile off. "Keep away. Go away." I've seen photographs of yachts alongside rescuing ships, smashed and sinking, men crushed on the ship's hull.

"We're okay. All's well. Go away."

Of course they'd never hear. Down to the VHF. "Unidentified ships, unidentified ships. This is the schooner to your port. Do you copy me?"

Hissing of squelch. Nothing. Damn, of course the VHF is broken. Grabbing the hand-held walky-talky, putting it to Channel 16. Back to the doghouse; where are they now? Lights on, you fool, get the navigation light on. Switch by the roof, there it is, been a long time since it was illuminated. On with the strobe warning light. Lights of the ships closer. Phosphorescence shining back at the masthead light.

"Security, security! Unidentified whalers, unidentified whalers. This is the sailing boat to your port. Do you read me?"

No reply. Perhaps they're not listening. Is the hand-held working? Maybe they are hove-to and sleeping. God, why must they be where they can be swept down on us? Up hood and out into the screaming night, staring as the lights rise and fall and become blotted by the surf. Must be whalers, who else would be here? Could be warships, of course. But they always answer calls. Unless they aren't friendly. No, got to be whalers. Calling them again from the doghouse, back into the sleet and spray. Phosphorescence mocking from the hull, jeering from the shrouds. "You are my sunshine, my only sunshine."

Bryan Ferry going round again. If I went overboard it could be like the *Marie Celeste* up to date, with the ship empty, music still playing. They are getting closer, definitely. No, no, it's all right, the first ship is further off now. No, it's just that we were thrown off course then. No, I don't know. It's impossible to tell, but if I stay out here I'll drown from the spray. Stuff them. There's nothing I can do. We're not making enough speed to change anything whether we stand still or change course. Run us down and at least it'll be the end of this crazy voyage. An end to the doubts ahead, of the Horn, of trying to stay sane. I love you Carol and you don't understand about this voyage. And now I'm going to die and you won't know how I went. Will you wonder how, or care? "You make me happy when skies are grey."

That's how I introduced you to friends; meet Carol, she's bringing the sunshine into my life. And you were. Does it actually hurt when you die? At diving classes they said lungs fill with water and the heart stops. You've got a couple of minutes possibly to save your mate if his oxygen fails. Does that mean two minutes of coughing and choking, 120 seconds of pain? If a ship cut through the yacht and I'm sleeping, it'd most likely slice me in two. Would the blow send me unconscious first, or would I be aware?

The sweat inside the clothes has cooled and now rubs with each step. I just feel so uncomfortable. So lost, so hopeless, depressed black. Water splashing about. If I take anything off, it will get soaked in the bilges. Can't be bothered cooking. If I go to bed, I'll be bruised again in that berth. Just one night off, that's all I need. At the pictures, or out with friends. Anywhere, doing anything, except sailing alone like this.

6

I know something is wrong. Eyes open, staying in the sleeping bag; maybe it will go away. I am not sure what it is, so I climb out. The temperature, of course, it's warmer. Warm water means we have come north again and so we are still not clear of the Agulhas area. Damn, damn, damn; if we get caught in rough weather here, poor old Captain Fantastic will know what struggling for her life is really like. Nothing on the horizon, just our usual saucer of sea, heavy swell, but not a strong wind. Can't see any ocean birds, so that must mean we are north of the convergence line. Please, God, keep the fronts away. The barometer remains steady; well, that's a good sign down here. Nothing can change without the barometric pressure altering too. Looking at the compass we're off course and then I see that Anthony Rowley is broken again. This time it's a sheave which the starboard control line runs through. There's one in the spares, so I replace it and get Anthony Rowley going again.

I play with the high-frequency transmitter Icom radio and find some South African commercial stations. They are light and fun and remind me of home and I sing to the records I know. The jingles are almost identical to Capital Radio in London. How odd to be listening to DJs in their comfortable studios and me out here worried sick by what the Agulhas might do to us.

Heavy seas in the past storms grabbed the halyards on both masts and washed them over the side, so I made some nets for the rope ends to go into. Early into the second storm, I took the winch handles below. We couldn't afford to keep losing them. I tried to straighten a badly buckled stanchion, but it wouldn't move. A stanchion on the starboard side was bent, too, and I tried to imagine how that could have happened; perhaps the force of water when we started to come up after capsizing, or possibly a wave crashing into us.

The wind direction would not let us improve the course, so it seemed sensible to make the most out of the warmer conditions. At least it would clear some of the condensation, so I lifted the hatches to let air through the boat. I had hardly opened one over the galley than an opportunist sea threw a wave down. What's a bucketful between friends, eh, Captain Fantastic? Let it swirl around with the gallons we've got down there. Later I bucketed out the bilges again.

Darkness came in the late afternoon and a clear night, so I used the young harvest moon, Venus and Rigil Centaurus for astro sights. They worked out well and I felt pleased.

The propelling pencil needed a new lead today, which meant we have used four and a half inches of 2B for navigation, so far. I use this pencil only for chart work, just as if it might be enchanted. Perhaps it is, for all I know, and I am taking no chances. I have another pencil which I use to note the sextant angles when I'm on deck, and a third to work the tables. I take the navigation seriously, because it gives me such satisfaction when it all works out. The whole thing is black magic to me. It has to be impossible that the angle of the sun to the horizon can really tell you where you are; there's got to be some sort of guiding mystic's hand at work.

As usual after heavy weather, the charts are wet and the table has a little lake floating about on it. I use plastic bags from the food stores to put all the reference books in and that keeps them fairly dry. The water comes from the keel casing. I suppose the dryness through the tropics made the wood separate from the steel and a steady stream comes inside. It is infuriating because I know it is trying to reach the radios.

When the missionaries arrived in New Zealand, they tried to cure the Polynesians of living just from day to day. Now I have to try to embrace that philosophy. Worrying continually about the storm tomorrow deprives me of the pleasure of this day. I may well die tonight or next week. If I have any sense, I will try to enjoy now while life lasts. I invent daily slogans, with which to head the daily pages of the log. Today is the only important one in life. Today comes before tomorrow. First things first – first today. It takes more than a few brushes with death to remove a lifetime's teaching. Still, I will try.

A stowaway appears; I was making reefing lines for the number two yankee when a buzz sounded nearby. Unmistakable, a mosquito. I must be going mad; how could a mosquito appear on board? After all, they have very short lives, as far as I can remember. We have not been close enough to land for him to arrive as a foreigner. No, he has to have been on board when we left. Possibly as an egg. But where could he have developed? The only pools of water around were very definitely salty and he wouldn't survive in that. Now where's he gone? Don't go outside – the wind will take you away for ever.

Log 1500 hours: I've found him, he's sitting happily by the starboard skylight. Don't they have a lifespan of less than a week? In another location – on land – I might have made his life shorter, but here he's welcome. I'll call him Skeet and hope he stays for a while.

You're going to go hungry for meat around here, mate. It's all vacuum-packed. Except me, of course. Yes, you're welcome to have a bite any time you like, but please try not to squirt too much irritant into me. It's uncomfortable enough on board as it is without more aggravation.

When I was preparing the meal that night, I watched to see if he would come over for food, but he stayed by the door. He took some finding in the dark. "I wouldn't go out on deck, you know," I warned. "You get caught in an eddy off the doghouse roof, and you'll be swept away. I don't care how good a flyer you are, you'll never get back aboard once you've gone."

I put some fresh water in an ashtray I pinched from Brown's in Brighton. Maybe he'd get thirsty. I suppose if he could sense water, he'd know where to go. I put the ashtray in the sink and jammed it upright with the Long Life Milk. I left an arm out of the sleeping bag that night, in case he was hungry, but there were no signs of midnight feasting in the morning.

The barometer remained steady, but unease filled me; I looked round the boat for the cause, but saw nothing. I strained over the rails to see if the hull looked okay and put the binoculars on the triatic; I looked round the hull from within and checked the steering and Anthony Rowley's fittings. Something was wrong, I knew that for certain. But I didn't know what.

Dolphins are often seen as harbingers of trouble and now a school of small black and white ones came along. I shouted and whistled appreciation to them as I usually do, and accepted my disquiet as a mood. I had been in a precious state all day. Relax.

The next morning, with a loud explosion, the foremast toppled forward and started to crack. I stood on deck staring, unable to believe what I saw. The projectionist was running the wrong film; this was much too soon for The End to be shown. "Break, you bastard, break and fall into the sea," I shouted at the mast. "But don't hit the boat. For Christ's sake, miss the boat."

The mast stood there, waving, the foresail in the sea. I could see what would happen. If I tried to get the sail down, the mast would break and impale me. Wherever I stood, the mast was bound to catch me as it fell.

But I've got to do something. I can't just stand here gaping, waiting for it to go. The shrouds look so strong, they're going to force the mast to bury itself into the deck. And maybe take us all to Davy Jones. "Break, you bloody thing, and go into the sea."

Find the wire cutters, bring them on to the deck and discover they are the wrong size for the shrouds. What will I do when the mast goes? Only alternative is hacksaws. Find two in the tool box and put them nearby, ready. "Go, damn you, go. Break off. Don't force me to jury-rig you."

But the mast stays, waving erotically with the motion. Up to the mast again, let the halyard go and the yankee comes down. Bring it on board dripping and the mast is still standing. There are big pregnant lady stretch marks where she is gradually breaking. What'll I do? I can't stand here waiting. Get the tools, take the winches off, and the spinnaker pole cups. Anything else I can salvage? Can't get the winch bases off, but at least this will cut the cost of replacements. Replacements? Christ, the way that mast will come down, I'll be lucky to get time to launch the liferaft.

I untie the spinnaker halyard which is upwind and take it back behind the mast and tie another long warp to it, which I lead back to the cockpit. Then wind it up tight on a winch, waiting for the mast to go ping! and catapult away. But it straightens and stays there. What are you going to do, mast?

Log 0900 hours: The aluminium is tearing – and the barometer is dropping quickly. Got the broken mast tensioned as much as possible, but I don't have much hope. Don't see what else I can do. I must try to save it.

Log 1450 hours: It's sunset, hard to believe this early. Got the foremast pinioned with the halyards winched in, but it won't take the buckle out. If it stays till a calmer time, I may be able to rig some sort of running backstay. Worried if we had to change tack in the present weather. Hopefully the barometer will stop dropping.

If this mast drops, I pray it won't take some of the ship with it. Every crash of a wave makes my adrenalin race.

Log midnight: Sleeping in clothes in case our forward friend goes. Dropping barometer seems to confirm worst. So far jury-stays holding on okay. Mainsail down, but we're going too slowly without a foresail.

Log 0300 hours: Winds dropping along with barometer and with just a staysail we are only doing three knots. It's maddening. Our mast is still there, thank goodness.

Log 0600 hours: There is not enough wind to make us move with this sailplan and too much to put up the mainsail. Which doesn't add much anyway. So here we are at four knots, hit by occasional waves, waiting. I must be crazy. It's cold, it's wet, it's frightening and worst of all we can't do anything but wait. So much of the voyage is like a Defoe nightmare.

Log 1019 hours: Trying to stay cheerful. Bolt cutters ready.

Log 1100 hours: Deep thumps come from within the boat as we chop into waves. I check the steering, the centreboard; it's a powerful thud. Is it the mast wearing through the jury backstay, before it comes crashing down? And taking what with it – part of the deck, damaging the staysail stay, the other mast, too? There's a smell around here; it's me. It's fear; I know, because I've smelled it before.

Log 1340 hours: Barometer started its fall on Friday (it's Tuesday). I slept in my clothes last night and I've been ready all day. In another hour it will be dark. It's the waiting that is the toughest part. Worrying about the boat, steering, rust, self-steering and, not the least, me. The frustration of our sailplan, the need to move along, but we can't. Just sitting here, moving so slowly, waiting for all hell to break out. Hoping it mightn't be so bad. What a chump I am.

Log 1700 hours: We're doing some heavy bashing into cross-seas and obviously that won't enhance our chances with the mast. Each heavy crash has me staring forward into the darkness pessimistically, but it's still standing. Still poor visibility, drizzle and the roaring wind. So much depends on how bad this blow will be. At 37^δ we ought to be spared a lot of the brutality of the previous storms. I hope so for all our sakes. Mast, ship and crew.

By four the next morning the wind moved significantly. Was this the next front? The schooner cannot possibly survive with her mast bent over, as useless as geriatric genitalia. Then the wind started to die and rain came and the barometer began to rise. Now I needed to get the mainsail over to the other side, but could we gybe without upsetting the damaged foremast? We would have to do it soon, or our course would be all wrong, and I postponed the inevitable till three the following day. Then I moved Captain Fantastic round, and the mast stayed upright, and I opened a new cake from Gerry Adamson.

Log 1600 hours: I found it difficult to understand the weather today. A good following wind all morning, cold sector cloud, but otherwise not the sort of front weather I expected. A couple of hours ago, near sunset (1430), some vicious squalls came across with forty-knot gusts so I dropped the mainsail. These continued and now the barometer has jumped again two millibars, so I guess this is the strongest part of the front. Anthony Rowley seems to be able to handle it okay. At least for the present. It was marvellous to see the sun again. Good astro sights tonight, except for a star I couldn't recognise. It turned out to be Vega. Our harvest moon is in a gibbous state and it's like daylight (well, close to) when the clouds clear from her. Even Venus seems brighter than usual. We have been doing a good steady speed today. I asked God for a gentler front – and that seems to be what we've got. Here's hoping for the next few critical hours.

Saturn was in conjunction with Mercury, but the cloud cover upset sighting them. The front did not develop and I continued to make crosses on the chart. Not always a straight course, but now obviously pointing for Australia, so far off across the Indian Ocean. The sun went down and the moon climbed up and sank as the sun rose the next day. In the moonlight I could easily see knots I had tied and found I could even read, albeit with a little difficulty, the biography of Captain Bligh I was wading through. I was worried for the people at home as so much time had passed since they'd had word from me. A friendly ship could pass on a message if it came close enough, but all I saw were the ocean birds and an occasional squid which, squirting its way from a predator, landed on deck. Ugly beggar, and a reminder that giant squids surfacing at night are not opposed to snatching hapless mariners.

Log 1700 hours: Celebrations tonight for getting to seventy-seven days. Quarter-bottle of Moët for aperitif and a bottle of Giovanni's Verdicchio which I found this afternoon. Found some potatoes on their last legs and an onion that had little which wasn't rotting. I boiled them and put a beef goulash over that. Music and dancing, admiring the huge harvest moon. Earlier I'd been taking a sight of Venus when I'd suddenly seen a ship. I rushed inside for the VHF hand-held radio and called it up. No reply. I was concerned that it did not show lights as ships usually do from about sunset. I looked through the binoculars; more ships, a flotilla. Great! At last I would be able to get a message through to home. But the outline of the ships was breaking up and it became obvious the fleet was just a collection of clouds. I put the hand-held away and continued with the sights of planet and stars. It's spring next week.

The changing time as we progressed east sent me to bed early as I was getting up at about three in the morning. I saw some extraordinary clouds at this time, unlike any I had seen previously.

Odd phenomenon, I wrote. Dust cloud or bunched particles? It's well away from us, but being towards the sun is dark and unsettling. There's no wind and no land within hundreds of miles. Is it pollution come down from the heavens, despatched from some city, to descend here in the wilderness? If so, how many other patches of this poison abound? Do they ever expire or do they remain to build up over the years?

I had time to think beyond my own survival and I was surprised to discover I was opposed to nuclear power and the dumping of atomic waste. I had attributed opposition previously to well-meaning nutters, but now with hours to work things through in my mind, and without the false mental clutter of city life, I came to the conclusion that I was part of a generation which would become the most despised in civilisation.

For the first part of the voyage, my mind had been dominated by old conversations; I still had long mental conversations with friends. But now problems which I had filed away over the years kept coming to the surface. What did I really think about God, about death? What was I doing there in the Indian Ocean and why was I doing it? What were the real values in life and why, like so many countless others, had I avoided them? Booze, television, eroticism sidetrack us from facing fundamental issues.

I hate heights; I get dizzy, I try to hold on in panic, waiting for someone to help me. But there's no one out here and Captain Fantastic depends entirely on me. I've got to pinion that mast in place because I am certain now that if it goes overboard, it will take some of the boat with it. Immediately, or later, the boat will sink. There is no doubt about that, or that my chances of survival depend entirely on the boat staying afloat.

So I get the old wire halyards out of storage and prepare them to act as backstays. I will put them as high as I possibly can on the mast; if I can only reach part way up to the crosstrees, that's where I'll put them. I have brought some jumars with me: a climbing device which mountaineers clamp on a rope to hold a person from slipping backwards. I thought it a clever idea at the time, but it's going to be difficult to use them on a leaning mast. I tie the bosun's chair to the climbing jumars and gradually push myself up a halyard. The wind is light, but the mast moves about with my weight and the schooner leans closer to the water. I slide one jumar up, let it grab, force my bulk against it, relax the previous jumar and then slide that up. Inches at a time. If I get stuck, I won't be able to go up or down. I'll be left hanging here till my body rots. What a find for some rescuer. Would the boat run aground in Australia, with a skeleton caught on the broken foremast?

Higher, climb higher, and the horizon widens; don't look at the deck. Up more and I can see a light gust speeding over the water towards us. Captain Fantastic leans gently to receive it and we go forward a knot faster, and the gust moves on and we ease back to three knots. If I fall, it'll be straight into the water. And Anthony Rowley won't be stopping for me. Muscles not used to the activity are sore, but I'm almost at the crosstrees. Just a push more, and another. Out round the spreader, and here I am at the best position for the jury-rig. Hold on, then pull the first halyard up. I have a thin line to the wire. It catches as it comes but then frees itself. Round the mast, a shackle through the eye. Tighten it up; and now the other halyard. I've done it. I've got the halyards fastened on. All I have to do is to get down in one piece. Take a breather first and look around. The yacht is so slim beneath me; Mr Rowley seeking the wind with the vane, the lead lines turning the wheel; the gentle white water at the bow and our saucer so wide now, blue with hardly a white scar. A skua over there looking for prions to terrorise, a mighty wandering albatross appears from behind the staysail, a curious expression on his celtic face. I'm sure he's forgotten what he is supposed to be doing, mesmerised by the grace of his hang-gliding. The view from here is incredible. What a perfect position for looking for land; if I could get up here more easily, and less dangerously, I could see Australia come rushing over the horizon.

I climb down and a sense of satisfaction more than compensates for painful muscles and rope cuts. I hate heights, yet I've just done one of the things I've been most scared of in the voyage.

7

Nearly spring and the sun emerged with promise and I left off my Helly-Hansen polar wear and climbed into a pair of fresh jeans and a shirt. It felt marvellous to wear clean clothes and I was amazed to see that my body showed no signs of suffering from being wrapped up for so long. The only change I noticed was that the hair on my chest had grown longer. How extraordinary, I thought, admiring the growth in the remains of my hand mirror, and then I spotted a grey hair. That surprised me even more. Only one? I expected all my hair to be white after the hurricanes.

The birds made me feel that I belonged to their world now. Usually they fall silent as I approach, but today when we crept past a number of skuas sitting together in conference, they continued to be noisy and verbose. Their voices were quite high pitched, something like a parrot. You know you belong in a house when the owners conduct their arguments in front of you. I felt we had been accepted into their vast home. Skuas are vicious birds with no conscience, yet I liked them and enjoyed their antics. I could spot the extroverts and the shy members, those which displayed courage and the Judases. They are great gossips, like all ocean birds except storm petrels. Petrels have a rotten life, I think; they have no time to listen. They are too small and have the wrong wing motion, they are as unsuited to being at sea as I am, yet their brief lives are almost entirely spent on the ocean, except when they return to land once a year to procreate. I felt a tremendous kinship for the little petrels. The prions and skuas have a great friendship for the albatrosses and whenever these giants land, you'll find the others swooping in. Albatrosses, because of the vast distances they cover, are obviously the best equipped to provide news. Because of their incredible vanity, the albatrosses always sounded as if they were giving first-person reports; their despatches liberally filled with such comments as "the informant told me," "I can reveal exclusively," or, "as I flew in perfect poetry of motion, I alone was able to discover," and the like. The birds reminded me of people: the albatrosses of an old journalist friend, Peter Thompson, the plump pintado petrels of Ron Pell.

I talked to the birds. If people can talk to house plants without fearing for their sanity, I could chat to the ocean birds.

I had to call on God today to help out. I decided that if I took the square sail halyard, which is on the foremast, and tied it to a halyard on the aftermast, then I would have a triatic stay again. It was such a simple solution, why hadn't I thought of it before? I joined the two halyards together and, as I was hoisting them, I suddenly realised the flaw. I needed an extra separate line so they could be recovered in case it became necessary to ease the chafe, or to recover one of the halyards if the other broke. While I was working this out, the square sail halyard slipped inside the foremast and became trapped on a sheave. I daren't wait till heavy weather returned. I would have to go up the mast again.

The aftermast seemed much more difficult to climb than the foremast, and it was clear I would have to go right up. Part way, I realised that I would not be able to reach the top, not because I was scared, but because the mast fittings and the motion stopped the jumars from working properly.

Back on deck I decided to try to free the halyard by jiggling it to and fro. Eventually I had to tie the foremast halyard to a winch. The halyard became badly torn, but it freed and I thanked God for his help.

> Log day 82: Finished last of gin (which I loathe, but half bottle was left on board by Ron) so no more aperitifs, blow it. Finished *Jungle Book* and another cake. I'm eating a lot at present, but do my running each day. I think the main reason for putting weight on round my middle is that I am not taking anything like as much exercise as I would normally. No running up underground escalators, no fast walking in town, no rushing about. It showed up yesterday when I was wandering around unclothed, but eating is the only way to soothe my nerves.

Each of the boil-in-the-bag meat dishes carried a message in ink for me. It was part of the huge job Lilian undertook and she made sure that each of the helpers wrote something, an encouragement, or a humorous comment. Sarah Crookshank had been in charge of the lamb dishes and she won my unofficial prize for the cleverest. "Lamb for my lamb" was one, "dragging your tail behind you" was very appropriate on another day, the best was "I see no sheeps".

I'm writing this on deck, Herb Alpert coming up through the hatch, and the sea a mass of silver lamé. I looked out just after 2 am and the sun was already on the sails. It's very odd adjusting to the changing time. I go to bed early now; last night after I'd been there for what seemed like ages, I got up to water the plants. Looking at my watch, I found it was still only 10 pm. It's cold at night so I have been wearing a quilted jacket. I'm also drinking more tea and coffee in these colder parts. A school of whales passed either side of us today; they were eastbound, too. I think they were returning to their feeding grounds after spring mating, lucky devils.

While some brown rice was cooking for dinner, I shone a torch into the briny. What a shock, all the weirdest creatures. Much comes up at night, so the books say, hence the ocean birds feeding at night, but what an assortment of transparencies. Long thin traces, some like old wine pouches, some just like bits of plastic; masses and masses of them. A long fellow who looked like a belt with bright studs got caught round the rudder. Then a brother did, too, and it was some moments before they slid free. Turn the torch away and they all glowed with phosphorescence. A beautiful but horrible sight, so I didn't stay long watching them. The moon hadn't yet risen; it was really terribly black.

The brown rice was the worst meal of the voyage. Brown rice takes some cooking and so the salt in the seawater had become too concentrated. I had never thought to mention to the catering team that all cooking would be done with naturally salted water. I added garlic powder – it's supposed to be very good for you – and I think that finished it as an edible offering. I added peas and veal, but ugh! I ate most of it, though. I was hungry.

Lilian, who prepared the majority of the food list and did the buying, had provided six large containers of salt. In the whole voyage, I used no more than a quarter cupful.

A lot of discussion had gone on among the cake producers as to how much alcohol was needed to make them last. Frances Graham took the biscuit, you might say, with her cake. The morning I opened it, a rich aroma of brandy filled the boat. It was delicious and I ate two fat slices. I recorded in the logbook: Coffee to sober up afterwards.

I wrote on top of the daily page: Fancy going to the pictures tonight, or out for a meal? That was one of the problems on a long voyage, you don't get a break from death's company for even five minutes. She's always there, only the thickness of the hull away, twenty-four hours a day.

I celebrated three months at sea with strong pains in my head. I felt weak and had a constant thirst. The illness continued through the day and into the next. Sail-changing was a nightmare and I spent most of the time in bed. The pain spilled over to a third day and I began to get quite worried. I could not diagnose the sickness at all and worried if it might be the start of going mad. I now developed a temperature and I realised how vulnerable my lot was. There would be no help within a thousand miles, even if I could get a radio working. The headache eased a little and I was able to read a little more of Joshua Slocum's voyage before the turn of the century. By evening I was feeling much improved, even though a northerly gale made conditions lively for a while.

Log 0300 hours: It's spring, tra-la. Much rejoicing and blasting of foghorn. Drizzle, close-in visibility, but it didn't dampen enthusiasm. Suntanning cream and parasols distributed among crew. It's soaking inside the boat.

Falling barometer, rising wind. A dark, cold night and I put the sail change off for as long as I dare. With the strange sailplan our progress is like a bus overladen at the rear. No sail up front confuses the boat, but with the foremast so badly damaged, I only dare use a sail there when conditions are light. Now I have to do all adjusting on the mainsail and the one ahead. The wind is over twenty knots, so on oilskin jacket and out into the dark. I'll only be out for a minute or two, so there's no need to put on the quilted jacket underneath. I have worn it ever since we arrived in the Southern Ocean. It keeps me warm and its padding saves the body if I fall, or if I get hit by a stanchion, or a flogging halyard. But tonight I will save time and wear just the oilskin.

I've reefed the mainsail a thousand times; I know it so well I can reduce the sail by a quarter or half its size in two minutes. I go to the mast, free the halyard from the winch and ease the sail down the mast till it is at one of the reef points. Put the steel eye on to the hook; crank it hard on the winch, and fourteen loops to stow the halyard neatly. Down to the cockpit. Pull on the pennant that is at the other end of the sail, and that hauls down a similar amount, tighten it in with a winch, and I have reduced the sail by fifty per cent, bringing the schooner back under control. The wind may continue to increase, so I need to reeve a line through an eye on the top reef at the end of the sail. It is a simple job that's done so many times in ocean races. Not usually by single-handers, but I like to follow methods used by crews. I don't care always to do the easiest thing.

I bring the boom in so that it is over the cockpit and clamber up on to the boom, holding on to the leach for support. Reach up, through the top eye and bring the rope down the other side.

Phosphorescence spinning past below, the wind is cold; it's black all round. I'm about to step back into the cockpit when I slip. It's all right, something calls from inside, you'll fall into the boat. I see my feet before me, seconds seem to pass. Then I am clubbed in the back and the darkness takes me.

I am back in those pre-school years, reliving the first dream I ever recall. I'm in a forest being chased by a bear. He carries a club and comes closer and closer, but I cannot move; fear won't let me. He raises the club, I glimpse his evil expression, dripping fangs, foam on whiskers, the replica of a story-book ogre. I manage to turn as the club comes down: the blow catches me where the pain is now.

Gurgling, bath-plug noises near my head, water swilling in and bubbling, trying to escape. A crippling pain in my back. Blackness out there, just a glow from the navigation instruments in the doghouse. Wind noisy in the rigging. How stupid, how bloody stupid to fall off that damn boom. But the pain, God, it's too much to move just yet. Lie here for a few minutes. Can't do any harm. I've got my oilskin jacket on; got to stay here a few minutes. Then I'll think the thing out; I'll work out some answer for a broken back, don't worry. I'm not going to die here; no chance. Skuas peck out the eyes of dying mariners. First I have to get to the medical chest. Of course there is a medical box. I asked Stanley Halpin to recommend its contents, but he's such a good friend, as well as being a conscientious GP, that he did it all himself.

I'd listed the most likely injuries. Fractures I put as a number one risk. With a big boat, tremendous forces are involved. I feared breaking a leg on deck, not being able to get below and most likely dying of exposure. After fractures, I said, burns from cooking were a great hazard, perhaps I'd be thrown across the cabin on to the cooker. I needed drugs to stay awake if I was exhausted and trying to find land in fog. I needed to be able to kill pain if it threatened my life. To be able to suture a cut, to be able to inject myself if necessary. Stanley helped with suggestions and produced the magic box. Until now, I hadn't needed it. How do you strap yourself up when your back is smashed and the box is down there in the storeroom? I am paralysed. God, the pain; I can't move. The noise of the wind increasing, the water swilling through the cockpit drains reaches me now. We're in for a blow and I'm stuck here in the bottom of the cockpit. I can't move. A dose of morphine; kill the pain and I can think straight. Could you really stick a needle in yourself?

"Vito Dumas was preparing to amputate an arm that had become

67

septic," I had told Stanley. "It's so difficult to be prepared for everything that might happen on a solo voyage."

They had asked me when I did my National Service what I wanted to do for corps training and I'd said I'd prefer to help rather than kill other humans. I had feared that they'd put me on the burial team, but they'd trained me as an army medic instead. I had enjoyed it, but now I knew the problems that could occur if I moved: one wrong jerk on a broken back and I could be paralysed for life.

Numbness spread through my body. Must try to wiggle my toes. I've *got* to move. Yes, the left leg is moving; I think it is. Yes, I felt it hit my right boot. Good. My back's not broken because I couldn't move my legs if it was. But it hurts; my back. Darkness again and I imagine Carol is standing before me. Her hands are in red gloves, she has a woollen hat and a scarf round her neck, and she's holding a book.

"I think I'm going to die here, Carol."

"It's a nautical almanac which I've written in." She opens the cover of Reed's and I can see clearly the words, "All my love always."

"I'm dying, Carol. Help me, help me."

She leans over and kisses me. Her lips are warm. Then her mouth is hard, sharp, and she strikes my forehead. My God, the skuas, they know I can't save myself, they'll take out my eyes. Frantically I half-clamber, half-roll out of the water, shielding my face. I can move! I'm not stuck here for ever! As I breathe cautiously in and out, I see that it was not a skua striking my forehead but a winch handle which fell from the ledge. Slowly, very slowly, I work my way to the doghouse and down the steps. I sit in one of the airline seats British Caledonian gave to the voyage. The pain now confines itself to my right side and is much less. I get a pot of milk going on the cooker and sip cappuccino with honey and two Godiva bars. Don't want to use any drugs if I can help it. The barometer's just slumped three millibars. Wind is thirty knots. God, I'm going to have to drop the mainsail altogether soon. But I sit in the chair for two hours, watching the flame on the cooker, listening to the noises of Captain Fantastic, waiting for the pain to ease.

I can only shallow breathe and it is the back of my chest which is sore. Diagnosis: broken ribs, probably several, but no sign of blood, so unlikely to have punctured the lungs.

Take great care not to fall again and don't exert yourself for a few days. Then you should recover and be all right. Thanks, Doc. I put the quilted jacket under the oilskin, good and tight round the ribs, then slowly go on deck and drop the mainsail as we are in a gale now. Crabwalk along the coaming to adjust Mr Rowley, cursing as I go. So dangerous to have to climb along this coaming, and also very painful on the damage, but the ribs seem to accept the treatment. Eventually I go to bed and the quilted jacket saves the ribs from being crushed further on the edge of the berth. It really must be the most uncomfortable berth in the world, for it hasn't been designed with enough clearance for me ever to lie flat with my seaboots on.

I can't reach the floor on port tack, because the berth is at too sharp an angle so it's a fight to get out. On starboard tack, I lie right in the leecloth itself. The folds in the plastic cover of the squab have been designed for unhappy ribs. I can't turn over with my boots on because they get trapped under the ledge at the bottom and there's a piece of wood that juts out near the top which always catches me on the forehead.

The barometer rose a little, then started to fall again, and the gale went and a new one came along and the air below was thick with salt. I bailed eight gallons from the shallow bilges, but the pain in my chest made it a long job in the Force 9. Will we ever see Australia? How many more gales will the boat take? What if I puncture a lung? I find the last apple from the case Gerry Adamson gave us and it tastes good. Bless you, Gerry, for caring. Not bad after ninety-three days at sea. Dinner wedged in by the cooker.

It's a thousand miles to Perth, but we won't be going as the crow flies. I found some strange water creatures attached to the genoa sheet. They are like little snakes, with claws for holding on, but there is no apparent head. I listened to the Top Twenty on BBC World Service and afterwards switched over to medium wave, just in case I might find an Aussie station. Suddenly there was a radio station from Perth with a country programme, and I'm listening to Jeff Walk playing the Irish pipes. So unexpected and such a romantic sound. I wonder what Lilian, being Irish, would have thought.

I've been ninety-five days on my own and now I must go to civilisation to have the boat and me repaired. I wanted to do the double circumnavigation all on my own, but I need other people to sort out my problems. Now that it is inevitable, I look forward with a sort of desperation to seeing humans. But once I am reunited with humanity, will I ever be able to go off on my own again?

8

Time was playing extraordinary tricks. Dawn began at ten at night around the clouds ahead. At 0200 I was trying to get my first sextant sight of the day with the sun high; watching a family of whales journeying past. Bulls lazily following the herd, mothers shepherding the young as they flung themselves out of the water, spinning in the air and crashing back on to the sea. Their home, their environment. Sometimes the young whales dived head-first into the water, or just played space-shuttle until they ran out of momentum and fell noisily on to a wave. Occasional perfect belly flops. Enjoying themselves. What a lesson for me. Here was I doing what I enjoyed most of all and yet my happiness was constantly marred by worrying about what *might* happen. Weeks were rushing past, yet how often did I think, I'm having a really great time? When did I last smile? I was given the intelligence to know when things were good for me, yet these young whales were giving me a lesson in making the most of it.

A great bull whale came close by; he was as long as *Spirit of Pentax* and as he broke the water, I could see the scars of many battles criss-crossing his back. Notches on a bedstead. I grabbed the 8-mm camera to film him, then put it down again. It would not be possible to portray the complete oneness with his environment of this mighty beast, nor the aloofness with which he dismissed the gaudy piece of driftwood sailing by. I felt that he recognised Captain Fantastic as part of his world, but we were newcomers to town who would never really belong; he just put up with us politely. I always felt I was a guest of the ocean's inhabitants, so I had resolved not to fish on the voyage. I wanted to be able to get right round the world twice knowing that no living creature had suffered because of my presence. Except for the goose barnacle, who has always been number one enemy for ocean mariners. He sticks to the side of the hull near the waterline and grows, sometimes to astonishing size. He is bad news if you want to go quickly:

he and his like often came under attack from my deck brush from above.

The weather chart for early spring showed severe storms could be expected off Western Australia so I kept a good eye to the barometer. As we crept closer to the continent I began to worry about the dangers to be expected off a lee shore. It was the first time I had fussed about that since the South African coast, three thousand odd miles back. All that way with a broken foremast. It had to have been the longest egg and spoon race in history.

> Log 0840 hours: Wind increases but we're running, so I'm not going to change sails too early. Tried to repair leaks by the chainplates. I was throwing some paper out through the starboard hatch when the hatch cover fell back on to the deck with a thump. When I next looked at the barometer, it showed a rise of fifteen millibars. Fortunately I remembered the hatch cover crashing back and realised that the thump must have caused the barometer to jerk up. Odd to think that this device which almost rules my peace of mind should be so fragile and so easily damaged. Good sun sight this morning and a great find – half a bottle of Beaujolais. Immediately I opened it to let it breathe before dinner – assuming all hell hadn't broken out again by then.
> Log 1000 hours: Red reef in main and tightened the jury-rig triatic, which is a very great worry. Ribs still very painful.
> Log noon: The barometer continues its slow descent. Is this a local low, or ? Prepare dinner of beef and spinach and the beaujolly. Jack's tape playing. It's almost dark now. Strange world – all these miles and we keep on going. Finished a biography of Francis Drake, which I enjoyed.

I could see similarities in Drake's sailing and my own. I know that I am an ordinary person: it was not from conceit that I identified with this stocky privateer who rose to public greatness, but because the way in which he pushed his vessel on, and his determination, often touched a familiar chord. His reported speech to that tough bunch of mariners at Port St Julian in July 1578, as they faced the rounding of Tierra del Fuego, was very close to home:

"By my troth, I must needs be plain with you. I have taken in hand something I do not know how in the world to carry through. It passes my capacity. Even to think of it deprives me of my wits."

I wrote this into my logbook and marked it on a bulkhead beside the chart-table. If the great Drake could feel like that, then there was hope after all. My boat was not much better equipped than his. He had a crew, but in his attempts to go further into the unknown, he suffered from that negative force which emanates from an unwilling group. There were advantages in being on your own. You made it or not on your own mistakes, your own decisions, your own stubbornness. But there were times I hated being alone; when I would have given anything to have someone, anyone at all, present.

The epitome of loneliness has to be a toothbrush on its own in the bathroom. My brush rack was a wire on the doghouse ceiling. Of course many people don't bother about their teeth at sea. But I did as I considered it an important part of my health. I didn't want to find my teeth dropping out or my gums going septic. When I asked my dentist, David Beany, how I could clean my teeth without rinsing my mouth out afterwards, as I would have to conserve my freshwater supplies, he said that I need not use water. Brush in the usual way and forget about rinsing. So that was the way I did it throughout the voyage and my teeth survived. Every three weeks a new brush turned up in the food parcels; as a solitary toothbrush spelt loneliness to me, I always kept my old ones and added the new one to the collection hanging from the doghouse wire. In this way I kept at bay that hollow empty feeling which I'd often experienced in London, even with nine million neighbours.

> Log 1343 hours: Barometer dropped one, then goes up one. Diurnal variation or finer weather? Amazing to see Captain Fantastic zooming through the water, right on target for Perth. Really good dinner – the Beaujolais was just right. Odd going to bed at this time. We do need a ship so we can pass on our position to those at home. It's so long since they've heard from me.
> Log 2030 hours: Get up to correct course as the staysail was snatching but as soon as I am dressed the course improves itself and the staysail settles down. Barometer's dropped three millibars. Oh, what now . . .
> Log 2200 hours: Barometer steady. It's dawn! Up adjusting Mr Rowley.

It's the ninety-seventh day and I put the number two yankee on the broken foremast. When it had first cracked I'd thought it unusable but now I was more used to the idea, I thought it might manage small sails. The wind is behind us so it seems wrong not to put something up front. It is a beautiful day. A long time has passed since I've seen such a clear sky and such a promising sun. Promising because it's not really hot yet. As this is 33°S and the sun is at 4°S from 1000, I expect it to become warmer. I take advantage of the sun, sitting up on deck by the bagged heavy staysail, reading Willy de Roos' *North West Passage* which is very interesting. His preparation rather puts ours to shame. The old ribs have been extremely painful today – if possible I must get them X-rayed in Perth. I keep feeling we are going to see a ship. I look out more than usual – perhaps we will soon.

Captain Fantastic.

A cold front making its inexorable way towards us.

Grey and silver, the inevitable colours of the Shrieking Fifties.

The Southern Ocean.

Land on the horizon, but not for calling at, as Captain Fantastic rounds the Horn.

Drying out the bedding in the Southern Ocean swell.

Taking off the beard in the South Atlantic en route for home.

Log 1100 hours: The sun goes down leaving a fabulous sky. Good planet and star sights, Jupiter and Mercury have left us and are now (I believe) in the morning sky. Sadly missed; they were good company. Oddly enough, fear of what may happen after Perth keeps coming to my mind. But first I must make Australia, then find out what the sponsors say. I can't see the repairs being completed in less than two weeks, but I daren't stay there too long. Sarah definitely wins my label award; last night I opened one for veal, "Veal meat again" she wrote. Today it is lamb and asparagus with a bottle of Giovanni's wine, plus a quarter of Moët as aperitif. All very fluid.

Log 2100 hours: Heavy dew over the boat. Mr Rowley very stiff to adjust – had to bash him several times.

Next day my Aptel radio direction finder picked up the Swan River aero beacon for Western Australia. The wind now increased till a gale was blowing, the disturbed sea started to fill the schooner. My spirits sank and I put off a necessary gybe for several hours

Log 0100 hours: In fragile shape today. Maybe disappointment over change in the weather; it's not a typical Low and if the characteristics are not easily identified I find it worries me. I hate this vile weather, I'm not a must-be-soaked-to-the-skin-to-be-happy sailor. Big sea, partly overcast. I'm knocked down a few times while trying to reef the mainsail. The barometer is up one millibar, as usual I keep looking at it to see if it's going up any further. Meanwhile I make a huge list of what needs doing in Perth. I must admit I'm worried about the sponsor's likely attitude.

As usual with a gale, a good charge of electricity was going into the batteries so I decided to devote some time to trying to get the Icom to transmit. Up to now I'd only used it for listening in to pop stations near South Africa, to the BBC World Service and to eavesdrop on ham chat in the Atlantic and Indian Oceans. Working a rig is divided into two parts: getting the transmitter-receiver to the right frequency and using an antenna tuning unit to get the right amount of signal out of the boat.

I got out the instruction manual and pedantically followed the book in every move. I listened in to the twenty-metre band and found an Australian voice saying: "CQ, CQ, CQ. This is VK6SW, CQ, CQ, CQ. This is Victor Kilo 6 Short Wave calling CQ and standing by." His VK call-sign meant that he was an Australian and the number six put him in Western Australia. The rest of his talk meant that he wanted to chat with anyone in the world who was listening in. A ham in Malaysia replied but VK6SW did not hear him and started calling again. What a crazy world, there was the Australian sitting comfortably in his house beaming a signal up into the ionosphere, a man on the other side of the equator replying and

73

hams right round the world listening in, and here was me who really desperately needed a contact, with a rig that wouldn't work. Ah well, I had plenty of power, I'd try calling again.

"VK6 short wave, VK6 short wave," I began and went once more carefully through the lengthy calling procedure in the hope that I might be heard. I released the transmit button and there was the Malaysian also giving a long response. Damn, damn; I'm the one who needs a reply the most, not you, mate.

"Maritime mobile station, this is VK6 short wave. Call again. I missed your call-sign."

Was he calling me? Could there be another yacht replying? Give the Aussie a blast, sport. I was so excited, I could hardly get his call-sign through, and I repeated mine several times and my name.

"Hi, Paul, the handle here's Bill. Great to make the contact. What's your position?"

Unbelievable. After all this time a voice speaking to me. I repeated my response just in case he was talking to a station out of my hearing. But no, it was me he was contacting.

"Bill, I can't tell you how fabulous this is. I've been out of radio contact for ages. People need to know I'm alive before they worry too much. Jack Huke needs to be telephoned. I'm sure he'll be relieved to hear. Bill, what's happening in the world? What's your QTH (location)? God, you can't believe how good it is to actually speak to someone."

"Missed most of that. The signal's not good, but if you give it to me a bit at a time, we'll be okay. Now talk slowly. Go ahead."

Talk slowly when I haven't talked to anyone since, well, since for ever. It's so unbelievable to hear my voice talking like this; sure, I speak to the birds and everything on the boat, but that's different. God, don't go away, Bill. I need you to tell me about Fremantle harbour, that island in front and the reefs. What it's like to be able to see people all the time and sleep with someone, to go to a pub and out for a meal? Are all Aussie girls big strapping sheilas? Bill, I want to see what a tree looks like again.

"Yes, sorry about that, Bill. Will try to talk slowly. It's very good to be able to talk to you. It's been a long time. My QTH is 32°55'S, 103°20'E. About 635 miles west of Perth. I left England ninety-nine days ago."

I tell him about the foremast and ask him to contact London, but I don't mention the ribs today for fear of worrying those at home. I'll tell him tomorrow.

It gets dark quickly, but my spirits soar and I forget to go to bed. Although there is a lot of work to do on the boat the next day, I am watching the clock waiting for our time. Then it is 0800 hours and Bill is there and he reports that Jack was excited to hear the news and that a Pentax representative will be meeting me at Perth. Bill, who turns out to be a pilot, knows navigation and is able to advise me about the approaches to Fremantle. The relief is great and we arrange a schedule for tomorrow, but now reception is poor as there is not enough propagation between us. I am 230 sea miles from Australia, a day and a bit away from civilisation. I don't expect Australians to be particularly interested in me, or helpful. Why should they be? Still, if Pentax will support the project, I should be able to repair the boat, with or without public interest.

I look around me, trying to visualise the boat with alien eyes. What a mess. There had been no certainty that I would ever make land, so I had hoarded everything. The plastic bags the food came in were handy for protecting films, and books, but there were hundreds more that filled one of the pigeon-holes. I'd even kept the envelopes from bon voyage cards put on board at the start; there were pieces of paper from the food parcels, broken shackles, pieces of ruined rigging wire, corks from the wine bottles, wire from the Moët champagne tops, wax from the cheese. Nothing left the boat if it could possibly have a use. I kept all the used matches. After all, the boat was made of wood and matches were wood, too. If I needed wood, wire, paper, well, none were to be found at sea. There were no handy corner shops. I'd better start to tidy it all up.

Anthony Rowley is broken again and the repair takes a long time. A weak front moves through, heavy downpours souse the boat, but I can hear radio stations all day and at night they are particularly good. I quickly learn to recognise the first female voice I have heard since Madeira each time she comes on. She is Libby Stone, a morning DJ, who has a phone-in programme. While the problem of survival is my lot, I hear of Perth controversies, a man troubled by a neighbour's rooster, bees swarming on a telegraph pole, modern clothes, and many calls about children being pecked by magpies. Miss Stone does not comment herself, she seems a long-suffering sort. Except once in the magpie drama.

"The reason why the magpies attack girls," says the strongest Aussie accent I've ever heard, "is that they mistake them for boys. Boys of today grow their hair so long that the birds can't tell the difference."

"It's not only magpies they are confusing," she replies, and I think it'd be great to meet someone with a sense of humour like that.

The front drives us along at eleven knots, but soon I am forced to reduce some of the mainsail. It's too far to go yet to be risking a second mast. Now I can smell Australia, I feel people are near, that I am not being deluded by my navigation. I am on target and life is only a few hours off. I stare at the horizon, but haze blocks the view. Up on to the doghouse roof, nothing, back down. Out with the Aptel, a sextant sight, then turn the transistor to find the direction of the broadcast station. Search for the loom of Rottnest Island lighthouse when the day goes. Nothing. Wind getting up again and a heavy sea and a radio station saying there is no wind in Fremantle. Well, there's plenty out here, mate. Below for dinner and a snooze, then up on deck to see a ship has passed us close by, unnoticed. Put the navigation lights on; better late than never. The Aptel says I am getting close to the shore, unlit in these parts, and that I am too far north. Reluctantly go about, and run down the coast with a slight westing into dawn. Still nothing, except the big sea and a near gale. Listening into the weather from a coast station, I hear:

"Sighting and contact report requested of seventeen-metre British yacht, *Spirit of Pentax*, en route Plymouth to Plymouth, diverting to Fremantle ETA 9th October. Yacht believed to have broken mast and only occupant to be injured. White hull with word Pentax on hull. Red sails. VHF and ham radio equipped."

Log 0124 hours: Day 103. Land-ho! Rottnest Island, about ten to fifteen miles, port bow.

But the island is low-lying and it is really only five miles off. The wind is dropping, so hoist the lighter sails and take off the clothes I have worn for ages and change into fresh ones. It feels good. Fancy putting the alert on the coast station, I really didn't think they would. Rottnest Island comes closer and I realise it is the first piece of solid earth I have seen since the Canaries, over there on the other side of the globe.

Somehow we've got down round South Africa without running into anything and crossed the Indian Ocean with its evil reputation, all with just the sextant to give us our position, and the Aptel for confirmation near land. How incredible that such a simple thing could work. Amazing that I've been where William Bligh, Captain Cook and Sir Francis once sailed, my heroes for so long; like them, I've found my way, using the same sun-to-horizon angles. Has the world changed so little?

This navigation is magic; I can't see any logic in it at all. To think just ten years ago I was learning to sail.

By Rottnest Island the wind goes and we slat around in the swell, watching a heavy surf wrecked on rocks. The island resembles a prison, flat, with grim buildings, yet for me it is good to look at. Real solid earth, rocks and sand so different in colour and shape from the sea. And beyond the haze, out of sight, are Fremantle and Perth, cities, mountains and deserts. But, most of all, people. I'm listening to a pop station and on the news they are talking about me. How vain to be listening to your own news. I tune to a neighbouring station, and a few minutes later I am the subject there, too. Good grief, I didn't think they'd care.

I see my first plane for months. It's a Cessna and soon it has found me and is just about at sea level. Give 'em a wave, maybe they're taking film. I can't think straight because I'm so glad to be making a landfall. Along beside Rottnest I hear someone in tears on my boat. Big boys don't cry. A warship passes by, then a freighter like a tin can comes along; in the distance an ocean-going fast launch steams this way, an angry bee stirring up the sea. Perhaps they might slow down and wave, and I'd catch sight of a human face. Suddenly, the launch spins on a sixpence and she's alongside. People on deck, men in shorts, smiles, women waving. My God, that girl's got no bra on. In fact, not much on at all. This can't be Australia. "Gooday, have a beer, mate?" It's got to be Australia. People, clean, smiling, fresh from civilisation. What's it like to make land? Had many storms? Are you going to continue with the double? How's the ribs? Have another beer? God, that girl's attractive, and hell, look at that one aft. So soft and gentle-looking. What did I want to leave all that behind for?

What have you missed most since you've been at sea? Asked by the one with the lungs up front."

I laugh. "Daren't answer that."

And they throw another beer over and say, Do you want a tow? And I say, Yes, from the entrance of Fremantle marina, but I'll sail that far, and on the radio beside me the news reports I've refused a tow and that the rigging is all down on the boat; to the uninitiated perhaps that's the way it appears. It's just so good to see these people who now decide to rush back to land with some film they've taken, but they will return soon. Through the haze I can see the mainland and they point to landmarks for the entrance to the marina, but all this Australian beer has everything in doubles. God, I'll be out of my mind by the time I get there. They rush off, and another launch joins me with an action replay of the questions.

The first boat comes back and a man shouts that he's from Pentax and they've got a surveyor waiting on shore and a new mast is almost ready.

Hell, if you think you're getting rid of me in a couple of days, you're mistaken. I want to live and breathe people for a bit. I've got 103 days of loneliness to catch up on. But I have to admire their drive.

Peaceful waters, the sun really hot now, breezes scudding across the flat blue, islands to the south, reefs protruding, the coastline; buildings reaching up, a ship slips behind a breakwater, yachts with white sails and tubby comfort below, another can of Swan beer. The Beach Boys, "Good Vibrations". Hear, hear! Good vibes all round. Dropping the sails off the marina and Bill Douglas comes alongside in his launch *Genevieve*. A rope over and smiles. "Welcome to Australia, sport; it's all right, use our line. How's the old ribcage? Don't you worry, mate, we'll have you on dry land in no time." We ground going in, but what the hell, yachts moored, clank-clank of rigging in the wind, water so smooth, yellow brick clubhouse where they'll hide you from the elements and you can forget the cold fronts and the water ruining everything in the bilges. A crowd on the jetty, clapping as we go alongside. For me? No, I should clap for you; you've brought me in from *that* out there. Happy people. Staring at me. Is he mad, is the lone pom crazy after all that time at sea? He's not mad, but he's crazy to see you all. God, it's so good to look at your faces, see your eyes and hear you being encouraging. A TV crew tries to argue with the customs man but he steps firmly on board first and we go below to a wad of written questions. My passport's out of date. Not surprising. Didn't expect to be landing anywhere. A chorus from the jetty: "His passport's expired."

"I don't know what this'll mean. You can't land without a passport."

You'll have to chain me down if you think I'm staying here, I think to myself.

From the jetty: "Poor bugger's got to stay on board."

"But it's Friday. He'll be there all weekend."

"Shit, that's not a fair go."

"What about his ribs?"

Finally the customs man agrees that I can go on to *Genevieve* for a few cans of beer while he makes some phone calls, but it has taken too long for the television crew who have taken off for the boozer.

I step out of the boat on to the jetty, and the jetty doesn't move. I meet Bill Lowe from Lloyds and Jim Hugo, Pentax's man in Western Australia. I press a kiss to the jetty and a crewman from *Siska* says he'll tie the sails down and secure the amazing Captain Fantastic.

"We'll go to *Genevieve* for a few beers while they sort out the passport," Jim said, smiling. "Then, if you like, we can provide a bath, bite and a bang." Could they provide a better welcome once through the pearly gates?

We went on to *Genevieve*, the beer flowed, someone opened a sideboard and a huge television set popped out, and we watched the lone yachtsman arriving in Australia. It confirmed that I was in God's own country, as they say.

9

Jim's car moves on to the motorway and we are doing much more than Fantastic's ten knots. The incredible magic of petrol causing an engine to turn wheels has almost escaped me. Yet I know I could drive without even thinking about it, although I've not seen or heard a combustion engine for so long. Will my lungs prove cleaner than everyone else's when I'm X-rayed tomorrow? The chest feels good, I feel good; though a bit mixed up by all the Aussie beer they pour down me. But it will take more than alcohol to put me out tonight. Have I not yet been long enough at sea to appreciate all the things I've taken for granted in the past? Other cars race past, people rushing on important errands: to the pub, home, to work, from work, to earn money, to keep up with the neighbours. No, no more thoughts like that; if that's what they want to do, if that's what seems important to them, let them do it. They want to live their lives their way; just as I do. God, it's great to be back in life.

We're in a Perth suburb and here's a dog, tail wagging, Jim's pet. Must be great to have something so pleased to see you every day. And here's the missus. Hi, Brenda! She's smashing; must be marvellous to have someone like that love you. And the sons. Hello, Jeffrey, hi, Chris.

Yes, I'd love a shower. I haven't washed since England. And you turn on a tap and fresh hot water comes out and there's no limit to the supply. Washing my hair, God that feels good, after so long. Soap suds and a long soak. Rodgers, you've put some weight on. Quite a spare middle there. A fresh towel; must smell it, gentle perfume. I didn't realise you'd got so white, old body. Still, a bit of Oz sunshine should bring up the melanin. Into unworn clothes, but they're stale compared with the towel. Locked away from the air in the bag.

Hi, folks, I'm out. That's the bath part, eh, Jim? Restaurant's booked, so back in the car and Brenda's perfume and soft hair. Crawling by the curb. God, Jim, you have trouble parking here, too? Here in huge Australia. No problem in the ocean, though.

The restaurant is Italian and our man at the door has an Australian accent, though he couldn't look more Roman. Great, the table's set for four. Is there some company lined up for me? But mustn't appear too keen; especially not in this chauvinist place. But it's very difficult to hold back, I'm just so amazed and excited to be with people again. One kiss from a perfumed lady and I'll be finished. Sure of it. We're through the first bottle of wine and we haven't begun the meal yet. Here's another with the main course, and, surprisingly, I don't think I can manage it all. I'm not used to several courses. Just one in Ron's lunchbox, the plastic lunchbox that Ron left on board and became my evening dinner plate. It's got high sides to stop the food spilling out and it is easy to clean. Must make a note to get another saucepan. We are talking about sponsorship and Jim is encouraging about the chances of getting the boat repaired and going again soon. Tonight I couldn't give a damn about the boat or the sea; but you can't tell people that.

Well, Jim, that takes care of the bite. No, we have some sweet, cheese and more wine, and still the fourth setting is unused. Another bottle of wine? Golly, the old plimsol line's slipping a bit. But what the hell, it tastes good and I'm not driving. Here's to life and love, Jim and Brenda. Tonight I can really relax. The sea can't kill me here; my bed can't flood, trapping me in a vessel spiralling to the home of the giant squids. Thank you, God, for all this. Hope I don't have to stand up just yet, the room seems quite unsteady. I hear laughing; it's me, it's all of us. Jim has been telling jokes and we're laughing together. It's great to be with friends, laughing like this. I'd forgotten how good it is. No, I don't think I realised before how important it is. We go to the car and leave the empty fourth place behind.

It's morning and there is nobody beside me. Night fantasies of that fourth place dissolve. I have breakfast with the family, then we go to Fremantle to admire the schooner with the crowd gathered round. A television news team ask questions, then over to the yacht club to be cheery with two women in the bar over more Aussie beer. The girls want to see the boat. As they clamber through making distinctive Australian exclamations, I find it hard to believe this has been my home for so long. She already seems to belong to another age. I'm Merran, says one of Captain Fantastic's admirers, and I think I love you Merran and that perfume. And your friend, too. Brave to do the journey? Hell, no, I sail alone only because no one will come with me. Laughs and back for more beer, thoughts far removed from seafaring and Merran says, Let's meet the next day; Can't wait, I say, and they don't know how true that is.

Everything seems so unreal as I go shopping with Jim's family. Humans everywhere, sun hot on us; visit a doctor who prods, says the ribs are knitting well and talks about the hunt he loves, just outside Perth; they chase kangaroos instead of foxes, he says. A nurse in radiology pictures my insides and we learn that all is repairing. "But don't let them squeeze you too tightly," says the lady in white, and I cliché back, "Chance would be a fine thing."

Brenda and family are sorting through the voyage clothes, reeking in the back-garden sun, ready for the washing machine. People and places become hazy and surreal as more of the endless drinks take effect; I am dimly aware of talking to newspapers and seeing someone familiar on television again.

Then it's dinner with Merran and another girl and a Chinese menu. I order something unpronounceable hiding in garlic, but later Merran says she doesn't like garlic, so I neatly switch dishes with the other party who has father's car and says she will run me home afterwards. She looks like she's just come in from the beach. No one seems to wear make-up; you wouldn't describe her as chic, but you'd have to agree she looks jolly healthy. My attention has been for Merran but a conversation, out of hearing, has me whisked off with the third person, who says she thinks I'm very brave because she couldn't do it herself as she hates being on her own and well, really, she just loves you-know-what and doesn't seem to be able to get enough. But the wine and rich food and the direct attack challenge my composure and I do some very swift backtracking as she pulls the car to a rapid stop. It's important I get home not too late, I say; after all I am a guest at Jim's place. But she doesn't seem to be listening. Stop, for God's sake; I'm going to be sick. And she lets me out of the car as if it's an ordinary interruption. I can't say I need to be gently helped back into civilised ways, so it's easier to find my own way home. An angry engine, her car, passes up and down the street, then she gives up. I emerge from the hedge, grateful no dingos were lurking there, wish I had a sextant to help me find my way back to Jim's.

Obviously it's going to take some doing to stay healthy and in one piece on land. I'm already foundering inside. Here people go visiting armed with cases of Swan beer. They must all be share-holders, or deserve to be. I want to shout that I'm so happy to be among people I don't need booze to pep me up, but it's their hospitality and, like a certain lady, they don't understand no thanks.

Next evening a man turns up to say he's an attorney, acting for a syndicate, which wants me to race a local yachtsman. An Aussie has left to go twice round the world. I am to pursue him, catch him and take a film of him.

This annoys me: it was my original idea, I did the initial planning and now a man from Western Australia wants to copy me, turning my solo voyage into a big adventure film of a race. I say politely that I am not really interested, I'm just off to a party. He replies that a large sum of money is involved. How large? I enquire mercenarily. It is a ridiculous figure, much too much. I say I'll think about it. But money is no good to me; once I get to sea I want to forget all about the profit motive. I want to go round the world twice because there is something in me that says I should, not because of bits of paper that won't change a thing out there in the oceans.

I take a cab to the tavern and am surprised when the driver won't take a tip. The pub is a barn crowded with people and smoke, overflowing with beer glasses. There is a folk singer and the patrons, mostly young people, are singing loudly about hedge-hogs. A healthy specimen near me smiles, so for the sake of conversation and rustic interest, I say, Why sing about hedgehogs, why not platypuses? She replies, it's not hedgehogs, it's head-jobs, you know, blows, the Great Australian Bite. The direct talk knocks me into silence. She's drinking pints to my halves.

I was not feeling well when the telephone rang next morning. A newspaper reporter asked me whether I was going to race the local yachtsman, but I said I had not decided. Before I could go back to sleep, Jim called to suggest now would be a good time to meet on the schooner to discuss repairs, then Pete Sanders rang from England to see how the sails were standing up to the wild condi-tions. Pete quizzed me on each of the sails for about fifty minutes, with suggestions about improvements we could make if there were to be a next time. Give over, Pete, I said. No next time for me. My head hammering. Then a quick interview in a radio car about my reaction to the "syndicate's race offer" and a taxi to the marina.

Jim introduced me again to Bill Lowe of Lloyds who had come down to greet my arrival. An ex-Warwickshire man living in Perth, Bill had begun the Parmelia Race alongside *Spirit of Pentax* in 1979, but had had to retire early with rudder problems. He now pro-ceeded to complete a survey of *Pentax* and then offered personally to get her ready for the sea again. His survey report was worrying, to say the least.

The anti-fouling might have lasted three more weeks, which meant that if we had not been forced into Perth, progress would have become gradually slower, as barnacles and organisms began growing under the waterline. He pointed to the chainplates where the metal joining the shrouds to the boat had been nearly destroyed by the severe conditions. He said the mast was a write-off and a new one was being prepared. Bill was genuinely shocked by the state of my berth and the fact that I could not see out of the cockpit.

Insurance and the sponsors would cover the work necessary, Bill thought, and he offered to supervise the repairs without cost, using volunteer labour. Over the next fortnight, Bill became a valuable friend and an adviser I would have been lost without; by using volunteers where possible and shopping around for equipment and spares, he saved the sponsors hundreds of dollars.

Jim also remained a real mate even if he led me astray at mealtimes with too much drink. All his family helped. It was in Jim's office that I first spoke to Pentax after the landfall. I was worried about what they would say. Laurie Moore, the executive handling the project, was calling and he had the power to say, Enough's enough and we're quitting. Sportsmen are in a vulnerable position with a sponsor because there is seldom anything in writing. Pentax could drop out at any time. But Laurie was encouraging, saying the company was pleased with my progress and glad I was recovering. "We want the boat and yourself right before you go on, and, Paul, money's no object in getting it right."

It was a fabulous gesture from Pentax, but I never did take Laurie at his word; we still tried to be economical. My parallel rulers were broken; I tried to get more, but considered they were too expensive. However Jim discovered a smaller pair in a shop one day and, as a replacement paraffin lamp had turned out cheaper than expected, he bought the rulers.

Spirit of Pentax now sat out of the water at the Fremantle sailing club and every day groups of visitors stopped to look at her. She was in public demand and the media reported her well. I might work on the boat in the morning, then break off for an interview, be taken out for lunch or work with Bill.

The anti-fouling was applied correctly and the chainplates welded. The local spar factory worked on the new mast and Bill arranged for the boom to be strengthened. We painted the saloon and cabin white and she began to look much better.

Merran came to the boat and offered to help and began working through the shopping list with Brenda. I was pleased to see Merran again and soon we were going everywhere together. God was being very kind to me.

I was also introduced to Libby Stone on her morning show, another gorgeous Celt like Merran. On the air, I said that hers was the first woman's voice I had heard since Madeira and that I had fallen very much in love with her. Libby dried completely at that. Soon the interview became even more unusual for the conservative Australian Broadcasting Commission because I rushed to her side of the studio and gave her a warm kiss. But I think it went well and a surprising number of people referred to it during my stay. Brenda said afterwards: "It's the first time I've ever heard Libby Stone stuck for words."

Captain Fantastic was almost ready to go and meals in the evening with Jim and Brenda, Bill and his wife Gloria, were coming to an end. It was early spring in Perth, the best time of the year, and I would be very sorry to leave.

A local ham, Cedric Woods, a university lecturer in electronics, took the high-frequency rigs away, repaired them and found the fault. The antenna tuner had been wired wrongly in England and was trying to push the signal back into the Icom. Only a very small part of the radio signal had actually been leaving the ship.

One wet evening Merran and I were dashing across the boatyard trying to avoid a soaking, when a wiry figure leaped in front of me. "You are from that boat?" he boomed at me in a heavy German accent, pointing at the schooner. "You are going round the world? I am going around the world." He thrust a handful of fingers before my eyes. "I am going round for the third time." And then he disappeared into the darkness. I thought, What an eccentric.

Mr Rowley had now been taken to pieces, serviced and put together again, but Bill Lowe still felt it was far too weak for such a voyage. The makers flew their man across briefly from Sydney, and he had some extra steel welded on to the gear; Bill also instructed engineers to carry out more strengthening.

The problem of the broken barometer was solved by Port of Fremantle Rotarians who gave me a new one after I spoke about my adventure at one of their dinners.

Captain Fantastic slipped back into the water and Bill Lowe with a group of helpers went out for the trials. I was a spectator from the comfort of Bill Douglas' beautiful launch, Genevieve. Watching the others sail Spirit of Pentax was like seeing your best girl friend out with someone else. Mr Rowley was grateful for the audience and broke a cleat as soon as he came on duty. It was an indication of how things were going to be.

We tried the sails out and found the big reef I had ordered for the heavy weather staysail was in the wrong one.

At the end of the trials, a crewman on Genevieve fell overboard – was that an omen, I wondered – but they got him back okay. A party was held on Spirit of Pentax and the food was stored on board, but the night before departure, the meat, in an extraordinary Australian invention, started to thaw, so we had a barbecue for Bill and Jim and their families under huge English trees beside the Swan River, watched by its famous black occupants and pelicans.

In the afternoon Bill Douglas towed Captain Fantastic out to sea and soon Bill Lowe's own yacht, *Ingilgi*, took Jim, Brenda, their children and all the helpers off. Good Australian enthusiasm surrounded us in yachts and launches and the watchful eye of a television helicopter. Then Merran says, Take good care of yourself now, we kiss and she's gone, the breeze sweeping her perfume from the deck and from my life. I wave at these humans, my last faces for another year. But at least we've got a good snug yacht. Mr Rowley steering well, sails drawing finely, radio transmitter going, sunshine and that old familiar feeling of bar-tight nerves and seasickness.

As Bill Lowe left he said he would go back to fetch a chart I needed, so I dropped some sails to enable him to catch me up in his yacht. He threw a light line across and I pulled the chart over. "We were doing ten knots with the engine flat out," Bill called. "You've some speed. It looks well for the future."

Up sails, the space widening, and when a discreet distance away, being very sick. Cheers, Rottnest. Cheers, Merran; cheers, Aussies; I must be crazy to be leaving you.

10

The worst of the sickness passed and I tried to keep active. I didn't want to think of the good living of civilisation, of the gentleness of Merran, and the incredible hospitality. Britain seemed so far away, though it seemed to mingle with Australia in my subconscious. Now I had navigation to worry about; I had to get to know Captain Fantastic again, learn where all the sheets led to; and, most important, to get the bad weather sail arrangements worked out.

Our course was to head back towards the west for a good offing, then turn left, and once off the bottom left-hand corner of Australia, to turn partly left and head off down below Tasmania. Soon we would be in the Southern Ocean again. The wind was not helpful, of course, and came from the way we wanted to go. I was concerned about the reefs that abound down the coast, so we stood off too far and added many more miles to the voyage.

The first night I spoke to Bill, Jim and Merran on the radio and Merran said she would call again in about ten days to see that everything was all right. I said I looked forward to hearing from her, but as for everything being okay; well, we had gone over every bit of the boat, so what could possibly go wrong? I should have known better.

It took longer to reach Cape Leeuwin than I expected as we were still bashing into the wind. The waves were short, the type Captain Fantastic hates, and she battered her way on reluctantly. The second night I had my first sked (schedule) at sea with other radio amateurs; Cedric's work on the transmitters had been good. Now a whole new world opened to me and I made a host of friends, yet I would never recognise any by sight. Cedric got the weather for me from the meteorological service and passed it on each night. It was a marvellous luxury.

Cape Leeuwin began to drop away and the sea, a deep clear blue, one minute the Indian and next the Southern Ocean, was confused. I could get the local station still on the radio and could hear Libby. She had come down to the boat to farewell me; I missed her and the others and became quite homesick for this new place in my life.

I tried to find the cause of the heavy thumps when we went over big waves. The lifting keel had become twisted in its housing and a restraining bolt, more than half an inch thick, was bent. The forces needed to do this had to be immense. I checked the hydraulic lift and found that the keel had not gone down fully and so had been moving about in its casing. I let it go down the last half-inch, but the rollers holding the keel in place had been seriously damaged. I could expect trouble in the next gale.

I applied myself to other work round the boat. I baked some part-cooked bread that the Mother's Pride bakery in Perth had given me and it smelled delicious. I had two silversides which Brenda had cooked, so with vegetables and the bread, I was eating fresh food. The Goldenlay eggs from England were still very good, so for a fortnight I didn't open a tin on the boat.

Mr Rowley developed some growing pains and took my mind from the keel. I could not get him to follow my set course. He established his own. This was not a new error, in a way, because Mr Rowley had always tended to follow a different course when the wind blew harder; he had one direction for lighter airs and another when the wind got up. But now when the wind blew stronger, the wind-vane itself moved.

The Rotarians' barometer now started its first fall of the voyage.

Log 0000 hours: Light breeze putting catspaws across the ocean, smooth but not flattened. They talk about an ocean breathing – it looks like that. Waiting for the front.

Log 0224 hours: Gybe-ho! Sunny, hot, brilliant blue sea. Barry White on tape. A stowaway! A moth found hiding in the cockpit. My sail-trimming disturbed him earlier, then during the gybe he took off, but quickly discovered there was only water around. He made a valiant effort to reach the boat again, but a down draught from the main gave him to Davy Jones. Poor little fellow – he would have been welcome to stay.

Log 0816 hours: I wired up a speaker in the doghouse from one of the cabin speakers. Not hi-fi, but it should be a help. Merran has bought me some tapes and I'm enjoying them. Another two moths found. One poor devil had been crushed underfoot near the cockpit. Another is sunning himself in the doghouse. He's a slightly bigger version. It's blowing thirty knots now.

Log 1200 hours: New moon and Venus looking good. Blowing Force 7 now. Sea rough, but managed to cook sauté potatoes, onions, silverside and tomatoes. Dire Straits on tape.

Log 1740 hours: After dinner, it blows strongly and I drop all the main after progressive reefing. Then the rope leads come off Mr Rowley and

Dead-Eyed Derek won't work in his new location, so I steer for several hours. After some strong gusts I dash forward and drop number two and staysail. By great good fortune, or our Helper above, the wind abates and I climb out aft and re-reeve the lines. It takes less time with the new wheel drum. Then up sails and we're under way. I must reposition Derek yet again. Didn't sleep well last night and I'm feeling quite wrecked now.

Two hours later Mr Rowley's lines go again and it becomes another fault I have to suffer for a long time. The wind goes to a strong gale, but I keep a sked with Art who runs the Australian Travellers' net. Jim and Brenda come up, too. It is strange to be talking to them with the storm raging outside while they are in the comfort of Cedric's house, drinking Swans, they tell me.

Oh, that old familiar scream in the rigging. It brings back memories, but they are not the nicest. Not like those of land, Merran saying I love you and I'm going to miss you, those female non sequiturs, Jim saying it's time we had a drink and Bill Douglas and everyone always so hospitable. Now I'm out in the wind and trying to get Mr Rowley to go. I've been cunning and watched him for a while so now I know what happens. The wind-vane creeps up into the wind, instead of bringing the boat back on to course. I put elastic cords on either side of the vane and tie them to the backstays. Not very satisfactory, but the best I can do for now. You're a bastard, Mr Rowley; you know damn well you've got to stand up to this heavier stuff. It's the difference between ten knots and dawdling at five to six. The difference between doing a double circumnavigation in one dash and having to divide it with the seasons. So frustrating to be dropping the sails earlier than necessary because this bit of rubbish won't take it. God, do we need a miracle. A long one going right on round this ocean, twice.

I've got a big reef in the staysail now and that seems to work well; watching the storm from the doghouse, whipping the tops of the swell bright blue to dark grey, the sun hiding behind the cascades, trying to shine through. Boo, here he is again. Surreal, but what is real these days, at sea or on land? Alcohol-saturated thinking on land, as if we are all putting off the truth of now for something that is coming. But what does anyone know? The transistor tuned to Albany's Rainbow Radio, steps of waves overtaking, noisy, foaming, splashing amidships, moving ethereal stairs, and on cue Led Zeppelin fills the doghouse with "Stairway to Heaven".

At fifty knots and more Mr Rowley can't take it and the ropes won't hold the course steady, we ease to the wind, then the hull is being hammered by the giants, me clambering along, doing the crabwalk to Cat Stevens, to the self-steering; back on course, tighten the strings.

My keel is a giant centreboard plate, four tons of steel, twelve feet deep and now it is moving to and fro in its wooden casing like a knife-sharp pendulum. The bolts are no longer holding it in place. Four tons of steel swinging backwards and forwards, waiting to slice Captain Fantastic in two. There won't be any warning: she'll go straight down; won't do to be below if that happens. Or perhaps there will be a warning, a sudden gash in the keel housing, frozen Southern Ocean spilling in.

What's that scraping overhead? The staysail halyard has found the new triatic and is chafing itself through against it; all that work in discovering a way to have a triatic which can be adjusted from the deck and now it's fouling the halyard. Oh, you win some, you lose some.

Cedric on the sked. The front is 120 miles to the west and the wind will not be any less. Good old Aussies, trying to be encouraging; that's nice. After the front has gone, we can expect settled weather.

One hundred and twenty miles, so if it is moving at, say, forty knots, it will take five hours to get here. Instinct says expect a bit more wind, or is it just my groaning nerves that give the warning?

Log 1409 hours: Ahull. Self-steering is worse. Won't hold any course at all – other than on the wind. So down storm jib and lie ahull, leaving the boat to find her own position.
Log 0006 hours: Still lying ahull. Up for breakfast, then start thinking of a way to mend the self-steering. Tried to get a good sleep, but it's difficult when you are tensed up waiting for that fatal slam.
Log 0823 hours: All these hours working on Mr Rowley. The temporary answer seems to be the string to the backstay. Not entirely satisfactory, but at least we're holding a course.
Log 1410 hours: We were going well, six to eight knots. I was speaking to Cedric, Bill and Jim when bang! from the self-steering. The connector rod had broken and the rope leads were torn out of the new wheel drum, so down sails and a long radio sked instead. Amazing the people I spoke to; seems all the hams in Australia are tuned in to our problems. Bill Lowe has listed all the problems with the self-steering and promised to come up with an answer. Does this mean a New Zealand landfall? It was a good sked and I feel great because of it. So the sails can lie on the deck. I'll try to sort out the mess when it's light.
Log midnight: Working on self-steering after good sleep.
Log 0100 hours: Under way with storm jib and number two yankee.

The wind was back to forty knots and I knew from the way the barometer was rising that the wind would eventually decrease. I must try to do something with the keel rollers. Up to now I had been unable to move the tightening nuts on them, but with desperation helping, I managed at last to turn one nut, and then a second, which had the effect of pushing the keel from the back towards the front of its box which, I thought, would stop the pendulum effect but I wouldn't know till the next storm.

Before I left Britain, I had arranged to do a monthly talk on Plymouth Sound, the Devon commercial independent local radio station; now that the transmitter was working, I was able to call them up. Perth Radio put me through to the UK and I spoke to the DJ, Chris A'Court. Twice they tried to get me on the air, then Chris said a technical fault in the studio was stopping the call from going out.

However, I was able to get a call through to Pentax to speak to Laurie Moore who said the sponsors wished me luck and were well pleased with progress. Bill Lowe turned up on the sked with Cedric to say that he had spoken to the manufacturers of the wind-vane and gave me instructions for correcting its assembly. He suggested a NZ stop and said he planned to bring the modifications for the gear over himself.

What with Bill's news and the rising barometer, it was time for a dinner party for one, using the fresh food from Perth and a bottle from Giovanni's collection. I gave Gio a toast and three cheers. especially as he had been good enough to telephone me before I left Australia. It reminded me of how good friends can be. What was I doing out here alone? Some Australian port was opened after dinner and Bob Seger, another present from Merran, drowned the noise of the wind.

Log 1700 hours: Talked to the Albany net and the Travellers' net, who report that I can expect a High ahead very close to my track which is a nuisance as it will slow me down. When I was giving one of them my weather, he wanted to know how I could have complete cloud cover, yet had been able to get a sextant sight. "You could build a transceiver easily," I replied testily, "but I couldn't. Similarly I can get a sun sight when there's cloud cover. A man's got to be good at something." I tried moving the piece on the self-steering, as advised by Bill Lowe, but it doesn't appear to make much difference. When we're becalmed, I'll have a better go. At the moment it's overcast, cold with a light breeze.
Log 1344 hours: Been trying to get Perth Radio for the past couple of hours, but no reply. We were mentioned on the traffic list, so there is a call for us. How bloody frustrating.
Log 1411 hours: Get through to Perth Radio. The call is from Merran and she shouts "Paul" excitedly and then tells the operator she can't hear me – and I'm cut off by an operator who is tired and a Perth Radio op

who couldn't care less. And the course in these fluky winds is 270°. Exactly back along the track we've come. Frustration!

Log 1459: Wind goes south west; unbelievably good, so we wear ship and the wind goes to the south east. Not possible, you think. But I've just seen it happen. To hell with it – there's nothing for me to do. A school of whales passes in the darkness. By dawn we are becalmed and the sea drops quickly. Without rough weather to worry about, I ask the amateurs on the Albany net to contact Jim, who knows Merran's home number, to find out when she will ring again.

Now there is a large centre of high pressure right on our track; unless we can go round the outside of it, there will be no wind. It seems extraordinary, but in this part of the Southern Ocean it would be quite possible to be becalmed for several weeks. In the southern hemisphere, not only Lows and cold fronts circle the world, but anticyclones, too. It came as a great surprise to me every time a migrating High, as they are called, overtook me in the Southern Ocean. In this particular spot in the Great Australian Bight, the Highs often become stationary, which is hard luck for any sailing vessel that gets caught, trapped until the anticyclone moves on, or until the current in the Southern Ocean drags it clear.

I cooked an omelette this morning, or Pell-met as I often call them, after Ron Pell, who was always able to produce the most fantastic omelette when we sailed together, no matter what the weather. I was using a frying pan bought in Australia which I treated as if it were a new invention. For until Australia, I had just two saucepans, a smaller one for heating milk for cappuccino, and a bigger one for cooking a meal and heating seawater afterwards for washing up. This was a pretty simple post-meal function as there was just the pot itself, my lunchbox/dinner plate and a teaspoon. I used a spoon because the motion was too extreme for a knife and fork, and a teaspoon because it made the meal last longer. Eating and drinking were my only worldly pleasures.

We changed course to the south after the news about a High ahead. As I was about to wash up after breakfast, I saw a whale leaping through the water in the distance. I stayed in the cockpit to watch him, then realised there were many in his school. About half a mile from the boat, the school dramatically changed course and sped for Captain Fantastic. As they got closer, I saw that there were possibly a hundred or more of them and immediately remembered the trouble I had had with just one in the Trans-Atlantic Race, and I also remembered hearing that just recently a skipper off Perth had reported hitting a whale by accident, whereupon the creature had swum in a big circle, then come back and struck his boat, which had

92

promptly sunk. I've never seen whales act that way at all; I always believe that they do not have a mean streak in their bodies, but now was a frightening time to put beliefs to the test. We were hundreds of miles from land and if they were determined to sink the boat, what was to stop them attacking an inflatable liferaft afterwards? Assuming the liferaft did inflate as it was supposed to. There was no doubt they were aiming for us and to my horror the first to arrive immediately dived and passed under the keel.

My God, what can I do? We are doing three knots, not enough speed to dodge them, let alone give them a chase. If they want to kill us, we're lost; we're entirely at their mercy. I remember the theory that whales mistake yachts for other whales. So how to make Captain Fantastic seem unlike any other creature? I dash below to the cassette player, where Pink Floyd are playing, and turn it up full. The LP is "Animals". There can't be any whales in existence with Pink Floyd emanating out of them; it's a gamble. I grab the movie camera and start filming the beasts. There's nothing else I can do. The sea around is swarming; I've never seen such a huge school. More dive under the yacht, and carry on towards the horizon. Perhaps it is a sort of a game they have; a pelagic Simon Says. Simon says pass under the crazy whale with music coming out, and the participants dive under. Are they killer whales, likely to change the game to Simon says crush the crazy yacht? The film comes to an end, the last of the whales goes away and I turn down Pink Floyd. Got to conserve power in light airs. I am very grateful we are in one piece.

I have my own pet idea why whales won't attack us. Assuming they do mistake yachts for whales, they have to be impressed by our hull. Whales are the only species apart from man which places an importance on the dimensions of the male equipment. Photographs of catches in the peak of the whaling era show the old bull whales with enormous appendages. But none were twelve feet long. A sex-conscious whale, happening across our hull, must surely realise that any creature this well hung deserves to be left alone.

With the High to our left, I set Mr Rowley to keep the wind at fifty degrees from the bow which meant we always kept the correct distance from the centre. It was like feeling your way round the perimeter fence of a football field in the middle of the night. Soon we were moving along the High's southern side, so now we could ease away as we needed to go closer to Antarctica in order to get past Tasmania and on to New Zealand. With the wind eased, our performance increased and the schooner stood more upright. Getting me round the High satisfactorily had become an obsession with the amateurs and the metmen, who were giving me advice twice a day. Too much really for the limited progress of a yacht, but I could see it might have far reaching effects if sail ever returns to commercial shipping. Meteorology has become a much more exact science thanks to weather satellites, so the old problem of sailing ships becalmed for long periods could now be avoided.

It is surprising that sailing ships have not returned, now man has the knowledge to make yachts go upwind, for the reliable airstreams of the Atlantic could be used for traffic between America, South America, Europe and Africa. In actual speed terms, many sailing ships went faster than modern freighters. Of course the overall performance on a long voyage would be slower, because of changing winds, but the saving in fuel has to be considerable. I know we don't need ships taking smaller crews, but a modern rig on a commercial ship would hardly need more than a dozen hands.

It's a very black night and I'm trying to get Mr Rowley to hold his course better. Still very light airs around this High. Then I see a light. It is on the starboard beam for a few moments and then fades. As a matter of course I check the compass for its bearing and stare into the night. I can see those odd shapes the imagination teases us with, but no light. Part of a fore and aft light? The disappearing stern light of a ship? Someone on a liferaft? I've not seen any ships since Cape Leeuwin. I take the big torch, a present from Perth, and flash it in that direction. No response. I switch on the strobe light. No response. Should I chase that way in case it is a liferaft? But I'll never see it if they don't use a light. How far off? Impossible to tell at night, not knowing the strength of the light. I stay watching for an hour and then realise we are a good six miles from the point of sighting and whatever it is has to be well over the horizon. Strange, though. My instincts suggest it is different from anything I have seen before. A UFO? Unlikely. I'll never know; it doesn't pay to think in that way when you are on your own. Better to believe what you really do see and answer the rest with logic.

The wind is lighter by dawn and I pinpoint our position with a shot of a planet and a star. Strange clouds hover on the sea itself. They are black and appear to be composed of steam. The sun climbs from behind one of them. *Tena koe, e koro; haere mai, haere mai.* I'm chanting to the sun as the old Polynesian navigators did when they covered huge distances without a compass. I always address the sun and moon each day I see them. The Ron Pell birds are back, the pintado petrels and long-legged Wilson's petrels which I call butterfly petrels. They are ocean misfits like the storm petrels, and me, and they run along the water, picking up tiny organisms like a

94

gardener weeding. I offer some of the bread I've just rebaked. It's delicious with butter and honey and the smell is good right through the boat. Here, have a gorge on this, petrel. But the butterfly petrels are disinterested. They have a role in life that they have submitted entirely to; they don't need distractions. The pintados are not so choosy, however, and a group disperses the bread, bobbing on our slow wake.

Log 0358 hours: Wind comes in from south, straight up to fifteen knots.

Ease the sheets and we're doing a good speed on our course for Tasmania. The weather people are saying, Go to 42° for consistent winds, but yesterday they advised 41° and the sixty miles' difference is a lot for a yacht. I'll play it by ear and stay on this course. Twice now they have advised against me going south of Tasmania, saying the sea will be very big down there. But that's our route and we will just have to cope. I hope they are thinking of the size as landsmen and not experienced mariners. Big seas themselves are not a great problem, unless they become confused.

A storm on the sun has affected a lot of the radio signals here on earth. What an amazing life when a bit of rough weather more than ninety-one million miles away can affect us. It was the part of my amateur radio studies that impressed me, the black magic of radio waves and magnetic storms. There's a great deal going on around us that we never actually see. Well, we can't see God, but there has to be an overall substance. Anyway, I know for certain from my voyage that God built the world for one species, and that's man. Everything else is subservient to us, and some have terrible existences, like the storm petrel. Others like the albatrosses, so proud of their fabulous gliding abilities, enjoy every breath from birth to death. Their task is to keep the seas clean, which keeps the air clean, which lets man live. Of course the system isn't clever enough to dispose of atomic waste.

Log 0700 hours: How different this part of the voyage is with daily radio contact. Whether this is for better or worse psychologically, I'm not sure. It's very handy for weather reports, but it stops my solitaryism from setting in, which is possibly a good thing.
Log 1340 hours: Flat calm after that great run today. Good meal of fresh food, but left a lot of the silverside. I think it has been around a bit long. A bottle of Lilian's Beaujolais to help it down. Yummy.
Log day 13: Extraordinary vessel under the lee; we must have crossed tracks without me noticing. Maybe he's a fisherman, but he appeared to be bristling with communication equipment. Called him on the VHF but no reply. I got through to Merran at last and we had a good chat.

It was great to speak to Merran. I do so need an anchor-woman, someone who cares for me. We all do. I don't know how I survived the first three months without a live relationship to refer to. Merran says she will try to make New Zealand, if I have to stop-over there. She loves me, she says, and that feels good.

Art who runs the Travellers' net – such a good friend, I do like him – says the wind is expected to lessen. It is blowing Force 5 at present so I am trying to hold on to the number one genoa. The part-baked bread is going mouldy and Jim advises to take the loaves out of their plastic bags, which I have done. As they swing in the nets, the space below fills with breadcrumbs. I have started to bake them all to try to stop the mould.

Log November 10: I spoke to Bill Lowe with VK6CD and we decide on a New Zealand stop-over. The choice is Wellington or Dunedin. Rod said tonight on the radio that the meteorologists are now recommending that I cut through Bass Strait between Tasmania and Australia. They say the sea south of Tasmania is "very rough". Thus the choice is between a lee shore with an unlit island or rough seas. I think the rough seas have got to be the better bet.

11

We are well into the Roaring Forties, ocean birds, and no sign of man. Helly-Hansen polar wear on with the anti-sweat liners: they seem very effective and keep out the cold. I wear Henri-Lloyd oilskins over the top all the time. Tomorrow we may see rough seas and I'm nervous about what we might find, but I feel it can't be worse than anything we have been through so far. But trying to find King Island in Bass Strait, notorious for poor visibility, has got to be a much more difficult encounter. As it gets dark, I peer out for the loom of lights from Tasmania. I wanted us to be further south than where I think we are. Cloud cover has stopped me getting a satisfactory sextant sight, and during last night we went well off course, which was my own fault, really, for not checking the compass. It is so cold at night now that I look round for shipping from inside the doghouse. To go to the compass requires several steps through the wet and the spray. And I need a torch with me because there is no compass light. (When people ask me about world records I must say that – a double circumnavigation without a compass light.) If there is not too much cloud, I can recognise a star and then know if we are going in the right direction. The old mariners used to worry about the coast of Tasmania lying ahead because it rises suddenly and very steeply. It has taken many lives.

I daren't sleep tonight worrying about the approaching coast so I am daydreaming below when there is a big windshift, and the mainsail is caught aback. Captain Fantastic falls to the opposite tack and everything's confused. The frying pan has shot across the boat, pursued by the Long Life Milk from Scotland, a couple of Pentax mugs and some fittings from the cooker. On oilskins; cold spray, sea threatening the coaming. Come on, Captain Fantastic, stand up. But the steering is jammed over by Mr Rowley and the mainsail sheet is too tight to be freed. Lights astern, a ship is there; can she see us in trouble, even though we have no lights on? Unjam a lead line on the wheel which frees the steering, then kick at the mainsheet to force us round so the wind will take the sail across. I'm not frightened; we've been through this before and the sea may be almost pouring into the cockpit, but I know there's a safety margin. Scold the boat for crazy angles: admonish Mr Rowley. Above, the clouds are breaking, there's Rigil Centaurus; it's a small front going through. I drop the remainder of the main and bring her on to course, mugs and pan crashing back below. The sea very black, the ship's stern lights showing. Call on the VHF, but there is no reply. Any lights ahead? No, Tasmania stays out of sight. We're on course, but I have to steer. The lead lines have been broken, one snapped by the tremendous force exerted. I steer from the dog-house, keeping an eye to Rigil Centaurus. Pointer, point me the way. It'll be good to see land again; but it's just blackness all round.

As dawn comes, I drop the staysail and yankee, repair Mr Rowley, then hoist sail again. Soothing Barleycup with hot milk and a Godiva bar and contemplating the trouble with the wheel. It has become very loose on the mount, but because of the new drum put on in Perth, I cannot get at the wheel nut. The bolts holding the drum in place are difficult to reach and I am reluctant to attack them. I may not be able to repair the wheel and I may lose the use of the drum; a system that partly works is preferable to no system at all. But the wheel has been getting looser each day and there will be a crisis soon.

The keel is still moving, I can feel it shudder right through the boat, and I don't know what to do about that. A possibility is to go into Hobart, but at this rate we are never going to get round the world once, let alone the second time. No, got to keep moving. On the sked now I say, No more news from me till I am past Tasmania and have a few of the problems sorted, and I go on deck to put up a bit of mainsail as the wind weakens. It is quite light now, but ahead on the horizon is a dark patch. My God, could it be? No; yes, Land-ho! Land-ho! Tasmania, it's got to be. Well, it had better be Tasmania or my navigation is going to take some explaining away. Through the hours, the patch of darkness comes closer until it's a sharp mountain range which we'll need to go more to the south to avoid. The water so blue, a Japanese fishing boat nearby, 8-LEM; he doesn't respond to VHF, but comes over for a look. The mountain gets bigger and it becomes a pale baby boy blue with a white beard. The swell is large, but Captain Fantastic carves her way through easily. We're doing a good nine knots. The steering is a worry but it feels fabulous to have her going so well. And it is so good to see land coming up like this over the horizon.

What about the big seas ahead? But as we get closer to Tasmania I am overwhelmed by the extraordinary nature of things that lets me sail on a saucer of ocean and every so often brings along a lump of mother earth. This is the most spectacular landfall I have ever seen. Just as Cook saw it, just as mariners in their clippers witnessed it, as they tore past under a press of canvas.

Now I see the south-west corner, as I get closer. I can make out trees on shore, some sand and rocks. The land rises so high and we are surrounded by birds, huge albatrosses and thick flocks of prions, all a light grey, each marked with that distinctive W across their backs. Squalls cross the sea ahead and I watch them race up Storm Bay and across the land. Somewhere underneath is Hobart and people. Ahead is Eddystone, a rock mass which bothered Bernard Moitessier back in 1968, but we go much closer, watching the changing relief at nine and ten knots. Tearing past. A squall comes close and I drop the sails to let it pass ahead and then up sails and on. The water becomes a greenstone hue, the land gentle pale blue, white foam roaring at Eddystone. Colours so good on the eyes, a precious oil painting exhibit exposed to me only, Captain Fantastic adding to it with the sunburned tan sails. I think we must look smashing as we ride past. We clear Tasmania by nightfall and a lighthouse is the only evidence of man. The sea is becoming much heavier and the Roaring Forties are blowing well. Congratulations, Captain Fantastic, we're in the Tasman Sea.

Another notorious stretch of water, but it is so green and breathtaking that I will break down soon from the beauty of it all, the world so vast and incredible to see this way. It's cold out here, but it is better to try to repair the wheel now. A problem will take our mind off the overpowering grandness of our lot, so down sails and unbolt the wheel drum, which comes away more easily than I expected. Then I can see the wheel nut is loose; I take the wheel off and there is no damage. Thank you, God; and it all goes back together okay. Soon we are back to nine knots, foaming through the big sea. Who's afraid of the big bad ocean, eh, Captain Fantastic, when there's scenery like this? It's dark now, and a can of Emu goes down well to toast our last glimpse of Australia.

Log 0939 hours: The change in time takes some getting used to. My watch stays on GMT for navigation, but my day starts yesterday. Getting up at 8 am today is really 10 pm last night. I called up Hobart for weather and to report my progress. They said there was a call for me at Melbourne and it was Merran. She says she'll be going to New Zealand. That's good. With the wheel repaired, the self-steering seems much better now. Well, we're off the wind, too. I changed the storage round, with an eye to trim and weight. All the tonic water left us, as did the old eggs which were beginning to smell. One this morning was definitely senile. I looked forward to the phone call to Jack this morning, but it was lost. I went in on the pre-arranged frequency but that was busy. The next frequency Melbourne suggested was not commercial enough for my signal. Next a 12/13 megacycle split, which is difficult with the Icom, and that was hopeless. Try Sydney, they said, on eight megacycles, but there was no response. I tried their 12/13 megacycle calling channel but a long conversation was taking place with someone who didn't speak Japanese and a gentleman who spoke little else. I'll try tomorrow.

There's a big swell running in this green sea and for company we have huge wandering albatrosses, pintados, butterfly petrels and the grey prions. A giant petrel came round for a look – what a strange near-completion creature he is. We saw some black and white dolphins off the south of Tasmania yesterday, so it is difficult to be lonely here. However, I was in a down state this morning and have since worked hard all day and it has helped. I did try to fix the keel, but the locking nuts for the rollers won't turn at all. There was quite a bit of keel movement today.

Log Tuesday 0242 hours: Fine rain came through, then it became sunny. Had a good talk with Jack in London about the rollers; I got him out of bed. And to Merran earlier. I was down a little today, no doubt thanks to the falling barometer, but the links with these two friends helped. I wasn't going to keep any skeds today, but I came up on the Travellers' net and was greeted so warmly that I felt I had been wrong to leave them for a day or two. VK3YK, Doug, immediately went off to get the weather, which gives much of the same for the next twenty-four hours. The result was I kept the light genoa poled out and then had the number one yankee poled out all night without having to worry about what might come along. But for the weather advice, I would have reduced sail, so we must be going faster as a result of these forecasts. I had a bottle of Anne Mason's wine yesterday, but no wine today because of the possibility of having to do a sail change. I need my wits about me for that, even though it is all second nature now. But the Southern Ocean is waiting for me to make a mistake.

Thick cloud cover has left us without a sun sight for a couple of days so it's a shock to find we are being set to the south. We are down to 46° 30′S, and that is very close to the Shrieking Fifties, which is an even more treacherous part of this much feared stretch of water. It wouldn't be quite so bad if the boat were free of trouble, but the keel which jars and thumps more strongly now could open us up in a heavy blow. The rough sea had me feeling quite ill this morning. Ahead of us lies Stewart Island, and to the south the Snares Islands: I need to sight them in order to reach New Zealand. If we pass them by, it will be difficult, if not impossible, to get back against the Southern Ocean drift and the prevailing winds. I sit out in the wind, but it takes more than wishful thinking to coincide a clear horizon and a glimpse of the sun.

There must be a way to stop the keel moving. I lie down on the deck staring down the keel housing and discover the damage is greater than I dared imagine. The rollers on either side miss holding the keel by several centimetres. I have to find an answer. We're bound to be struck by a storm before long. That's the way this part of the world is. Doug in Australia and Ron in New Zealand are both aware of the danger we're in now and are keeping in touch with meteorologists in both countries. They should be able to warn me if bad conditions are approaching. Which means I shouldn't get caught below if hell, and the keel, break out.

Tonight I see an Aurora Australis; footlights at the theatre, huge beams of white light but they are quite stationary. Later I see a solitary light to the south, then it disappears. I stay on watch for a while, but the little white light does not appear again.

Log Friday 0225 hours: Hard work with strength brought of great fear and we have three top rollers against the keel. I think the fourth must have been damaged in the pounding near Leeuwin. Are these three enough to stop the pendulum? Grabbed a hasty meridian – and another blow. Win some, lose some. This shows us pushed down to 48° 20'S. Impossible, I insist, but I know really that it is all too likely. We are being set to the south. I took the sight with a very poor horizon so perhaps it was well out, but the whole thing saps my strength. While I was working on the keel, we were shooting along at bursts of ten knots. But all this has me in an emotional state, when I stopped for a cup of tea a little while ago I was fantasising – erotic and very real. My mind searching for escape.

I am approaching New Zealand waters worried about deteriorating weather, far from happy about the state of the keel. Our course through the water, according to the miles ticking away on the log, is well ahead of the sun sights but then these can't be relied on as visibility is bad. I hope to reach New Zealand near Stewart Island, which I plan to round and then sail up the east coast, like Robin Knox-Johnston in 1968.

But without the latitude provided by the meridian sight, I can't be sure where we'll arrive. Possibly well south of the Snares, as we seem to be being set strongly towards Antarctica. The Aptel radio direction finder picked up the Puysegur Point beacon and that helped confirm the dead reckoning.

Log 0725 hours: You wouldn't believe it! Doug reports that a cold front is advancing this way and as far as can be told, winds in excess of thirty-five knots. They couldn't say how "in excess of". I can see it happening as we go across the shallow waters of the continental shelf which should add to our problems no end . . . what with the North and South Trap and Boomerang Breaker reefs, the unlit land and the rotten visibility. Changed clothes today, so that should make me feel better. Hoping for a good star sight tonight. Oh, these optimists! Still, you have to be an optimist to survive down here.

The wind increased in the morning as the front approached and I climbed on deck to change over to heavy sails. To the north a few miles off sat a huge iceberg. I couldn't believe my eyes for a moment. It had to be a dream. But, no, it was a large mound of greyness. That's not an iceberg; that's the bloody Snares. Can't be; got to be. Christ, we've got here in a hurry. This has got to be a speed record of all time. I hurriedly changed the sails. The Aquair had been working hard, but in these stronger conditions it was better out of the water. The wind was already shrieking in the rigging. I took over the steering and headed us closer to the islands. I could see now the effect of the Southern Ocean drift, as we had been carried several miles to the east during the sail change. The Snares began to look more like rocks now and we passed a few miles off, calling *tena koe* to this lonely barren satellite. Few people of my generation would ever see them. They were a well-known signpost to the canvas sailors.

We were past the Snares and heading into cloud too lazy to stay in the sky and the wind was over fifty knots and rising. The sea was surprisingly flat for a storm; I wondered if the current across here took the aggression out of the wind. The keel was holding firmly, though that could change the moment we hit rough water. So far, so good, and I held on to our canvas as the wind was now just behind the beam. Captain Fantastic loved it, strong wind, flat sea, she kept up a consistent eleven knots. We were one again, me at the wheel, guiding her on, encouraging her; she with a bone in her teeth, white water screaming along the hull, still clever enough to show no quarter wave. Go, you beauty, go. Aren't you the most incredible ship about? Go, go, my fabulous machine.

The visibility was reduced to about a mile, but we had about sixty miles to go to Stewart Island and the dangers of the off-shore reefs. I took a direct compass course, and relied on the drift to push us clear of the dangers. Eventually, a dull outline appeared through the fog, a low range of hills. Stewart Island, fabulous. Much closer than I had expected, and I altered course to clear the reefs. A few miles and white water exploding ahead, the Traps. Closer again than I would have expected. It should have been a warning, but I was too excited about reaching New Zealand. It seemed impossible that I could actually sail a yacht all the way here. From one spot on the globe to a place on exactly the opposite side. I didn't question why there was no east-going current.

We cleared the Traps on a grey, grey day and the wind slowed down. Our speed came back to eight knots, seven, five, three. The wind went away and we bobbed in a grey ocean with a grey shore nearby and a grey sky. The environment had prepared itself for the arrival of the front and was waiting. Captain Fantastic slopping on the water, sails banging, cups rattling in the sink. Captain Fantastic waiting, me waiting. Two hours and we were still becalmed. Four hours, five. Will it be a storm? Will the keel break free and treat us like a can of pilchards? Six hours. The shore stayed near, but I didn't worry. That might be Stewart Island there, but this is the Southern Ocean and the current in this part of the world goes east. God arranged it in the beginning of time and nothing short of the end of the world could stop it. I knew we were in shallow water, but without an echo-sounder I couldn't tell how far down was the bottom. We'd done without it for thirteen thousand miles; we'd be all right. I looked for the local pilot to read about tides, but I could not find it. I got on to the radio and called Awarua. The weather report showed that the front had stopped, so there was no movement of air likely until it, or something else, shifted.

I called my son Christian in New Plymouth. I hadn't seen him for years and it was great to be talking to him so easily. He had been following my progress around the world and had all the clippings from the local newspapers. He said there was tremendous interest there in my arrival. I said I might make Dunedin in about thirty hours when the wind returned. It was one of those statements I regretted.

The next weather bulletin came up on Awarua Radio and I spoke to a young operator who knew of me and said to be careful not to go too close to Stewart Island. I wouldn't be the first vessel to come to grief there, as there were so many outlying rocks.

"I'll be all right. I've got charts of the area with me." Something else I was to regret saying.

Now it was night, we were still becalmed and hadn't moved, as far as I was aware. I had expected to drift a mile or two to the east, away from New Zealand, but was not perturbed that we had not done so.

I cooked a good meal that night, had a bottle of wine to celebrate being so near to where I was brought up, and several cans of Emu during the sked with Australia.

Waiting for a front always makes me nervous, and I put my present feeling of unease down to that. There was no reason not to relax, and every so often I put my head out into the mist and looked about. I could make out the lights of a fishing boat occasionally, otherwise everything was very still. Even the sails hardly banged at all.

It was a very dark night and Captain Fantastic was a few hundred yards from a reef and closing quickly. She should have struck, but some guiding hand seemed to push her to one side and she whispered past. The sea was still, so there were no tell-tale breakers.

I came up on deck, looked around. Nothing to be seen, blackness and the mist. I might as well turn in. Beneath the keel, where a few hours ago lay massive depths, was now scarcely twenty feet. But I still was aware of nothing, except a growing unease. Damn the front, damn it leaving me here in the ocean slowly being pushed away from New Zealand.

Now a High was building up rapidly over the Tasman Sea, forcing the front away to the south. The first of the new airstream, north-easterly winds, was catspawing itself down the coast towards us. They breathed gently on the large area of canvas I had set and joined the tide in sealing our fate. I turned in my sleeping bag, excited by the prospect of seeing old friends again, of being with my family.

On the north-eastern corner of Stewart Island two great claws of reefs reach out, always happy to tear the bottoms out of ships lost in fog. They were grim killers in the days of the early settlers, but for fishermen they provide a good breeding ground for crays and scores of different types of fish which enjoy a lifestyle denied most creatures on other continental shelves. Here they live in rich waters where there is always a handsome feast, from beginning to the end of life, for all the inhabitants. Albatrosses have a big colony nearby, so good are the fishing grounds. Skuas and pintados live here in crowds.

In between the reef claws is another outcrop which has grown above the water and now hosts a measure of native bush. A lagoon sits in the middle of this deadly hand and under cover of the mist Captain Fantastic was slipping into its grip.

Close to the land, the temperature rose and I got out of the sleeping bag and took some clothes off. It seemed strange for the weather to be getting warmer. I looked around. Smooth water for a foot or two, then thick wet mist. Hope I don't drift too far from

Stewart Island, I thought. And went below and climbed into the sleeping bag again.

With the scarcely discernible breeze pressing against the hull and sails, the schooner went backwards across the length of the lagoon. Possibly almost a mile. Now an unseen helmsman found a narrow inlet beside the shore and steered the boat stern first into that.

It started to get light, so I climbed slowly back out of the boat and looked about. Mist. Then something grabbed my heart and squeezed. I knew something was desperately wrong before I saw it.

A solid mass came through the mist to starboard and as I grabbed for the wheel, I saw land on the port side, too. It was impossible. At that moment, a sickening boom came through the boat as the keel hammered on to the reef. The light swell lifted us and down she crashed, steel against rock, Captain Fantastic reaching out with her keel, trying to push herself off, the water shouldering her further on to the reefs on the shore; the north easterly arriving at one knot now, sufficient to push her mast-tops towards the trees, which appeared as the breeze dismissed the fog. The elements were happy with their trick. They had duped the schooner, got her on to the rocks and now only the sea was necessary for the kill. The swell picked her up again and shoved her hull first on to the bank; steel sliding, scratching on rock, the wooden hull rammed on to protruding teeth; a heavy thump from the rudder as it finds the ground. Captain Fantastic sliding down the rock face, screeching, fingernails on glass, then the tide picking her up and returning her to the ledge. Heavy crashing under the keel, the rocks smashing at the hull, the rudder groaning with the force, and beginning to slide on the pintle. Swell receding, the schooner trying to follow, a hooked fish in panic for the water; then shoved again further on to the bank. Native bush a hand grip away, cicadas awakening in the dawn, death cries of the schooner.

Calm seas, brilliant white hull, the words *Spirit of Pentax* in huge red letters. Here is a tourist sight for albatrosses and fishermen to wonder at; me on the deck in bright red polar liners, unkempt beard, heart breaking with the ship. Who would believe this if they saw it?

Can't get the anchors out: they're under a pile of sails and more; they haven't been moved since Britain, the other side of the world. The chain is beneath the floorboard amidships. I'll never get that out in half an hour. But I've got to do something. There's nothing that can be done, except put out a kedge anchor. Jesus, we're clear of the water on the receding swell. But the seventh wave comes back and is strong enough to lift the hull high. And drop her on to the rocks, to scrape and gouge.

Captain Fantastic on her side, the pride of the Southern Ocean. Despite all prophecies, despite Peter's forty-sixty bet, she made it past the Cape of Storms in the winter of the Southern Ocean. Smashed down by two successive hurricanes, yet she got up and saved me. Now on her side, exposed for the coup de grâce.

12

Red sails on the reef, white keel reaching twelve feet towards the sea. The impossible had happened, she was clear of the water, attacked only by occasional swells. These affected the rudder; heavy smashing of steel, the tiller arm forced higher over the counter, as the whole of her equipment was pushed upwards. The wooden paddle of the self-steering was chipped, but clear of the rocks now. Captain Fantastic resembled an exhausted stranded elephant.

I climbed along the deck and dropped into the forepeak, fighting angrily to clear sailbags so that I could get at the anchor. I did not know how I could do it, but somehow an anchor had to be placed well off the reef so when the tide returned, I could try to pull the schooner clear. Perhaps a westerly wind would come and help us. Yet that was only a part of the miracle necessary. She would have to be directed correctly to slip out through the small reefs which held her, back into the ocean. How could I alone possibly get the anchor out at all, or in time? The inflatable dinghy would be cut to pieces on the rocks. The position was hopeless. But I had to do *something*.

At last the anchor was free and I climbed up to the deck, to hoist it out. Around the corner a mile off, a fishing boat appeared.

I could not believe the sight. It had to be a mirage, but yes, it was a fishing boat, piled high with crayfish pots. I began to wave, but the boat continued on course. Now I wished I had a rifle with me, a few shots in the air with a Lee-Enfield would get their attention. Or I'd pound into some cray pots till they noticed. What an extraordinary scene this must be from their boat. A large schooner on her side, and a red leprechaun dancing on the sloping deck. Maybe they'd think it was a nightmare and clear off. Ahoy! Ahoy!

The fishing boat changed course and came at us. Now I could see two men, one on the foredeck, one driving from his doghouse.

"What's the problem?" A friendly New Zealand accent.

"I need a tow off." The boat coming closer, trying to find a route through the maze.

He comes in bow first. I have a rope ready and heave it to them. It drops short. Pulling the warp in, coiling it, the rudder smashing down again. Throwing, and the foredeck man catches it this time and makes fast. The fishing boat pulls, taking up the slack, Captain Fantastic scratching on the rocks, then the rope slackens. Don't say they're going to give up.

"Undo the warp," the skipper calls over.

"Why?" God, they are going to abandon me. Or want to argue about a salvage claim.

"She won't come out this way, but she might stern first." Hell, he's right. The forefoot would catch around that clump of rocks if we continued head first; not enough room to turn her round. I take the rope from the sampson post and rush it to the stern, round the outside of the shrouds. The sea finding more of the hull to bash increases its attack on the rudder. Bowline round the backstay chainplate.

"Okay."

"Right."

Careful of the rudder, sport. If she falls back that will be the end of any steering. But the skeg takes the weight, and she slides like a toboggan on the rocks, moving effortlessly. Captain Fantastic, you beauty, you. The fishing boat gently goes astern, then eases off. It's as if the boat had been tricked on to the shore while God was nodding, now he was awake and apologetic and was lifting the hull to ease her into the water with all the helpers he could muster. The roar of the fishing boat's engine, then idling, the scraping of the hull. The long keel pushing out a spastic's boot, useless without deep water underneath, trying to avoid the rocks. Then Captain Fantastic stands upright and the fishing boat pulls more strongly and she eases into deeper water.

I go to the wheel and turn it; yes, our steering still works.

The skipper came out of the doghouse. A stocky man, in his thirties perhaps, suntanned smile. "I'll give you a tow into the lagoon a bit more, then you'll be all right. When you get the sails up, we'll let the warp go. It's deep enough water through to the sea, but try to stay in the middle."

He's not going to talk about salvage? "I can sail out through there, you say?" I replied, still dumbfounded by this generosity. The law's on your side, cobber, you can claim this yacht.

But John Fewster wasn't that type of man. I was back among kiwis. He was happy to help and said it must be great to sail around the world, it was bad luck to be caught in the reefs like this. "Jees, it could happen to any joker." He was rolling a cigarette, his engine idling, as *Spirit of Pentax*, on the end of a limp towrope, sailed down for the tow-off. We could have been two cars parked on the side of a back-country road, stopped for a spell, a smoke, a few words with a mate.

A group of penguins swam by, clerics on an outing. Native bush down to the reefs. Nothing had changed since Captain Cook was here. "This is the first time since October there's been a calm here," he said. "Most of the time it's been blasting fifty, sixty knots. Just bloody bad luck you got caught out." He lit the cigarette and I could smell wax matches. I hadn't experienced that since I left New Zealand twelve years ago. "There's a fair old current rips through here, goes right through this part and out past the reef at the other end." His mate let go the warp. "If you've got any problems, call us on Channel 16."

I still couldn't believe he was not going to press for salvage rights. He might have got a new fishing boat out of it. I grabbed the last of the Australian beer and most of the wine and gave them to him with thanks. Crikey, he said, embarrassed, and insisted on my taking three crayfish. We exchanged waves; up sails and with the tiller arm stuck well above the deck, the schooner left the lagoon. I sailed clear of Stewart Island before we hardened up on the wind and shaped course for South Island. What a fellow, I kept thinking. There's still hope for man while people like him live.

"What we need now are fair winds and a smooth sea so we can make Dunedin in one piece, eh, Captain Fantastic?" Not much more than a hundred odd miles to go; with luck we could be there tomorrow.

In the Tasman Sea the High continued to develop and the pressure rose steeply. The isobars encircling this mammoth anti-cyclone became squeezed at the perimeter. Unfortunately for us, the edge ran down the east side of New Zealand to Stewart Island. The wind moved ahead; this meant we would have to zig-zag up the coast. A strong tide began pushing us up the shallow water between Stewart Island and the mainland, but fortunately the strengthening breeze helped us fight it.

I regretted again not having an echo-sounder. Poor visibility made sighting the island to the east of the straits difficult, but I would have known how much water lay below us with a sounder. We ran the risk of going aground again a long way from the coast. Nothing for it but to short-tack, a difficult manoeuvre now that we had running backstays. For a while it appeared we were not going to beat the tide, but eventually I could see South Island and was able to gauge that we were progressing. Then I was close enough to make out sheep. I was entering highly evocative country, the years fell away as I relived holidays on this coast, swimming in these cold waters, climbing, fishing.

By evening we had made the right-hand bottom corner of New Zealand and started to climb the east coast. We sailed into the land, then out to sea, then in again. It was a slow zig-zag journey and it was going to take a long time to make port. I put the crayfish into the water now, hoping they would be happy off the mainland. I didn't want to eat them out here, although crayfish are delicious.

Near nightfall we were making land again and the scene was exquisite; a painting of sixteenth-century New Zealand, long before the arrival of the *pakeha*, the white man, with their huge sailing ships. I could see swamps, a stream, water spilling over a cliff, cabbage trees imitating palms, and ti-trees. Scrub and ferns, the smell of the bush that overwhelmed and hypnotised me as a child fresh from England. Bush so dense it needed a compass, where huhu grubs offered a hungry boy food, where you felt agoraphobia one moment and stifled the next. Baby crays in the streams, fantails and bellbirds in the stilted trees; starving mosquitoes, buzzing aggression when you came upon the swamps. I was sure I could hear a tui now. I sailed in close to the cliff, surf crashing on rocks, the noise immense when I closed the rock wall, then . . . "Stand by to go about. Lee-ho!"

And Captain Fantastic falls to the other tack, from forty degrees heel one side to forty the other, pulling the sheets round, the sails cracking across, tighten the weather backstay. Four winches in use, doubling on the primary Barlows before jamming off the backstay. God, we can do with some extra hands for this. Then looking back. At the bush, so green, a thousand different greens, now producing the one magic colour which visitors never forget. The sheer cliffs, surf, white water tearing past us, eight knots, rapidly putting the land behind. This is living.

The sea is getting up and the jerkiness helps the rudder to edge back down the pintle and soon the tiller arm is at its right height. We tack out in the approaching darkness for two hours, then tack in. It's a slow business, but there is no alternative. If we lie ahull till the wind changes, we'll only be swept further away. No, keep going.

On the sked tonight, Ron has to act as organiser because so many hams are waiting to talk. Where are you, they ask, but I have to say I am not sure. Somewhere off Catlins, I think, and I describe the landward side of the previous tack. A National Parks Board ranger comes on the air to name the bay.

"Put your lights on and we'll go to the coast and see if we can spot you," says Matt at Owaka village.

"You've got to be kidding."

"No. It's only a few miles down the road."

"I can't do that. It's a hell of a lot of trouble for you. Before long I'll pick up a lighthouse, then I'll know where I am for sure."

"Go on, put the lights on and we'll look out."

"Well, if you're sure. As long as Captain McLaren doesn't find out at the London School of Navigation. It's not the recognised way of piloting."

My brother Chris is with a ham at Gore and we talk for a while, then Doug's there from Australia, and Matt comes back to say they can't spot any lights to sea. Ron says he has the weather now and unfortunately the north easterly is going to get up some more.

I make this tack a longer one and we go out for thirty miles, then begin the return course and the wind goes. I change down to the light sails and the wind returns, still nor' easterly and increasing. Gradually I'm changing down to the heavy sails. We meet the land again near the mouth of the Clutha River and head off back to sea. I get through to my parents and say, Might see you tonight. But the wind gets up to a gale and I have to use the big reef in the staysail. The sea becomes an angry green and now we cannot point as high. This will add hours to the voyage.

Life on board becomes much more uncomfortable. We are beginning to take water and a regular stream crosses the saloon floor and is a lake on the leeward side. Damn, my sleeping bag is wet. Everything is getting soaked. Mr Rowley cannot cope, so I am steering all the time. I listen in to the Travellers' net and I report to Ron and Mac in Dunedin that my ETA is now the next day. I am getting very tired and as the tacks are an hour long I can get fifty minutes' sleep every two hours. I daren't close my eyes when we are heading towards land.

We make land in the morning south of the Taieri River. This means for all the great distance of our tacks, progress is poor. Ron and Mac report that no change is expected in the weather. The nor' easterlies will continue for several days. Mac suggests I find Green Island, a little further along the coast, and anchor in the lee of that.

After Stewart Island, I want nothing to do with islands, to weather or leeward of any land. The only safe thing is for me to keep sailing. And hope the damaged rudder won't drop off in this sea.

During the day I steer from outside. It is bitterly cold, except when the sun comes through, but I can stay awake better. The wind has whipped up the sea so wave tops now break off and bulldoze downwind as rollers. I've never seen this before. It must be caused by shallow water; they are dangerous and keep slamming us and dousing me. Thank God for Henri's gear, which keeps most of it out. I've been forgetting to eat. When did I last cook something?

By nightfall I see a strange outcrop which Mac recognises as Black Rock. It is no distance to Dunedin now, the way the gulls fly, but the gale is giving the schooner a terrible time. I feel exhausted and wonder how I can possibly continue. I stayed awake for three days and nights in the Trans-Atlantic Race, but that wasn't after months of living on nerves. At nightfall I begin a long tack to seaward and crash in the frozen, sopping sleeping bag. I haven't had the oilies off since Stewart Island; they reek and are wet from sweat.

Sleep pushes down; fighting to get a yacht off rocks, struggling to right the boat after we turn over in a storm. Carol saying, Meet my new fella, affectionate with him, malice for me instead of love. Angry shouts bring me from the sleep and I clamber out, heart thumping, but there's no one there. Just me and the boat and the black sea. God, was it me shouting? A cup of coffee, comforting; underneath I feel itches and rashes; I hate this. But up on deck, the edge has gone from the gale and the sky is clear. Rigil Centaurus, Mimosa, and Sirius the blue creature, the most beautiful gleam in the heavens, the brightest fixed star.

Ready to go about. Lee-ho!

No loom of the Otago Heads lighthouse, waves and swell, and rollers thundering. It's dawn and Supertramp on the stereo and I know Dunedin is there and I'll get there no matter how tired I am. We've got this far, and survived every dirty trick nature has pulled. I can *feel* people nearby.

Land-ho! Hell, it's Green Island, only about thirty miles up the coast on that tack. But I close the land and tack in small zig-zags and now we can see Dunedin so aesthetically laid out. God, there's my old school, a miniature Edinburgh Castle on a hill. And the beach we went to in leather jackets, on motorbikes, with bottles of Speights. Drinking like butch boys, egging the sheilas on. The mountains and wild country I tramped through, always open spaces and too much beer, beach and sand, the green sea and the wind.

I sail in towards White Island; the scenery is so breathtaking I have forgotten the cold, the water spilling over the bilges, the gale and exhaustion. I am reborn, watching huge shower masses form over Green Hill. I sail close to the beach.

"*Pentax*, this is the Ravensbourne Boating Club. Do you hear me?"

"Ravensbourne, this is *Pentax*. Yes, I copy you. I expect to be at the rendezvous in two hours."

"Cripes, we'd better get cracking."

At Otago Heads we are given bearings and transits for the run-in through cross-seas, and in we sweep. Still water; to the left where Robin Knox-Johnston went aground. Speeding towards us two launches, packed with people. Stand by for the onslaught of New Zealand beer, I murmur, and sail towards them.

13

Captain Fantastic positively smiling as we make the still waters inside Otago Heads. If she had a tail, she would wag it off. I feel the same. Somehow, by the most extraordinary fluke, the schooner and I had reached the opposite side of the world. If I had plunged a long nail through my globe at home, it would have come out at this very place. What an incredible world; now I know it must be round. And here are launches rushing up, smiling happy people passing over a warp, then keeping their distance. They can't decide if I am crazy through being alone so long, or downright dangerous. I wave to them, Come over close, but they stand off. One launch either side now.

"What about some New Zealand beer?" I shout. "I've come a long way for one."

But the noise of the launches stops them sharing my exuberance. There's Mum and Dad, and there's my brother Stephen. He's grown a lot since I last saw him. And a very attractive woman there – she's got to be a reporter. And on the launch to our starboard a television team. But how are they going to film from that far off?

The harbour looks magnificent. It might be honking away outside, but here the hills are green and fresh, protecting the water. I make signs for a local beer, I continue to wave to come closer, but they stay away. I know I must reek but this is ridiculous. I want people near. So below to search for a bottle of Moët and plastic glasses, then open the bottle in the cockpit. The television crew are no strangers to this, and they come over. Cheers, hello, great to be here.

"It's marvellous to see people again," I say, but they just smile back. Perhaps it's a language problem. "Won't you come on board?"

Yes, they think they might, so the launches slow down and the team clambers on. Shaking hands, a peck for the lady sound recordist. This is better; this proves it can't be a dream.

Word spreads quickly. The lone yachtsman isn't completely mad after all. The other launch closes and more people come over. Soon Captain Fantastic is covered in hospitable New Zealanders, eager to know about the voyage, but a little reserved. It's several miles to the top of the long narrow harbour, but by the time we get there we're friends and not reserved, thanks to champagne. We go alongside a crowd at a harbour wharf. Welcome and well done and smiling hospitality; others helping to moor the schooner, people stowing the sails, clearing the decks. The customs man takes a few seconds to complete formalities and Immigration is no longer. They know I will be happy to get ashore. Not half, I won't be.

There are many hands to shake now, and well-wishers hoping I will stay for some time. They really understand hospitality in this part of the world. I try to make off with the lady reporter from the *Otago Daily Times*, but she is not so easily misled. I walk into a bar on my own, and the clock could be going back. So little has changed in these places. The garden hose beer dispensers. The names, Speights, DB, Waikato. The dress of the men, the way they look, which I try to define over a glass of beer, but can't. The talk of racing and rugby, their jobs. It's home for me, and I am instantly attracted to it, yet strangely fear that it may trap me. The looks towards me in this male stronghold are not so hospitable. I'm different, I have a Pom accent of sorts, I need to be weighed up.

Then the family catches up. Brother Stephen more mature, mother and father looking younger if anything and excited to see me. And sister Janee who flew from the North Island as soon as she heard I was expected today. And she doesn't look changed, just better looking. I feel so warm towards the family that the wrench of abandoning the southern route is all okay. For the moment anyway.

Bill Lowe and Gloria arrive from the airport, straight from Australia; it's good to have them here. We eat lamb in the hotel restaurant and drink New Zealand wine. Times have changed since the six o'clock closing days. You'd be lucky to get more than fish and chips after the pubs chucked out and the patrons threw up. Now there are carpets, sophistication and attractive waitresses. Most of the people near us look as if they have just stepped off a Scottish high street, in spite of being here for generations. The talk keeps up at the table. How was the steering system, the self-steering, do I think Bill's adaptation will work? Anyone heard from the sponsors? God, Bill, I'm pleased you could make it.

Last night I was exhausted, wondering if we would make land; tonight I am elated, sitting up talking to my parents about brothers and sisters, long-lost cousins, cat-breeding (one of their hobbies) and occasionally about the voyage. But the sea is a painful topic – it's all a bit too recent. It's late. I cannot stay awake any longer. My bedroom window overlooks the harbour and above the hills opposite are Acrux and Gacrux and my pointer friends. I can sleep deeply tonight; I'm really safe here.

We all arrive at the schooner early in the morning, but the Ravensbourne Yacht Club have beaten us. Their leader, Palmer Bryant, has a team ready. "We'll get the gear out and dry it and sort out what needs to be laundered and repaired," Palmer says, heaving sailbags to Paul and Colin Amos. "Then we will get on with the carpentry and the engineering. We're working on the assumption you'll be staying a week."

There was Martin, one of those gems you might hope for, but never expect to find. One of Palmer's group, he was an electronic wizard, a ham, crazy about sailing, who ran a Sea Cadet unit. Young, lean, shy; you find his type helping in the kitchen at parties. Bill Lowe appeared from below. Bill as usual was one of the first each day at the boat. It is Australia all over again.

People turned up at the quay and offered help. A dark-haired man named Michael called down from the wharf: "I'm an engineer and I can spare two days at the weekend." Bill marked him down for working on the steering. Later Michael left a Madonna from him and his wife. A man who didn't want to give his name asked me to take his fireman's hat badge. "It's looked after me in some pretty tight spots," he said. "I'm sure it'll do the same for you."

Over the next few days, the jetty was never empty. People came to stare, to dream, to pass over bottles of beer, or vegetables, and ask if they could help. Thanks to television, Captain Fantastic's working party became local celebrities, and wherever we went there were calls of encouragement, and often people would stop us and wish me luck on our visits to the Seamen's Mission for lunch or the Prince Albert pub for refreshments.

Merran flew into Dunedin three days before I was due to go. She looked so good that my heart got out of timing, vasomotor hyperactive, and I nearly collapsed. It took some doing to disguise the fall and hide the emotion flooding to my brain. Merran's arms around me, the smoothness of her skin, soft hair, her perfume. How could I go back to the loneliness at sea?

We spent the rest of the day together; I don't think we talked all that much, and certainly not about the sea. Ahead lay the Southern

Ocean, the ice limit and the fog, then Cape Horn. And a second circumnavigation if the boat held together. Now there were just the two of us, and those blue-grey eyes were all I needed to see.

That night, Merran heard plenty about the voyage, as I had been asked to address Palmer's yacht club. I expected a handful of people at the bar. We walked into the club, and before me was a packed hall. I was nervous, but I didn't need to be. It did not matter what I said; they were all friends and supporters and it was obvious they had been with me in spirit throughout the voyage. They were an incredible audience.

My son Christian flew down from the North Island. I didn't recognise him at first. He had become a young man, just out of school, and remarkably good looking. He was intelligent and strong, too, I noticed as he worked on the schooner. We became great friends and I wondered suspiciously why God was being so good to me. Parents, Merran, Christian, brothers and sister and so many friends. If I were going away to die, I couldn't ask for a better send-off.

I postponed the departure by a day, which gave me longer with Merran and Martin more time on the boat. Martin found the trouble with Dead-Eyed Derek. After taking the auto-pilot control unit to bits and announcing nothing was wrong, he traced a fault to a cable. This had been causing Derek to work too hard off the wind. He experimented with better positions for Derek's magnetic control unit.

Martin put tiny reading lights round the boat to save power, overhauled the ham transmitter, and gave me an outside listening position for the high-frequency rigs. He went through the entire electrics. Almost every night, Martin was the last to leave the schooner. It would have cost a fortune for his time and experience. But he wouldn't accept a free drink and sounded embarrassed on the radio later when he said he had received a thank-you letter from Bill.

Jonathan Brown and Bede Beaumont took the keel rollers apart and fabricated new fittings.

The night before going, a brewery threw a party for us on the boat. But I was very nervous about the departure, so, like most parties held that close to the event, it was no fun for me. But I don't think I was the only one who wondered if this strange, anorexic sailing canoe could withstand the might of those foggy wastes.

When Merran left Captain Fantastic the next day, I knew it might be the last time I saw her. She promised to phone, but ten months of

117

waiting on what may be a dead man is a long time. I knew it was selfish for me to hope she would wait. But the point of it all would end the day she stopped caring.

14

A large crowd gathered on the Rattray Street wharf, well-wishers from the city in office grey, from the country in agricultural green. It's so good of them to come down and farewell us, staring at the schooner that has travelled so far without an engine. At the local boy who made good all those miles and is now leaving to go twice round the world, to pass by this country again in the autumn. "Rather him than me."

Martin takes us in tow, Merran reassuring beside me, Captain Fantastic bristling with well-wishers, who are animated and cheery as we start. All of us waving to the people lining Otago harbour, a last word to Radio 4ZB over the transmitter which goes out live, slicing through the still harbour water. I go below to put on the polar wear and the oilies. Gloria Lowe making coffee for friends. I try counting them so I might remember all those on board during my next few nights. The first ones are the worst. I get to twelve, and I've counted someone twice. No, I've forgotten someone. Then it's eight, now it's fourteen. What the hell; I've Merran and Bill Lowe with me and they have been so good. So extraordinary that in a quarter of an hour I'll be left here on my own, washing up their coffee cups. They'll be returning to reality, to familiarity. I'll be going into a new ocean with a reputation even more evil than the seas before.

An ocean where waves put up by earthquakes travel at astonishing speeds. A place of incredibly deep Lows. You need to be a positive thinker to enter the Southern Ocean below the Pacific, or one who doesn't think at all. Forget the problems. You've got a good boat now. With a self-steering that will actually work.

A flat sea off the coast and people transfer to Martin's boat. My parents waving; wish I felt their confidence. So much can go wrong; forget about that. Big hug from Gloria and just me and Bill and Merran left. Bill takes me out of sight of the cameras. If I feel enough's enough at the Horn, he says, I should turn left for Britain. No one else can know the state of the boat after this leg across the

Southern Ocean, he says, so only I can make the decision. I know Bill is worried about the schooner and for some odd reason it lessens my fears and I remember the reassuring talk of local women on the bus in Brixton Road: a problem shared is a problem halved, they say. I've heard that a hundred times on bus 159, yet I have to sail to the other side of the world to believe it. Bill swings across to the escort and is gone. A last kiss, a last hug. "It doesn't get any easier saying goodbye," I try to joke with Merran but I feel as sad as it sounds. She's climbing down from the shrouds; she's on the other boat, the gap widens. I go to hoist the sails but the helpers have got them mixed, so I swap the headsail with the stay and hoist. No wind, sweating inside the polars, which I strip off. The boats tooting, waving, cheering, encouraging shouts. Still no wind; don't go, stay till the wind comes. But media film and copy has to reach the shore; the Lowes have to get to the airport.

Loneliness. God, this is when I feel it most, watching the others disappearing round the Heads, me bobbing in a swell. A slight puff, and up main and steering for the wind, getting a knot on the log, then two. I call Martin on the radio and say thanks. But they have been so good to me, so hospitable, that the word is not enough.

How incongruous, this feeling on the inside and the fabulous scenery of the Otago coast. Green water, a bloody gash as a school of red krill laze at the head of the tide. Too weary from doing nothing to get out of the way of the birds. Albatrosses and skuas gorging themselves, too weighted down to do more than paddle out of our way.

A fishing boat, the *Sceanna*, comes close and offers a crayfish for supper and good luck for the voyage. No, thanks, I call; haven't got my sea legs yet.

Me and Captain Fantastic still news on the radio stations, which turn the paragraphs inside out to bring them up to date. So great for people to care about adventure. Perhaps more people will feel the attraction of the great outdoors as a result of all this. Thunderclouds climb down from Flagstaff and douse Dunedin then aim for us, squalls and headwinds, calm, headwinds, darkness, light ashore fading. Mr Rowley ungrateful for the rebuild on land, tearing his lead lines through, which slip off the alloy wheel aft, breaking the clamcleats. But I screw on two large cleats in the darkness, and reluctantly the gear reports for duty and takes over. There's a sked with Mac and Ron and it's good propagation and they say the film taken on Monday was shown on television tonight. Really good, they report.

Can't be bothered cooking, but I have tea and see that Gloria has

Arriving in Fremantle, people at last, above, left. Right, Australian farewells. Below, under way once more.

Albatross, skua and butterfly petrel, above; an inquisitive school of whales, centre; and below the aggressive steamer ducks of Port Stanley.

Christmas night is disco night in the Shrieking Fifties. Below, Evi about to walk the amidships warp in Stanley harbour, and afterwards.

Chartwork and DIY repairs in Cape Town, above. Below, journey's end.

washed the coffee cups for me. Bless her. I lie down for a few minutes, but soon we're off course as Mr Rowley slips his lead lines again. I use some colonial words to him and refix lines. The Force 7 blowing shows up bilgewater and as I scoop it out, I see that there's a lot of paraffin floating about in it. I check the containers, but the lids are tight. The rain exposes the leaks and despite all the work in Dunedin to stop them, the old faithfuls are back dripping in the navigation area and over my berth. I would very much like to have a dry boat for this leg, which will be the coldest and roughest.

By the time I redirect the drips and make some more tea, dawn shows ahead. Astern there is no land; we're back on our saucer of sea and the music on the radio is not so clear. The wind returns to the most usual Southern Ocean airstream – south west, thirty knots. I get a large sail up and we are doing a good speed. A thumping noise comes from the keel occasionally. I can't guess what could be causing it. The rollers certainly appear to be holding and Captain Fantastic feels pleased to be going again. I wonder if she understands that the next land should be the Horn; maybe she doesn't know the stories, or maybe she's confident. I can't say I feel very happy about it.

I take the meridian and it gives our latitude well south of Dunedin. I want to give the Bounty Islands a good distance as they are often hidden by bad visibility, says the pilot book. I'm rather cautious about islands these days. How odd to think William Bligh drove the *Bounty* around this ocean, possibly sailing over this very piece. I wonder if he stared fascinated, as I do, at the butterfly petrels, their dainty walking on water. I feel great compassion for them; they're so like people in my neighbourhood, accepting class and not trying for a better deal. Mustn't grumble. I can hear these petrels saying it, too. I call out: "New Zealand's only a hundred or so miles back there. You could live on a cliff and there's stacks of fish in the water." The petrels haven't time for tea and a chat; there's none of the lazy skuas' philosophy; pass the day in company and then steal from another fellow rather than bother yourself with fishing. No, the petrels won't accept any other life and nor will my neighbours. I was invited to stay in New Zealand; I know my parents and friends would have understood. And I know, too, that life is much too valuable to be risked in this way. Yet I've come out, too, Petrels, and I'm driven to continue with what I must do. I just hope I will be satisfied when it's through.

No sleep last night, so I try to close my eyes now. But with this motion the piece of wood beside my head keeps getting in the way.

I'm going to have a massive bruise soon; I don't seem to be able to avoid it.

Log 1400 hours: Not at all settled into shipboard life yet. Worried by the leaks that showed up last night, over both bunks, too. There's water in the bilges amidships – that's new – and the old leaks have shown up in the after-shrouds. Cold out in the wind.

Log 0700 hours: Got the water out of the bilges, bent on the number two yankee and the heavy staysail, ready for a big blow. I repaired the rope net in the cockpit, tightened a lifeline and generally laboured. The big seas here surprise me. Maybe it's that I am not used to the swell after a week in port, but it seems huge compared to the wind strength, with tops that surf away. What can it be like in a blow? I might say, I'm not in any hurry to find out. Feeling quite precious and vulnerable today. I put potatoes and onions in the pressure cooker for tonight. The cooker is handy for the sea, but I do hate washing it out afterwards. The top of the cultivator which Francis Graham gave me to grow seeds in (and I have not used) left us today and I watched it growing smaller in the wake. That would be my fate, too. Please don't fall off, Paul; that's what it said to me. Noise in the keel most odd, as if there was a loose extension well down.

Log 0758 hours: Self-steering lines come free; reconnected. Having a Speights, listening to the radio and watching the sunset. Ra has found a cloud belt to hide his exit. Soft orange colours. Towering swell.

Log 1426 hours: Up to look around. Self-steering lines off. Reconnected lines and changed headsails in strong gusts.

Log 1854 hours: Third time I've got up to reconnect steering lines. Big sea running, so put below the changed headsail and as it's a gale I have reefed the number two yankee. Size of some of the rollers is unbelievable for the wind strength. One hit us as I was putting the lines back on the self-steering. Wet shoes. One was so big and threatening that I rushed into the doghouse as it roared along and expected a knockdown. Fortunately we rode over it. The self-steering won't let me sleep. I can't find the fault that causes the lines to come off. It's so wearing and frustrating.

Log Friday: Reefed the staysail and re-reefed the yankee after some of it broke loose. Rough going, the breakers are downright frightening. Meridian puts us at 48°S, so much for staying at 46° which I had planned to do. Overcast in the sky and in my soul; not at all well or happy yet.

Fog, rain, my breath misting. Looking out for the Bounty Islands, but it's hopeless in this poor visibility. Big seas, big gusts. Trying to hold on to reefed staysail and number two. We reached thirteen knots in a surf earlier. It is so unpleasant here one might as well go as fast as possible. Discovered that the self-steering had developed its old trick of edging up to windward with the wind paddle. I've reconnected the rope leads many times in the last few hours. Many birds are around, mainly skuas and grey prions, and a big clump of seaweed wandered past. A bit disconcerting, you might say, as this is usually associated with reefs. And reefs can pop up anywhere in this part of the ocean. I've had a hell of a headache for a while now, but I am eating and I managed to get an hour's sleep before lunch. Once past the Bounty Islands I would like to return to a level latitude as we are being drawn south too much. That ought to make the berth and sleeping more comfortable, providing that leak over my pillow has disappeared. Oh, Merran, where are you? If nothing else, this voyage has shown me I'm just a mere man. And every man needs a dear one he can worry about and love.

On the ham sked tonight, Lou is present and he suggests the trouble with Mr Rowley is caused by the elasticity of the lead lines. He said he had wondered about the rope I was using and had put some pre-stretched cord on board. What an incredible gesture, a thoughtful present with no thanks sought. The hams in New Zealand have been working on other problems and Martin was there to suggest reasons why there is no input reading from the solar panels. Ron has arranged the most incredible back-up team for me. The link tonight lasted an hour and a quarter and afterwards I went to bed and slept well, pushing part of the soggy pillow against the offending piece of wood. Up several times during the night to look for the Bounties, but half the time I am doing well to see the bow, the fog is so thick.

By morning the wind has gone and the ocean has become quite flat; it feels good to be able to walk about without going from one handhold to the next. We are surrounded by a huge flock of the light-grey prions. Such dainty birds, it doesn't seem possible that they could survive the rages of the Shrieking Fifties. My bird book says they flutter about in their extraordinary way to avoid being picked off by the skuas who welcome a variation in their fish diet. But it seems to me that their jerky flight and poor fishing abilities are caused by a complete lack of patience.

There was a good deal of mail for me in Dunedin, but I didn't open it till I began this part of the journey and I ration myself to one letter a day.

As we got near 50°S, the barometer confirmed we were in an area of extravagant weather. Overnight it climbed seven millibars, and then dropped twelve, to arrive at a thousand millibars by the following day. Twenty-four hours later, it was at 985 mbs. I had never seen such a low barometer, but the pressure kept falling. The temperature dropped, too, and now my breath was misty all the time and when I took my hands out of Henri's gloves, they quickly

123

numbed. Changing sails was especially painful. The fog had thickened and in clear periods I could see the foremast. We were able to keep up an average of about seven knots on the wind.

> Log 0200 hours: 981 mbs, down two. I've got the weather plotted on the chart now and it shows a Low of 985 mbs on my route. There are two possibilities for the drop in the barometer: either the barometer is hypersensitive in extreme ranges or I add the four millibars I believe it to be out in mid-range, and the Low is over us, more or less. Whichever, it is very disconcerting. Ron's weather report shows the Low to be three hundred miles from where we are, or my estimate of where we are, because of the fog, so it is all very puzzling. Heavy storm door in place, anyway, just in case. It's a thirty-millibar drop since Saturday morning, two days ago.
> Log 0110 hours: 980 mbs, down one. Fog, rain, cold.
> Log 0300 hours: 978 mbs, down two.
> Log 0426 hours: 976 mbs, down two. Break in fog shows a little sun and shower-type cloud, strung together at bottom. Most odd, but possibly indicating closeness of the front. So that's a little encouraging – if anything can be with the barometer so low. Listening to Electric Light Orchestra. Picked up Naomi James' book to read her account of this area. Looking for reassurance, I expect.
> Log 0744 hours: 974 mbs, down two. Well, it's still dropping. If anything was designed to shake a man to his core, this has to be it. The barometer's got to be wrong. Or we're about to slide over the edge of the world. Quite a rough ride, but it could be an awful lot worse. We've not got much more wind than thirty knots. Green sea again, but not many birds.
> Log 1200 hours: Barometer steady. Pin comes out of self-steering wheel drum, so up to correct that, for the second time.
> Log 1700 hours: 978 mbs, up four. Reef in number two yankee and it's a quiet ride while we wait for the front, for hell to break out. Fog has returned, but that's okay as it is such a treat to see the glass rise. But, please, let it do it gradually.

The drop in pressure was far greater and had settled much deeper than for the hurricanes off the Cape of Good Hope. Admittedly that was the winter and this was the start of summer. However, we were now at 50°S, and we could expect no mercy. I anticipated the worst, and went to bed, to try to get as much strength in reserve as possible. I slept soundly for six hours and awoke to find the wind had dropped to Force 5, the sea had lost some of its bite, and the barometer was continuing to rise slowly.

After breakfast, the fog was with us again and the barometer was dropping quickly till it reached 970. I felt I was aging rapidly, and the worry was not helped by having to bash upwind – something that is not supposed to happen in the Southern Ocean. I slept on the navigation floor as the bunks were soaking.

Then, as if a wand had been waved over the boat, the barometer started to rise and the wind leaped round to behind us. The schooner sat upright and Mr Rowley threw his wheel-drum pin out, possibly in surprise. Everything below was cold and wet, but Captain Fantastic and crew passed a vote of thanks to the Chief Looker-Afterer-Above for putting the wind back in the right place.

The sun came out and the fog went away and the wind slowly built to a gale and then went back to thirty knots. The barometer continued to rise and drop and rise at the rate of about one millibar an hour. I'd never heard of anything like it before.

Matt came up on the ham sked and reported that another lone yachtsman, David Scott Cowper, who was circumnavigating the other way round, was getting near my longitude. I tried calling him on the radio, but no response, so when I spoke to Matt later I relayed an invitation for David to come over for Christmas dinner. It had to be an extraordinary experience to meet someone this far from civilisation. He was about six hundred miles north of me, where winds are more inclined to be from the east, not that we were short of them ourselves, so I estimated that our paths would cross in about ten days. We would need settled weather and a great deal of luck to be able to meet.

The barometer started to plunge again, but I felt sure it couldn't go as low as it had before. We had avoided the fierce winds that accompanied the previous Lows, but it was unlikely we could hope for such good fortune again.

Log Thursday noon: 993 mbs, down three. Long sked with Cedric Woods from Perth, who'd mended my transmitters for me; so good to talk to him again. Gusts are getting up here now, a Force 6/7, so I guess the mainsail will have to come down, but I want to make as much progress as possible while conditions are moderate. Today's work included tightening the rails, reworking some of the broken genoa nets, preparing new self-steering lead lines. I must remember to service the port genoa winch; it's one I missed in the last maintenance burst. There's a growing pile of genoa sheet which has been worn through and the backstays are looking chafed. We need the right conditions for some of the servicing. Balmy days, that's what we could do with.

Log 2039 hours: 982 mbs, down nine. Good night's sleep, despite falling pressure. At one time when I got up for a look-about, there was a most unusual sea. Quite flat with small corrugations. You'd have thought we were charging through sheet ice. Very grey. It's raining now and grey and cool.

Log 2350 hours: Fog, rain and cold. Barometer stands at 975, down seven millibars. We're on the wind again at an acute angle. Reading, standing up against the pigeon-holes. Breath misting, it's so cold. The rapid and extreme drops in barometric pressure are stunning. We have been so well looked after in not being hit by correspondingly extreme strengths of wind. I've seen what the swell can look like here at fifty degrees at Force 6. What it could become, I just hate to think.

Over the next three hours, the barometer dropped eight millibars, and then five more two hours later, as the wind moved through sixty-five degrees to come behind us.

Then the barometer dropped one more millibar to reach the pressure of the Low; 961 mbs. The wind moved another twenty degrees to be in the south west. The barometric pressure was unheard of. I did not know it could ever drop that low, not even in the most intense hurricane. I gybed Captain Fantastic round and still the wind stayed at Force 5. I waited half an hour. No change, so I kept the sked with New Zealand and Australian hams. I was talking to Cedric when the wind struck. Got to go, I shouted, pulling on the Henri-Lloyds.

The wind-speed meter was jammed over sixty knots and the scream in the rigging was monstrous. Mr Rowley went off watch immediately after bringing the yacht side on to the elements. Now we were lying right over, pinned to the surface of the sea by the huge weight of this wall of wind. Put your harness on, I called to myself, even though I knew there wasn't time. I had to drop the sails before the sea poured over the coaming and down into the cockpit.

I clung to the windward lifeline and pulled myself forward. The wind pressed my cheeks into the facial bones. It was impossible to look into it for it threatened to poke my eyes out. Even my nostrils were flattened. I grabbed the yankee halyard and let it go, the sail snatched and held, freed, whipped furiously, then snatched again. Me darting from the foredeck, pulling at the sail, to the mast to free the halyard and back again. Eventually the sail dropped into the sea. The schooner stood out of the waves a little now, as the wind had less to thrust at. Back to the after-mast and let the halyard go. Forward to the stay and pulling at the sail which comes down part way, but no amount of heaving will move it. I can see the halyard is free at the winch. It must be caught at the top of the mast but not all the money in all the banks will get me up there in this weather. The boat has come upright now, but the loosened staysail is cracking about. I have to dodge the sheets, one smack from them now could easily break my arm. There was nothing for it but to let the sail flog itself to death. I returned to the cockpit to get some sail ties, to try to stifle some of the terrible crashing of the sail in the storm. As I passed the after-mast, I saw the halyard was knotted at the mast-sheave. That was the cause. I freed the knot with frozen, bleeding fingers. Now back to the stay and the sail came down. In the cockpit, the instruments showed the wind remaining above sixty knots.

I went back along the deck to tie down the sails. Now sitting there I watched the storm lashing the seas in a way I had not seen before. These were not small waves being scraped into larger ones. Instead, the wind was boldly lumping the sea into great folds, like some giant hand karate-chopping plasticine mounds. The water, stunned by the immense blows, staggered downwind in the same moving mountain. The tops became too heavy and collapsed under the massive weight, but late, so that half the mountain slid with it, with the booming roar of surf. An avalanche shook the nearby waves as this mountain passed us, great jets of water filled the air, were caught by the hurricane and ricocheted over the oilskin hood. Then the air was dry until the next monster fell over.

Captain Fantastic lay at the mercy of this incredible show of nature's forces gone out of control, but we were like a bottle, floating, tossing, moving with the might, never resisting. And as the schooner was shoved by mighty unseen shoulders, she went with the blow, there being no reverse curve, no counter force to try to stop the assault. We skidded down a wave, came upright, slid and skied forward, bashed, sliding, skidding now. Always nimbly going with the force. On board it was frightening, holding on as the surface of the sea seemed to disappear below us, but we were not shuddering under the blows. I was excited by the scene, knowing I was part of this incredible exhibition for a one-man audience, yet I did not doubt that we would survive this particular storm. I could see her reaction to the monsters all around and I was filled with admiration for her courage and sheer genius. You can't fall in love with an inanimate object. It's not logical; we're too modern for that. But whatever was the correct word, I felt a deep affection for her, I was in awe of this man-made creature which I alone had forced to this dreadful part of the ocean, yet in return I was being saved from certain, frozen death. Inside, water slopped about, reaching for dry clothing, at the hanging edge of a very damp sleeping bag. But it was only water from the bilges, not the deep ocean which waited to crush us and take us down.

I managed to get a rope round the wheel to dampen the steering, which was spinning from lock to lock. We couldn't afford to lose the rudder this far from help. Mr Rowley looked wrecked on the stern, ropes off, water paddle at an angle. He'd be safest left alone. The generator was spinning well, taking advantage of electricity out of the adversity of the storm. The air was bitterly cold and tops of waves leaped upwards near the cockpit and jumped in on top of me, determined to soak. But they didn't get through.

I climbed back on to the deck and retrieved the winch handles, one at a time, from the pockets on the mast, so that if we were turned over, we shouldn't lose them. Then back through the screaming noise to the cockpit, slow determined paces. For God's sake, don't slip. Into the doghouse and the heavy storm door closed.

There was nothing else to be done. In the navigation area, I shoved aside the plastic curtain that kept the water off the stereo and pushed in an eight-track of David Bowie. Up loud. And went back into the saloon and made myself a large mug of tea. As I sipped it down, "The Man Who Sold the World" competing with the Shrieking Fifties, I reassured myself that we would be under way soon; that we had seen the worst of it. But I was wrong.

15

I didn't expect to sleep, but my subconscious must have accepted that there was nothing else I could do. Inside oilskins and boots is not a good place to doze; the atmosphere soon has steam condensed and the inner clothes clutch at you and every movement is wet, scraping. At best, damned uncomfortable. Several hours passed; the storm was my continuous lullaby. Strong gusts, easing; then a furious outburst. Air is a fluid, and the similarities of moving air, particularly in the Southern Ocean, can be seen with water. The storm was producing waves of wind, and these giant rollers were the result of acres of heavy cold air that crashed from the sky to the sea. In the rigging, these great gusts were a noisy panicking chorus, moving up and down the scale as directed by the stronger waves. The wind generator harmonised, and often seemed to announce the strongest gusts before the chorus picked up their cue to shriek in the rigging. Sounds of surf through the hull and sometimes a deep heavy thump, as the top of a wave dived too late and came to a splintering halt against us.

In the saloon, the water swished from one side to the other, always exaggerating depth; always reaching out for the electrics, for the transmitters, which were the easiest for saltwater to destroy. The electrics fortunately too timid to even dip a big toe to test the temperature.

The drips from the keel-housing stopped me going back to sleep. How long would it take the pillow to become saturated? I knew then it was time to get out. This sort of contemplation can drive you mad.

Dawn showed everything dripping. A foot or so of bilgewater, the queer sickening rhythm of lying ahull. I looked at the barometer and my heart was gripped by fear. It showed a nineteen-millibar rise. A sight that would have terrified sail mariners racing their canvas machines through these wastes. "Rapid rise after low," says the old maxim of barometric pressures, "sure sign of a stronger blow." This was much more than a rapid rise. The barometer had reached an all-time low and now had risen much too quickly. The sea, foaming and furious, did not deny it. Captain Fantastic, groaning under the weight of the rollers, was getting tired. I logged: Bilged out roughly; water everywhere, but we're still here. Scared stiff.

The barometer rose another five millibars. The wind was registering on the anemometer now, so it meant the storm was moving on. I clambered out into the freezing cockpit and meant to fix the self-steering; extreme conditions or not. But it was hopeless. As I sat on the stern, legs either side of Mr Rowley, we would be twenty feet above the water one moment, and then up to my knees. I listed the faults: the connector rod was bent and would need straightening, a plastic end-fitting was smashed, a drum control-line hole was physically torn out, the starboard control line almost snapped through, and the water paddle's steel jaws bent.

I need a less bucking platform to make the repairs, I logged. It means we'll have to sit around for another ten hours or so, I suppose. We're taking a lot of water from somewhere. The navigation floor is awash and I regularly have to pump out the saloon. Donna Summer playing to a wet, cold cabin, with the pipe from the bilge pump stretched across the floor to the forward port side. All very incongruous. Felt ill before, but spending most of the time in the bunk, starboard tack, so it's not comfortable to say the least, with me lying in the leecloth. Very cold in the wind and tough on the fingers. The boat's rocking about on this huge swell, but very few waves actually crash into us. Even the rolling, breaking waves go underneath. Most of them. We have a few knockovers and the water alternator outrigger has been damaged.

One of the most horrible events of the voyage was about to happen. Two hours to go to the sked with the hams and I felt hungry, so it was time for the evening meal. In heavy weather, I usually got out the Goldenlay for the Pell-met, but today I decided I would have a proper meal and to hell with the sea. I clambered along through navigation to amidships and found a potato, a couple of onions and a stringy carrot. Back to the saloon. Normally I prepared the vegetables in the cockpit, but that would be too risky now. So I scooped some water from the bilges to wash them with, chopped the vegetables up, and boiled them in bilgewater. When they were almost ready, I replaced the water with a beef casserole from a vacuum pack. Waited about six minutes, then dinner was ready.

I made a pig of myself and ate too much, but I thought the

conditions warranted it. Only a good meal would make me feel a little human. I found a bottle of New Zealand beer, and that helped it all down a treat. Ron's lunchbox had been retired and I now ate directly from the pot. This lessened by one item the amount of washing-up necessary and the higher sides were better for this ocean. But I still used a teaspoon to eat with; I am a slow eater by nature, but with a tiny implement the meal was well drawn out and the pleasure of it all, with an appetite heightened by constant fresh air, was taken to the limit. I resented a sudden windshift at mealtimes and occasionally left Captain Fantastic on a poor course while the meal lasted.

Now, as the storm screamed outside, I was too bloated to do much except stay propped up, squeezed in beside the cooker where I would not be thrown across the cabin. Would the skipper care for tea, or coffee? Yes, I'd have coffee; much more restaurant-style. Now, would I have coffee made with water, or with the Scottish Long Life Milk? Milk won, cappuccino with a good helping of honey and a bar of Godiva.

My feet went suddenly cold and as I looked down in the darkness, I could see a wall of water about three feet high, pouring into the saloon from aft. For a moment I just stared, unable to move, thanks to the meal and because of the awful fear which stabbed at my stomach.

Jesus, God, we're sinking. Even as I watch, gallons of water come in. The level here in the saloon has to go up four feet, that's all, to start filling the boat. The stern gland, it's got to be the stern gland, the plug of wood that replaced the propeller must have worked loose, perhaps disturbed by the grounding in Stewart Island. No, I would have seen that when we were lifted in Dunedin. Wouldn't I? Well, Bill definitely would have; Bill misses nothing. God, how to get at it? It's under the cockpit sole, down in the cellar. Pump, man, pump the fucking bilge pump now or we're doomed. Then think where the leak is. What you can do about it. Are you crazy? If the water's getting in through the stern gland, we're done for; we could never keep up with that rate. God, it's still pissing in; it's got to be a hole. We must have been holed somewhere. But we heard nothing; no heavy bang that would have announced it. Get on the bilge pump, for Christ's sake. You've got to do something.

Sure, do something, and that has to be the liferaft. Got to get that over the side and in one piece; do that soon enough and we can get enough gear on to improve the odds. What a bloody laugh. The moment you get off the boat into that you're bloody dead. You always knew that. You weren't even going to take one, you said it would be so hopeless in this ocean. They talked you out of that – just as well now.

For God's sake do something. Look at the bloody water; it's lapping over the bulkhead into the navigation. God, how much time? Five minutes? Ten? No, about four minutes at this rate. God, help me, God, I'm in a panic and I can't think straight.

Then, pump, you fool; pump because you've got to do something. I don't want to die. Get the damned liferaft over the side then; that's what you've got to do. Look at the bloody water rising! My poor sleeping bag. The thing'll get really soaked now. Liferaft first. Remember, you've gone over this enough times. You've got a plaque in your mind. It's headed:

Alternative Travel. Leaving? Then take: sharp knife, liferaft, survival suit . . . oh, God, the survival suit. Should I get into it first? No, no time; put it in the raft.

Weld bag (Philip Weld was always talking about calamity bags during the OSTAR; the bag with emergency rations), and then, if time, more water, charts, sextant.

There's more, but I can't remember. Oh, Jesus, yes, the emergency radio with the aircraft frequencies. That's the only hope here.

Untie the raft, as it sits up-ended in the doghouse. Push the storm door open. The noise is suddenly overwhelming. Am I going out in that? Hurry, hurry, you bastard, or we'll be lost. Rollers speeding past the transom, thundering surf. Not so many now; it's much better. Another rolling down, lifting Fantastic and boiling up again to leeward. Pulling the storm door shut. I know I can't survive in that. The liferaft won't stay upright; not for a bloody damn second. We're fucking lost, and no one will know why, and I don't know what to do.

Then, bloody well pump. At least you'll delay the end. Isn't that all that life is; putting off the inevitable? Back to the saloon, water calf-high. Pump, pump, for God's sake. Christ, hope the bloody valve doesn't go. What'll happen when she goes? We've got the forepeak stuffed with plastic bottles. She should bob around with the bow above the sea. Jesus, that'll be a fat lot of use. But it's something. It's a damn sight better than being in the briny yourself. Freezing to death, breathing spume. Pump, pump. Would I pray when I was dying? Would I ask him to save me? No, I don't think so. I don't think I've got that cheek. Pump, pump the bloody bilge pump.

When the end is here, I'll take the exit pills. It won't hurt, they said. You just go to sleep. Some say you have a beautiful dream.

But how do they get word back, I'd like to know. Pump the bloody pump.

We're beating the water level. No. Yes, we're beating it. Can't be; not if it's a hole; how could you? But we are, look at the level for yourself. Even as I watch, while pumping, the fluorescent light is reflected on the floorboards. We're going to survive. I didn't realise before but my arms are just about falling off from this pumping. Stopping, dashing through the doghouse, pushing the door open. The big flashlight, shining it on the topsides, looking for a gash above the waterline. None port. And starboard? No, no gashes, no dark marks on the white hull. Then what can it . . . Oh, Christ, look at the counter. The bloody lazarette cover's been knocked off. A dirty great wave has knocked it off and filled the lazarette. There's a quarter of it full now. I grab the cover and fasten it back down.

All okay on deck. Back below, shutting the storm door. Doing up the liferaft cord. Pumping till the floorboards come clear again. Don't think about it; you've got to get it out of your mind. Now, compose yourself. Off with the Henri-Lloyd jacket. Get comfortable. Well, relax then. Now, skipper, what about a nice cup of cappuccino; have a bar of Godiva chocolate. To celebrate. Celebrate what? Oh, yes, we're going to put it out of the mind for a while. Have two, a milk chocolate and a dark chocolate. And an extra spoonful of honey to calm the old tummy.

Consoling hot milk and back to the bunk, to close the eyes and forget It's now that counts. Not tomorrow, not a moment ago.

It's getting light. Out to wade through the bilgewater. What did I take my damn boots off for? The barometer. It's up another fifteen millibars. Rapid rise after Low . . . Get a grip of yourself, skipper; the boat's here in the widest expanse of water in the world. She'll go anywhere on the globe you direct. So be the mariner again, not the thinker.

The wind eases to Force 10, then 9. I redrill the wheel drum and reinforce the holes with pieces from the auto-pilot spares pack I had from my old trimaran. New lead line to starboard from the self-steering, new connecting rod and new plastic connector. The water paddle is well out of alignment so I hang off the stern, dodging waves, and get that pointing the right way and I tighten the cursed paddle top-nut. Up to the foredeck, she's bucking like a stallion, and up yankee. Back to the wheel.

We're under way after thirty-three hours and thirty minutes of lying ahull with dropped sails, wheel tied, leaving the boat to find her own position. How I wish that it will be ages before we need do that again, if ever. It's been one of the longest of the storms; surely it must be the last of the bad weather. I stay at the wheel to make up for lost time, pressing on hard and when the wind is at a 7, I get the staysail up. It's odd watching the sea going down and by dusk there are still tall waves and the incredible pyramids which tower and collapse. But there's less cascading now and I remain fairly untouched.

Tena koe, e Marama, I hail the moon rising and greet Sirius, who is useful to steer by. It is too dark to see the compass. Then the clouds move over again and the fog returns. I am cold and stiff from standing in the one position. Mr Rowley on, then down below to warm up. I just make the sked with Ron when there's a bang from Mr Rowley and a plastic connector busts again. Ron gives me the list of people listening in to wish me luck, but I have to say I must go back to repair the self-steering. Mr Rowley has forced us over in a gybe, so I gybe us back again and find I have to tie the wind-vane to stop it creeping up.

Where is all this water coming from? I get a torch and climb down into the cellar; a lot of water is collecting there. I search for leaks, and I can't find any, but up in the cockpit some fibreglass is lifting, and I can now see that a lot of water is getting under the cellar lid. I have pumped out the cellar; there's not much more I can do. The saloon floor is very wet and as we roll about the water is swilling from tack to tack. Mr Rowley keeps taking us off course, so I presume the staysail is upsetting him, and drop it. It's supposed to be a speed run, this, Mr Rowley, not a kindergarten day out.

Log 1200 hours: Wind is gusting to a 9 again and the barometer has dropped ten millibars since we started. Had to put the port control line back on the self-steering and tighten it all up. Late dinner of onions, tomatoes and beef goulash. It started off as cheese Pell-met, but I thought I would use tomatoes for variation, then why not an onion, and finally the omelette didn't happen. Bottle of Speights to help it down. I'm tired now; been a tough day.
Log 1548 hours: Barometer down three millibars. It's a gale, gusting Force 9. We're down to a reefed staysail. As I was hoisting it, after putting the reef in, I found the halyard was on the wrong side of the new triatic. I dropped it, changed the halyard, hoisted again and the sheet fell out, so down it came while I hunted for the sheet, tied it back on and raised the staysail for a third time. I decided to drop the yankee when we were shunted over a bit far.
Log 1744 hours: Barometer 989, down two millibars. Self-steering connector rod goes again and we've gybed.
Log 2051 hours: Severe gale. 986, down three millibars.
Log 2306 hours: Storm. 983, down three millibars. Lying ahull to try to

134

sort out the self-steering and to have a rethink. Surprised to find quite some play back in the steering.

Four hours later the wind dropped rapidly to thirty knots, so I put up the sails again and we ran off downwind, ski-ing happily with both man and machine pleased to be under way. I steered to make the most of the conditions, but as I spun the wheel to clear the large mobile mountains, I was surprised at how loose the system had become. There was no feel of the sea on the rudder now, and I had to turn the wheel several inches to get over the slop. When the sea got down a bit, I would have to go through the system to try to find the fault.

On my next sked with Australia, I found Doug had been talking to meteorologists who were interested in the conditions I was encountering. Few ships go through this part of the world, so they were getting rare information from me. "The trouble is," Doug told me, "you're in the area too early by about two or three weeks."

We were a large chunk of the globe apart, but propagation was excellent. It could have been a local phone call. "Yes, I can see that, Doug. I had planned to be in this part about a month earlier, but I would have been in a kinder latitude."

"Yes, a lower latitude for the first run would have been better for you and then you could have taken this higher one the second time."

"That's the route I have planned on my world chart," I said. "But I have no choice this time. While there's still a chance of having a go at the second circumnavigation, I need to cut the corners. A whole lot of this part now is within the possible iceberg area. But to go in a kinder latitude gives me further to go, and less consistent westerly winds."

"You're in a bit of a cleft stick then."

"It's a gamble. I guess it is just bad luck that I am being hit by this succession of storms. Another time they wouldn't be so close together and I could be getting further on. But despite lying ahull, we're still making good progress."

"Yes, it is excellent; you're really leaving the miles in your wake."

Good old Doug. I could always rely on him for encouragement. He had said he planned to follow me round the world on the airwaves, and every day he came up with encouragement and a good ear, no matter how much I moaned about my lot.

"I just wish we could get some better weather for you. If only we could hurry the season on a bit."

"The irony is that if damage caused by being here in the South Pacific too early in the year forces me to give up the idea of making a second navigation, then I will have to make for England, but it will be the wrong time of year to do that too, for I will arrive in the North Atlantic bang in the middle of the winter. Either way, I'll be in the wrong place at the wrong time of year with adverse weather conditions."

"For heaven's sake, if you can't continue, plan to stop in South America for a bit, until you can time your journey to coincide with better weather."

It's ten days to Christmas. I have managed to get sufficient sun sights to give me a position, but I can hardly believe it. I have been trying to get out of this rough weather by edging nearer to 45°, yet the sun says we are still at 50°. We must have been well south of it; it's a wonder we didn't run into any ice. The sights seem right; I've been through the tables several times, but I always get the same answer. Of course the sights themselves could be out; we've got a monstrous sea here, poor horizon and the sun is never really clear. Is the compass wrong? I could check that by getting a bearing on the sun when it sets and rises, but there is always too much cloud about to do it. I can't understand it. I suppose it brings the Horn closer. But this weather; boy, could we do with a break from it.

I've been down in the cellar below the cockpit. And I have found the fault in the steering. A bolt in the first universal joint has broken and come out. The whole system has been riding on a key-way. I have put a bolt through the joint, but I am not optimistic about it holding. I fear the next storm or the one afterwards will put paid to the steering altogether; I think the whole universal joint is going to come off. It is a crazy, vulnerable system quite unsuited to long ocean work. Jerry Freeman warned me about it in Plymouth. He said I must keep it well greased because it was not very different from a car steering system, yet it would have to survive in a maritime environment. Too late then, of course, to change it.

The barometer's dropping again and the wind is gusting to a gale. I have been out watching the self-steering, trying to discover why it keeps breaking the plastic connectors. I have a cottage industry going below now, with lots of the connectors drying after I had glued them. I'm keeping all of the pieces and, out of three, I usually get two second-hand replacements.

When the self-steering has to correct the course, and the water paddle reaches out for maximum energy, the connector rod bends and the plastic snaps. It is a very simple cause, but how soul-destroying. The boat goes beam on and we get caught by the seas while I'm hanging on back there changing rods. We've been hit by a few of the nasty roller-types now running and it fills me with absolute horror to think about what may happen when we get into the higher latitudes near the Horn.

The whole steering question leaves me sick with worry. How can I try to continue with the thing about to break? How can I battle my way back to New Zealand for repairs? For repairs, or for a new system that can take this punishment and a different self-steering gear? Cappuccino and chocolate for the stomach lining while I study the chart. It's three thousand miles to the Horn, and an equally long way to a Bill Lowe service station. Here I am in this purgatory unable to rely on the two most critical pieces of equipment. I could steer myself, and then heave-to when I needed to sleep, but these seas are too much. If I have to tiller-steer and by-pass the present wheel system altogether, will I be able to cope? Can Captain Fantastic be handled by a tiller in these huge seas? I had heard Mike Dunham talk about two men being needed on the tiller when her steering failed in the Parmelia Race.

The current and our leeway seem to have ended any chance of getting north to calmer, warmer seas where I might be able to repair some of the leaks. We are in a sorry state, the sorriest of the whole voyage, perhaps. I am forced to consider my destruction here in this awful waste. How many times can the boat be rolled over before she gives up? Could she withstand a pitchpoling? Could I? A radical and amusing vessel for a crew, she is wrong for one man in this ocean, because she's just too tender and throws me about all the time. Too many bruises, too much brutality and with a gale every day there's no time for recovery. I am being weakened because of her uncompromising design and because she, too, is being weakened by the sea.

I won't give in. I'll fight, but I feel like David must have felt when he saw the full potential of Goliath. I hope I'll find my slingshot and I pray my aim will be true.

137

16

Tonight I am jammed in the bulkhead door beside the transmitter. I have some notepaper on the bench under the reading light because so many hams turn up on the skeds these days it is hard to keep a track of all the call-signs. A contact with *Spirit of Pentax* this far down in the Southern Ocean has become sought after in the amateur radio world.

Bill comes up, across in Western Australia, but the reception is not always good and sometimes Ron has to go between. But I can hear Bill and Cedric fairly well.

Bill needs to know exactly where the fault is and the explanation takes the best part of an hour. Some unsuspecting ham in Sydney comes up on the frequency and he is quickly asked to move on. We change frequencies, up and down the band several times, but eventually Bill understands the problem. Cedric speaks about a telephone call from Merran while Bill thinks the problem over. Then Bill comes back and explains how to dismantle part of the steering, and what sort of jury-repair I could carry out. While the sea is still high, he recommends a temporary change. During the call, I have to climb down into the lazarette to make some measurements. It is very black on the ocean tonight. An overtaking wave crackles with phosphorescence.

From my description of the problem, Bill says he is confident that the repair he suggests will work. He says I shouldn't worry unduly about the key-way because it is very strong. I don't share his optimism, because I have seen the wear on it. However, I feel much better having talked to him.

It's dawn now, but I feel relieved and fall asleep. It's the best, most relaxed sleep since New Zealand.

I spend a long time in the lazarette. It's uncomfortable and cramped, but by the time I emerge, the steering is holding better. I have managed to pack the new bolt, so there is less slop. I put "inspect and tighten" on my daily maintenance list. The steering is far from corrected, but it is much better. I am going to have to treat it as a fragile piece of equipment, otherwise I doubt that I will get another thousand miles out of it. But the relief of not having to turn back to New Zealand is immense.

Log.0840 hours: Barometer 972 mbs, steady. Wind comes further north, but it's very light still. I should have the main up, but with the glass so low, I fear getting caught out by a sixty-knot wall. On the sked, Martin had some good ideas about the steering and suggestions about Derek. He rang the maker's agents in Auckland today to discuss the problem of hyperactivity when off the wind in rough conditions. With all those well-wishers, I feel guilty for letting myself get depressed. I've got to succeed in passing the Horn, even if it's just for the people who are working so hard to help me. Weatherwise, it'd be a great night if it weren't for the barometer. I told Martin that it had risen by .25 mbs. I know I shouldn't have said it, because just now when I looked again, it had gone back to 972.

Log 2249 hours: All but becalmed again, which has been the position through the night. I usually hate it, but now a calm is welcome since I've had enough rough weather to last a long time. It was very cold last night, even with all my clothes on – the usual state of affairs – I was frozen. I only felt warm again near getting-up time. I use the term "getting-up time" because what else can you say when time has changed so much. Sometimes it is dawn when I am going to bed. I told Lilian on the radio last night I now doubted I would go around again. She asked me why. I said because of the self-steering, steering, the leaks and the state of the vessel after so much punishment. I asked her to keep it to herself, my friend (and literary agent) George Greenfield and Jack Huke. I didn't tell Peter Cox about my feeling when our call came through, but spoke about the plan to try to meet the other lone sailor, David Scott Cowper, for Christmas. Peter didn't sound too enthusiastic which surprised me as I think it is a good Christmas story. Peter says Pentax will be handling the publicity more aggressively from the New Year and would I call him each week. I said I'll try but I wonder if he knows the difficulties. It would be easier to communicate were I out in space.

I opened some mail this morning. The recent excitement meant I missed two days of letter opening. The letter I chose to open was amusing, ironically. It was from the Bank trustee enclosing my will for signature. The trouble I'd had over this damned will.

It began when Eddie Ball brought a will form to Plymouth for me. The morning of my departure, I wrote the will in my hotel room and gave it to a friend to hold on to until I could find two people to witness my signature. She put it into her handbag – a fatal move, of course – and it didn't get signed.

After I had gone, the will was sent to Lilian, who admits she signed it for me so that if the worst happened at least my last wishes would be honoured. I was concerned about this, so in Australia I completed another will. In the first will, I provided for a good boozy wake to be held at Giovanni's restaurant in Crawford Street if I went missing. After all the help I received in Australia, I included a further provision for a wake at the Fremantle Sailing Club, as well as at Vecchio Parioli.

I sent a copy of this amended will off to Britain, but the trustee had by now discovered I had some of the original wording wrong. His letter had reached me in Dunedin, but I had not opened it till now. Included in the letter was the will I signed in Australia.

Now I was in the roughest sea in the world, the most dangerous part of the whole voyage, and in possession of the only two copies of my will, one in my handwriting and the other one corrected, neatly typed and awaiting my signature. I wrote a further clause for a good New Zealand wake at the Ravensbourne Boating Club, signed it, sealed it inside some plastic bags from the food parcels, and put it safely with the logs in a watertight container. If I did not survive but the yacht did, maybe some parties could be held and memories of me would still bring a smile to a number of faces for a little while. As with most people in this crazy world, I am not worth much alive in hard cash. But dead I represent a small fortune, thanks to the strange ways of insurance.

Log 0240 hours: Barometer 976 mbs, up two and a half. Good chat with Mac on the radio, then we changed to Matt's frequency where I spoke to David Scott Cowper. Good old varsity rugger blue voice, full of adventuring madness and not short of insensitivity, I shouldn't wonder. Still, hell of a lot of guts. I'd hate him to know how terrified I am at the daunting thought of the Horn ahead.

The wind was staying at thirty knots, so I decided to apply myself to the problem of the retaining pin which slides out of the wheel drum and disengages Mr Rowley. A duplicate pin was in the spares kit, so I began drilling a hole in it; by using a split-pin I will be able to stop it coming out. The pin is nearly half an inch thick, and stainless, so to drill it is a long job. This one proves to be stubborn, too. After several hours and a great many cups of tea, I was through. Out on deck, push the new pin proudly in – and it is too short. Who would expect a duplicate retaining pin in the spares kit to be half an inch shorter than the original? Trust the Frogs to make the pins different sizes, I wrote in the logbook.

As usual my eyes were seldom far from the barometer, which had been incredibly low for too long. Now it started to rise, but the conditions changed very little. The good news came from the hams that two intense Lows were the cause and one had gone to the south and the second had passed well to the north on an eastward passage. We had been spared another ghastly assault, gradually the boat began to dry, and the floorboards soon lost their wet slime. On the foredeck, continually swept by waves, a lawn of seaweed was growing.

I tried to forget the barometer in order to concentrate on pushing Captain Fantastic on. We carried enough sail, though I tried never to over-canvas her, even in lighter airs. Experience in this ocean showed how unwise it was; conditions changed just too rapidly. I was hoping to get a good photo collection of clouds for an exhibition in London and spent spare moments busy with the Pentax, which had been replaced in Perth. Birds were another favourite, and I worked hard at trying to capture their grace, and their personalities. The ME Super was good to use, and I found the auto-winder a help in the bird shots. Prions were particularly difficult to catch in flight, but would have been virtually hopeless without the winder.

"We've got a reply from the makers," John Tenhave announced on the ham bands. "If I sound in a buoyant mood, it's because it was our Christmas party at work today." Yes, he was floating well.

"I'll read it all to you in a moment, but they say that the problems are caused by your driving the boat too hard."

"How flattering," I replied. "I have been feeling a bit guilty about not pushing hard enough. But conditions are so wild here and so changeable, I'm not too keen to put up very much canvas."

John read the reply, which was not particularly useful, although they did offer to send some equipment to New Zealand. Well, it would be a help on the second run round. I preferred not to think that far ahead. Looking after today was just sufficient.

A baker in Dunedin had given me two large cartons of partly baked bread which was going off rapidly, so I had a baking session and managed to get them all done. They hung in nets amidships, but soon got smaller through continual rubbing, so that wet crumbs covered the stores and the alternative berth.

The Icom continued to work well so I was able to talk to Merran, but I knew it would not be long before only the hams would reach me. Activity on the boat became minimal. I either steered to save the trouble of continually correcting Mr Rowley, or I tried to read below, and dodge the leaks and drips that forced their way into the boat.

I had a library of books of all types with me because I wasn't sure what I would want to read. I had anticipated that novels, with stories well removed from the ocean, would be the favourites. But I found I preferred books to do with the sea, particularly sail. I did not read a quarter of the library; the boat and the sea held my attention too much. Most reading was confined to gale times. The Seamen's Mission in Dunedin had given me some books and my mother had collected some more. I had sorted through them, sifting out any of an erotic nature.

"How surprising," Mum had said. We were having breakfast in the house overlooking Otago harbour. "I should have thought a sailor would have insisted on them."

"I'm not a great spectator," I had answered, "and I don't want to be reminded about something I can't have."

It hadn't been a hasty decision. I had weighed up my feelings about sex and the single-handed sailor in earlier voyages and had decided definitely to ban what, in the army, they call Stick Books. If you are on a diet, there's no point in reading cook books, and I didn't want my mind to dwell on the subject. If a chance existed of my thoughts reaching a higher plane than is normally possible in urban living, I did not want to deter it. However I had relented over one book from the family collection, *The Happy Hooker*, which I read in a long, miserable gale. It was an equally miserable book, but I was determined to see it to the end. However, some of the middle chapters were missing and the last ones were repeated. It was a binder's error and perhaps a hint from somewhere that I should have stuck to my decision. It was the only book in the whole voyage that ever left the boat at sea.

We were 2600 miles from the Horn, blasted by more than fifty knots, then in light winds, then hit by a storm again. But the barometer stayed around a thousand millibars, which was a lot healthier.

Log 2100 hours: Breakfast of orange, toast, Brenda's home-made marmalade and tea. In a sleepy state today, after a good night. I had been up doing a sail change when the wind reached fifty knots. It was eerie as waves with phosphorescent tops broke around the boat and galloped off into the darkness. I shook the reef out of the yankee this morning and gybed us around, as we were heading for Tahiti. The cloud cover is edging aside and more sun arrives. Could it be almost another Monday again? And only a few days before Christmas? I'll have to get some of the presents out of the stores soon, so I can enjoy it traditionally. I remember so well the Christmas before last when I was on my own poring over charts for this voyage. (It was just before I met Carol and I was a recluse for a week in my flat; I think I was much lonelier then than now.) I hope I am in good form when we are making the descent to the

Horn and while we are going past. After that it is a dash for the sunshine of 40°S as at the moment my plan is to aim for Cape Town, then see how I am for timing. This weather is extraordinary. A screaming fifty knots last night and now a sunny Force 6. And rises of barometer with prolonged fronts. Perhaps last night's was a front, but at least they don't go on for days at a time. Touch wood.

It's the longest day today, my second this year, as June 21 was the longest day in the northern hemisphere for me. The barometer at 1024 mbs seems to be exaggerating the pressure. The Fremantle Rotary Club one gives us 1017. I feel it is more likely to be right, or am I trying to spare myself for when the big drop starts happening? With the glass so high, the crew were permitted wine with dinner. It went down well. Our position this morning puts us east of 129°W which shows we are moving along well. Mr Rowley seems particularly good now, which is a tremendous relief. Oh, long may it last. I have no answers to what will happen when we get into higher latitudes near the Horn – I will be terribly dependent on the self-steering. For so long I have dreamed of passing Hornos, but now it is getting close, I can't wait for us to be through and heading back to the sunshine.

I wrote in the logbook today:

Dear Father Christmas:
    What I'd like for Christmas most of all is to be home, safe and sound. Of course I want the voyage to be a success and I want to round the Horn. But most of all I'd like to be home with friends and Loved Ones.
Yours,
Paul
PS: Grant me this present and I promise to be good for a whole year. Well, very nearly good for almost all of the year.

I speak to David Scott Cowper again on the radio, but it looks like we are still too far apart for a Christmas meeting. He tells me that the Horn is not always rough and I just might have a good passing. He is encouraging and I am grateful for that. I say I have estimated our arrival at the Horn for January 9. (By the Grace of God.)

Art is a friend of Doug's who comes up on the bands often. I know him quite well. In my mind's eye, he is a real digger sort, salt of the earth, but quite possibly an accountant and I guess about sixty or so. But today we have a long chat and he tells me he is seventy-four. His wife died in January, but they have a son who is a physicist at Cambridge. They visited him in 1976 and toured England and Scotland. Art is a retired railwayman. We talk about places he saw on the tour and about welded tracks and British Rail. He used to race pigeons but he returned to his old hobby of amateur radio when his health forced him to quit work early. He's had four coronaries, he says. I know Art so well, his voice, his sense of humour, the nuances in his conversation and his way of thinking. Yet I'd never recognise him if we passed one another in the street.

"If I were you, I'd go outside Estados." It's David Scott Cowper on the radio. He sounds like an RAF Spitfire pilot, but there's warmth behind the crispness. I had asked him about cutting the corner after the Horn and going through the Le Maire Straits. It's a pretty deadly stretch of water. The tide goes at fourteen knots at times. Get it right, though, and it has to be an incredible escalator. "I'd stand well off, before you head north."

"The recommended route is to go straight up to 40° and then cross on that latitude," I said.

Draw a line between South Africa and the Horn and the route is lined with icebergs, so sailing ships would always follow the South American coast till they got to the Roaring Forties, then continue eastwards.

"Do you remember when we met?"

"No, I don't think we have, David."

"Yes, we met in the Round Britain Race. You were becalmed at the Fastnet Rock and we were there, too."

"Good grief, were you on *Galway Blazer*?"

"I was with Jock McLeod. When we got close, we hailed one another."

"I remember it well. I told Jock I'd buy him a beer when we got to the Hebrides. The moment he saw me there he insisted on his drink."

"What was it like when you passed Stewart Island?" he asked.

"Thereby hangs a tale, as they say."

It was a good sked. We were on similar longitudes and planned to speak just before Christmas Day. But atmospheres intervened and we did not meet up again for a long time.

In from steering for a late lunch. It's freezing out there. High cloud is blocking the sun, so the wind from the ice is unwarmed. I found Mum's cooking amidships in a plastic box, plus a good letter. I had a couple of cupcakes with lunch, plus some Scots milk, Dunedin coffee, Perth brandy, and Australian honey: rather international. I got out the quilted trousers for the first time. Oh, Henri, they're excellent; I haven't changed my polars since port, hoping to make them last a month, then I'll get into the heavy stuff from Helly-Hansen.

We're charging along at the moment and I'm wondering if we should reef. But it's so good to be making progress, it seems a shame to alter things. Mr Rowley is coping so perhaps I'll leave it at present. I hate getting up in the night to reef – now it's so cold – but I think I dislike tampering with the speed even more. My nerves are quite on edge; no doubt because we are so far inside the berg limit. But if we don't cut a few corners we're going to be a long time getting anywhere.

Fog, rain, what a rough ride. Swinging from side to side, having boiled eggs and toast only by sheer determination. And at the end a particular lurch spills the egg-water over the remains of the loaf. Trying to use the bucket is ten times more difficult, and the wild weather has stolen the wash-bucket; yet another one gone to Davy Jones.

Meridian, or noon, today is at 2003, which is 8 pm really. Perhaps the sun might come out today. The floor is awash in the main cabin, despite pumpings. The area in front of the cooker, in the draught of the heater, looks dry. So the heater must be doing some good. Had it on through the night, but it seems warmer today.

Slept quite well for eight hours, though never really soundly. I feel tired now. I often fear that sleep is a way of burying my head in the sand, ostrich-style; very dangerous for me and the voyage. But the whole thing is crazy; inside the berg limit, racing along hour after hour, without so much as a quick look round sometimes. And now it's foggy so there's nothing to be seen anyway. How many thousands of miles of ocean have we crossed and never seen? During the night we were surging at ten knots, a good speed which would make an interesting outcome of touching something solid. It is amazing to be on deck at night watching us roaring forward. Mile after mesmeric mile, hour after hour, day after day and week after week. Can the world really be this huge?

It's merry Xmas Eve, with the wind at Force 9 and a difficult breakfast of toast, marmalade and coffee as the boat is being flung about a lot. Wet floors and bilging out, heater going and I'm leaving one ring lit on the cooker, too. Some strong gusts coming through, around forty-eight knots, and a full swell which topples us over at times. Then at mealtimes it's a matter of trying to balance what I'm eating and preventing a fall on to the cooker. Great dexterity rules. Hail is falling and overwhelming the other sounds, including Hazel O'Connor. With this huge swell running, there's not much for me to do, so I have been in the horizontal library with *Tracks* which I am enjoying. Reading in the berth is uncomfortable but I can't sit in the saloon to read, everything's too wet. I read standing sometimes, but I'm always being thrown around. The berth is mainly dry and I don't fall out, not often anyway. The heating arrangement is working out quite well. The floor's drying and so is my one wool hat which fell in the bilges.

I have been thinking about how I can press on with the voyage, rather than ending in the next ocean. But the trouble is the growing leaks and chafe damage. The steering and Mr Rowley, too, though he's been very good in this blow.

Friday, Christmas Day 1981: Rod Stewart with "Mandolin Wind" heralds my Christmas. It's sunny with big menacing squall clouds, and the gale is biting. But it is warm in the main cabin thanks to the heater. When it's going and I'm on deck working, I can smell it on the wind and it's homely, evocative of open fires and of the King Country, felling and collecting manuka wood for the farms.

A cold front crossing the area seems to have had second thoughts, for the expected continued rise in the barometer just hasn't occurred. In fact the barometer is thinking of dropping. So it has been low pressure, a big sea and gale winds with us zooming along on reefed staysail and storm jib for most of Christmas dinner.

It was very rough below and I had to hold on to my glass, bottle and food. Yes, glass. An actual glass glass which I have been saving for a decent occasion. Lunch was rainbow trout, Le Parfait, and a bottle of Alsace wine (with a Harrods label, no less). Our hero staggered to his bunk after this to listen to the BBC World Service and rose in time for the 0500 sked. This was disappointing because conditions were bad. However, several Christmas messages did come through.

A bottle of Speights disappeared quite quickly through this and then presents were found, small bottles of champers, so this had to be tried while Christmas cards were opened. All the while desperately holding on for balance. Dinner was onion, potatoes, garlic, tomatoes and a tin of poulet chasseur. I enjoyed it and a full bottle of New Zealand wine helped.

Our Boxing Day meridian gives us 51° 31'S and when we gybe our course comes round to the east, so it looks like we might be able to stay in this high latitude and cut the corner. Of course, we're right in the iceberg limit here, so a watchful eye is needed. At night it's blackness itself and visibility is right down as rain sweeps through on the forty-five-knot gusts.

It's fourteen hundred miles to the Horn and today is my birthday. At midnight I went on deck and thanked God for getting me this far. I tried to use a regular prayer, thinking it might be appreciated, but I could not remember any. I suspected embarrassment made me forget them, but embarrassed from or by what? Then after about twenty minutes of meditative study of our wake and our direction, I came below for some Moët and to open the cards. Most had been put on board at Plymouth. It was good to get those messages. At 0100 no less than five hams were on frequency to say, "Happy birthday".

I've got the mainsail up for the first time for days. It's a gorgeous day for this part of the world. Sunny, warm out of the frozen wind, with white "fluffy" clouds.

Whitbread Round the World yachts started from Auckland today and gave rise to the competitive feeling again. But I don't want that. This is for *me*, this voyage. I haven't heard any more of the Australian who set out to copy me from Perth recently. I suppose he's in the Indian Ocean. I do hope our paths do not cross; I don't want anything to do with him.

Log Monday: Where has the day gone? Greased and moved round Mr Rowley's control lines, port and starboard, greased the yankee sheets, keel top-bolts and the steering arm, as advised by John Tenhave. It's about twelve hundred miles to old Cape Stiff; just doesn't seem possible that we could be this close.

17

The fog is back. Stronger winds, then it goes lighter. Very grey this morning. I am cleaning up the galley, then amidships and now I've got the spare bunk actually cleared off. I find a birthday present under the mess. It's from Lilian and it's a sort of home-coming suit, white jeans, jersey, shoes, very Chelsea. What a super thought.

It's a dark night out, well dark as things get in this latitude at this time of the year; twilight lasts for ages. Tonight I'm sleeping in a strange place, in the new berth; which is so wide I feel quite spoilt. I've serviced both genoa winches and I've put new sheets round, so now I have three pairs going forward. It's an experiment to see if I can get round the perilous task of re-reefing the sheets between the yankees and the storm jib. More fog and a slight swell now. It's warm when the sun comes out, but it's like being up a mountain, breath-misting despite the sunbursts.

I've been thinking that the only way I'll ever make up my mind about going on for the second circumnavigation will be if I can stop being scared for a while. And I need time to think without civilisation being so close, with fewer skeds with my ham friends, so that I am further from being reminded constantly of the temptation of people. Yet when Ron said through the atmospherics that they would abandon the 0100 sked because of poor propagation I thought, "Well, that's going to be the end of talking to them," and something not far removed from panic swept through me. It's true that the radio has made a tremendous difference to this voyage, not just from getting the weather, but the human contact. I know I will hate it when it all stops.

Will we go on for the double? I can't say. It's too much of a challenge to even understand. Let's go on and complete one lap and then weigh it all up. It's too late in the year for the double really. To chance it is to chance losing everything. But let's think again if and when, by the Grace of God, we complete a single round of the globe. It's such a big, big world; too big for the mind to cope with.

Damn this fog. How am I supposed to find my position? It's most important now the Horn is so close. I guess at a sight and it's way out, then a clearing happens in line with the sun and the horizon. I'm so delighted I take the minutes and the hour from my Timex but I forget the seconds. I go back again and a fog bank swirls a clearing to the horizon. I feel the great openness – the great wide outdoors that you find outback in New Zealand and on the ocean. Boundless.

The sight works out, it's near my estimated position. Well, actually about 950 miles to the Horn, the way the albatross flies. The sea is so flat and blue under each break in the clouds. By the boat it's dark, near the horizon silver and shining. We've got to be careful here. Mustn't be caught out by the weather which has a reputation of being fiercer here than anywhere. Bubbling noises of the hull easing through the blue, the gentle rattling of the water generator reverberating along the hull. A squeak in the rigging, a block thinks it's a land bird. Will the weather hold or will we be smashed by those hurricane cold fronts now we are so far south? We have to go closer still to the ice.

We can't end the year dirty so I have a bath, yes, a stand-up bath. First of the whole voyage and a fitting climax to the twenty-ninth day from New Zealand. Top to toe, well not the hair, that'll have to wait until the sea is warmer. Damn chilly business but follow it with a good powdering and into clean clothes. Yes, no expense here in the Southern Ocean. Helly-Hansen's red heavy polar gear – I look like Santa Claus but very warm and comfortable. We've even got a red riding hood. While the sun was defrosting the deck earlier, I took a book and sat on the heavy staysail and read for a little. Been wandering about shouting and hooting and going just a little bit mad between tasks. I don't know why. Perhaps it helps ease the nerves. Fog around all day now and it's much thicker and colder. We are close to the iceberg limit again. It is all so unreal. High pressure, flattish sea, no visibility, nothing like I expected. I hope we don't have to pay for this relatively relaxed period. It's very cold in the fog. I've cleaned up the heater and it seems most improved. One day we might return to blighty and sleep comfortably. I often think about that but I don't take the idea too seriously. Sheets and sleeping without clothes, someone else cooking occasionally and being clean. Do these ideas really exist? Obviously not or no one would ever go to sea. We are beating as the High moves on; the wind has come forward of the beam. Grey, grey morning. I bring in the sheets so the sails are acrofoil sections towards the wind. My efforts are watched by a huge albatross but I don't think he is too impressed. "Be all right," he says, looking at the red sails, "when the adult plumage arrives." I've had a good breakfast in an effort to

149

rid myself of this eerie unease that throngs me from time to time and this morning especially. It might be caused by frustration at only being able to achieve such a wretched course. I'm banking on the wind coming back to the west soon. If it doesn't, then we'll just have to harden up north for a while. I always do feel awful when the barometer starts to fall. It could be that I'm scared stiff, of course.

Chopped a great piece of skin off my finger with a winch handle the other day. Every time I touch the sails now it gets opened up again. Got the meridian. We're down to 55°S. The sun burned through just long enough, then stayed hidden. How I'd like to get out of this ice area; we are far too vulnerable for this sort of thing in these high latitudes. Brrr! into the quilted top and trousers, tearing my finger open again in eagerness. I don't want to be this close to Antarctica for a moment longer than necessary.

Now there are eight hundred miles to go to Cape Horn. More prions about than we've seen for many days and this morning I saw a skua friend. They've been missing for at least a couple of weeks. Everything's grey here. Sea, sky, sun. It's nearly 1982 but I don't think I'll be opening any Moët, it's too cold; watching steam rising from a teabag when I put it in my usual rubbish container, an empty milk packet. I was down on the cabin sole inspecting the saltwater inlet and some bilgewater splashed on to a finger and actually steamed; that's what I call cold.

A new year. Wear ship! I worked out our reciprocal course. The wind veered even further, so I confidently expected quite a good direction. Here we are 40° off the wind and we are struggling to hold 335°. Before we were at 120° at 45° off the wind, so that's 145° between the tacks. It's nonsense, it can't happen, yet it does. Ridiculously, she points well, disregarding the angle of heel. Yet we always have this trouble tacking. Fortunately it's a lee-bow time, so we should make a marginally better course. Well, the barometer's going down so possibly a different weather picture will emerge and we will return to the prevailing westerlies. Robin Knox-Johnston had a week of easterlies on his way to the Horn. Hopefully we won't be in for that; my patience isn't as good as his and we do suffer from this acute angle when we are on the wind.

Great sked with Ron, Mac and Doug, with Art in the background, and Cedric, too. So exchanges of Happy New Year. It bucked me up no end. New Year's resolutions, please; I'll try to be better and be more understanding with people. Wind-vane keeps turning on its own again; I have tied it on well to a wind-generator shroud. Some heavy pounding in this chop, shuddering right through the boat. Crashing along, jarring, and after some hours we've just about doubled back on ourselves. Thank goodness for the current; we're sixteen miles further to the east than we were twelve hours and seventy miles ago. That's showbiz for you. We have a gale and then it eases. I'm trying to adapt the leak–umbrella I have in the master chamber, maybe I'll stop those two wretched streams over my bunk. Some of the time I can't be sure if it's day or night. I don't seem to be sleeping very much but I think I must be playing a game of navigational suicide. I was dozing and I felt sure we were off course yet I dreamed a windshift corrected it for us. Of course, when I checked on rising, we were off course. When will I learn? We've been on a course of 100° and that's way out.

What a start to the day. Missed with the bucket this morning, opened a new nautical almanac and found pages missing, tore a page of the logbook by accident, failed to get the cooker going and filled the saloon with smoke instead . . . and accidentally left the wind generator off all night. The meridian puts us at 56° and, wouldn't you know it, into the ice limit again. This fog is such a worry in these iceberg areas. I got out the South Atlantic chart and thought about what happens after the Horn, God willing we pass happily. One moment I think, Definitely carry on, later I think quite the opposite. A particular worry is that to turn to UK now becomes a "he gave up" situation and the ordeal of the circumnavigation is forgotten or just plain overlooked. Still, it's a long time before I need to decide. Whatever direction, we are recommended to head north after the Horn and the iceberg limit goes up an awful long way. So we are obliged to go near the Falklands no matter what. I was looking into the fog and watching the swell. It has to be seen. It is so big. Your sea is so big and my ship so small . . .

Today the sun came out, went and then came back. What a difference that made. Too late for the meridian, but not too late to put a bit of life into the ship. The heater came to the top of the maintenance list. Well, just a short job; see if another pressure valve can be found and I should have known that I could rely on Les Carvel as there are two or three. Well, why not replace the whole burner while I'm at it? It's a simple job; if you've done it before it takes a few minutes. But if the heater's stuck in a dark corner and you've not had that experience, then it's different. It took ages, but eventually we got there. Still it wouldn't work properly. Obviously the valve by the pressure tank. I replaced it. Still no, so I worked down the various divisions on the pipe from beginning to end, beautifully installed but damned fiddly if you're in a big seaway. And of course the fault was right at the end. There was a spare so I was able to replace it. Then I had to stop the leaks at that fitting.

Two new washers, a lot of tightening, then trying different combinations – and yet another. Finally it's not leaking and now the heater is going fantastically.

My legs are covered in what look like bites. Itch like hell. Is it a coincidence that it happened after working in the store? Or is it something I ate? A creature was flying in there this morning. Normal reaction would be to swat it, but it's the only other living thing, so it is spared. Even welcomed aboard. I think it has come with the flowers that I have brought to throw overboard in memory of the lone, lost sailor Al Hansen. There are strange noises coming from the steering in the cabin area but I haven't located the cause yet. The sky such a delicate blue when the clouds go back. A big albatross came over and then some sooty ones, too. The heater has been going well so I slept and had a good rest tonight. We are rolling about under the big staysail and the poled-out number one. If I had the courage the big boy would be there, too, but it's not worth the risk in this ocean. I've been sorting out the fruit and restowing it.

Our latest position gives us 450 miles to the Horn. Now we are one month and a day behind the original plan. Not bad when we started two weeks late and have spent some time in ports.

The noise that happens occasionally from the steering seems to be the main gearbox under the pedestal. I fear it is seizing. I took Mr Rowley off and the system is very stiff. In fact, I had to use force to free it. This is a blow as I'm going to have to do something. I can see no way of preparing it at sea. If I had to stop I'd prefer Cape Town but now it looks like the Falklands. I use some rigging wire to improve my join in the main steering. I shall be eating soon and going to bed earlier so that I can get back to more daylight time. There's not much darkness here at present but it makes sense to use the natural light as much as I can.

How well looked after we are, with the weather at present. The steering is a major worry. I just don't know what to do. It's giving out rather ominous groans now and I think the noise must have got through to my subconscious because I dreamed I had landed. I turned on the transistor and was able to pick up a medium-wave station. One of the exciting aspects of making a landfall, or passing nearby. I heard "Don't Cry for Me Argentina" on, presumably, an Argentinian station. We have had brown and grey prions in our company for some time but today the silver-grey ones are back. I think I prefer the brown and greys; they are more inquisitive and friendlier. The dolphins have returned. They're black and white and they have been playing by the cutwater, some leaping from the overtaking wave into the stream just forward of the bow. We're doing nine knots at times but this must be a puny speed to them. It's great to hear their squeaks again. A butterfly petrel came past. It's good to see this old friend back. We've been through some barren wastes recently. I was trying to raise Falkland Radio when I heard a woman's voice on four megs. She could hardly hear me. A man said try eight megs. Well, in the background he was reeling off digits, so I looked up volume one and found what I thought sounded similar and there was Falkland Radio pretty clear, really.

It had been blowing thirty knots but now it's over forty and that calls for a complete sail change. It's becoming quite a challenge to the stamina. I thought I would recover with a cup of coffee but the cooker disagreed and a battle of determination followed. I think I didn't win. I had to turn the cooker off eventually; a skylight and a door had to be opened to try to get rid of the paraffin smoke. Had a great sked with Ron and I was able to tell him of the new problem with the steering. Cedric phoned Bill who came back with a possible answer. When the weather goes down I will try it out. They have told me that in the Whitbread Round the World Race *Flyer* is getting close to me. I have had to reduce the sails because the wind is now Force 9, but there is a gap between these very strong gusts and I have a great fear that some of the Whitbread boats may come along and see us undercanvassed.

I have at last got through to *Endurance*, the British ice patrol ship; Captain Nicholas Barker, who seems a very pleasant chap, has some advice to give me about icebergs; he says that few are going north of 50° at the present time. He suggests I stay in these high latitudes, which would certainly cut the corner for me. Grey day but visibility is much better. There's hardly any wind, the sea is quite flat.

I know we've passed the Horn's longitude but I go back to bed. There's nothing to be seen. Until you can see the Horn how can you say you've passed it? I get up for breakfast but have a look around first.

Land-ho! Under the lee is something solid. It's got to be the Horn. It is, it is actually the Horn. I can't believe it. A thimble sticking up under the staysail. We've done it, ship, man and his God. I'm truly grateful. The sun is trying to come out. You can feel the water is shallow. There are prions and butterfly petrels to witness our arrival. Incredibly I am seeing this outcrop of civilisation just as Captain Cook saw it, as William Bligh saw it, and it hasn't changed at all. It seems unbelievable that so much could go on in the world and yet these things never alter. I sail towards it and now we are only a few miles off. I get the flowers for Al Hansen and put them over the side. "Our Father which art in Heaven, Hallowed be thy name . . ."

I start again: "Our Father who art in Heaven, Hallowed be . . ."

I always forget the Lord's Prayer on this voyage and yet I think it would be right for me to say it. I have a Bible from the Seamen's Mission; perhaps I should read the Twenty-Third Psalm from it, though Pink Floyd do it better. But Al was a sailor, he doesn't need prepared messages.

"Al, these flowers are for you. It's a long time ago that you went but you are not forgotten. You helped inspire me and many, many other people. I hope you're happy where you are. These flowers are from New Zealand but the thought is from all round the world."

There was just him and a dog and a cat and they sailed west-about, the difficult way around the Horn. He was the first man to do it alone but he didn't get very far. Some time later his boat was found broken up on the west coast. "Goodbye, Al, maybe we'll speak on the second time round."

I take some photographs, use up a couple of films. I fly Henri's firm's banner from the backstay because I know he wants to be a part of this type of adventure. I then put the flag into the sea. I think Henri would like it that way. Then we move off. There's a big roll of cloud approaching and as it goes through, the wind jumps from fifteen to thirty-five knots. It's summer down here. In the winter a roll like that could change the wind strength severalfold. We've been lucky this time, Captain Fantastic and I. The wind leaped from north east to north west on that little front. I began to understand Cape Horn weather. Then I cut that finger open again on the damn main halyard winch.

It's time to celebrate, so we have a dinner party, New Zealand potatoes and onions and one of Barry's Christmas presents, boeuf en daube. It's great to be here at the Horn, but we don't want to be wasting time. Moët for aperitif, then a Beaujolais from Lilian for the meal. I let it breathe; no reason why we can't be civilised now. Here's a toast to you, Captain Fantastic, and the crew, a Cape Horner at last. I find a radio station and we are listening to disco music and Blondie. I sing, "What shall we do with a drunken sailor," and Staten Island is under the lee. But the wind is going and with a glass in my hand I watch the sunset off the Horn as it tries to impress the clouds. It's so surreal, it's quite beautiful and I'm moved. Later the hams come on and everybody, too many call-signs to take down, is offering me congratulations. It's great because our triumph is theirs; their weather forecasts, their words of encouragement when the going was really bad; then Mac comes on.

"I've only got one thing to say," he announces. The propagation is excellent; I can almost see Mac standing by the self-steering. "You bloody beaut. I knew you'd do it."

It's so good to hear it from him. He's become such a firm friend, always encouraging, always wishing the best for me. I feel we must have done it, if Mac says so. Ron has congratulations from David Scott Cowper who says we must have created a speed record. So I look up D. H. Clarke's book and it seems that we have. Bill Nance did the voyage from Auckland in thirty-eight days, Alec Rose from Bluff in fifty-five days, Robin Knox-Johnston from Otago in fifty-seven days and the late Nigel Tetley from Otago in forty-four days in a trimaran. Ours was thirty-six days, two hours and thirty-five minutes. I toast Captain Fantastic and pour a little Moët over her bows.

"So we win, Captain Fantastic, but it's all nonsense, of course. The only record is that I am still alive and surviving even though I know that at any second all that could change."

The schooner likes the Horn so much she's returning for another look when I wake during the night, so I put her back on course. Over breakfast Falkland Radio gives us the weather forecast and it's a good one, but the day is grey and overcast with huge albatrosses and those tiny butterfly petrels.

Ours is a record and Captain Nicholas Barker on *Endurance* tells me they have just broken a record, too – they have been the furthest south any ship has ever been, right down towards the South Pole. The ship's company pass on congratulations to us; us to them. I relay messages from Captain Tom Woodfield who I met in England to the masters of the British Antarctic Survey ships *Bransfield* and *John Biscoe*. I'm at the wheel and we're sailing along the coast of Staten Island. Radio Nationale is on the transistor. Parts of today are really good, watching this extraordinary island going along, listening to the music, some photography, planning ahead and getting out the appropriate charts. I know now I have been under the shadow of the Horn ever since I first planned this voyage; now I've done it, now I've got over the great hurdle.

It isn't going to be so difficult to do the second rounding, just give me the boat and I'll set the course. Tomorrow if the weather stays good I will attack the steering and try to repair it. Then I think we'll forget all about the possibility of going to the Falklands or Cape Town; I'll stay in these latitudes and head for Australia and New Zealand. I am very pleased to have come to a decision at last. The

155

wind is going, just puffs now. Staten Island, touched by the sun, looking like some weird lizard, yet strangely beautiful. I think of all those who died to get this far, back to when Drake was near here; all those who have died in the dreadful storms that tear through this place, yet here we are almost becalmed and drinking orange juice that we have brought from England, and by morning the sea is absolutely smooth. Very pale, blue-green, with little weed-like jellyfish. A feminine voice on the Falklands gives us the weather. How incongruous this sound, attractive, evocative, reminding me of all I am turning away from, of the gentleness I have almost forgotten, here in this great moving hostile desert.

Now for the steering. The box under the pedestal where the trouble lies is difficult to take off, but I prise it open, get the box lowered, and rusty water comes out. It will not go down any further. I can only peer in with a torch. I see rust, but I do not see any grease. I think the steering is being destroyed. I try to remove the whole of the system by taking out the forward shaft, but it will not budge. I do not have the necessary tools and it takes all my strength to move the shafts to allow the bottom of the base to go back and I can only get two of the four bolts to fit.

So now we know the truth, that the steering cannot possibly last much longer, and I fear it has not been helped by my inspection. But without it, we would have been lost before we got to the Greenwich meridian. I soak the gear in WD40 and get in as much grease as I can with a screwdriver. It is imperative that it does not rust entirely through, but I cannot be sure it will not seize completely soon. I send telegrams through Falkland Radio to Bill and Jack and the makers of the steering, telling them that I am forced into the Falklands, and ask the operator, who says her name is Susie, to find me a contact for a tow in.

We shape course for Port Stanley and now another extraordinary sound comes from the keel; it's a loud reverberation, like an oscillator gone mad, yet it seems to rise and fall with the gusts. I have taped the sound on my recorder and played it back to myself. Now I know it is not my imagination. Maybe it is a wire trace caught round the keel but it sounds too much like an electric motor to be that. The noise keeps sleep away for a long time. I have tried everything. I've stopped the wind generator from turning, but the noise is still there. I have stopped the navigational instruments from going, but that makes no difference. Yet it seems it must be caused by a wind-driven motor as it rises and falls with the gusts. I ask Ron for any suggestions about what it might be. He doesn't know. Perhaps they think I'm going mad.

Got to get to the Falklands, but the fog comes down thick and blinding and so close. The Falklands are no distance really but the wind is head-on. New Zealand all over again and we are beating. Ranging between 10° and 30° off course, then tacking on through the fog blindly. Somewhere there is Beauchene Island to be avoided. It stands well off the coast of the East Falklands which have treacherous tidal streams waiting to snatch at the unwary. I break the lead in the propelling pencil while I am doing the navigation. Golly, we have used another two inches. Four days ago we were at the Horn, but we do not seem to be able to beat this gale, which heads us wherever we turn. Our tacks are terrible. The sea is very high and grey. When it gusts over fifty knots, I heave-to. She just will not go upwind in a storm.

The transistor picks up the Falkland broadcasting station and I'm transported back to the days of steam radio by a church service, in which the minister is encouraging the people of the Falklands to embrace hardship. He speaks of the negative influence of people he describes as "hippies". I wonder what terrible freaks of nature the word "hippy" conjures for these people cut off from the world. Before many weeks pass I am drawn to the inescapable conclusion that this radio station is the worst I have heard in my life

This morning I told Brian Summers, the Falkland Islands' main radio operator, my ETA for Port Stanley was tonight, but I should have known better because by night-time we appear to be no closer.

The Islands' meteorologist, Danny Borland, with a strong Scots accent, reports that the wind is going to the south but we have heard that before and still the wind is ahead. With nightfall, the fog closes in again and I have to keep watch from the bows, the fog condensing and splashing from the sails. The blindness playing tricks before the boat, but at daylight the fog clears by half a mile and Beauchene Island comes up. The sea is heavy and it's forty-three days since we left New Zealand. Mr Rowley breaks again. The wind goes quiet and I put up all the light sails and then, when we find the Falklands, the wind increases rapidly to forty knots and I take down the sails and replace them with the Southern Ocean set. On the radio, MV *Forrest* says he is ready to come to get me, but I say we will sail to the outer harbour. By nightfall we have not made it and I tell *Forrest* we will wait until the following day. But the radio operator says: "No, we'll come and get you."

This is a small island community, he said, and they would not welcome the publicity should anything happen to me on the reefs around here. I said this was a very generous attitude and I was very relieved when out from behind the outer harbour lighthouse came a ship which gradually got bigger. It came alongside and passed over a warp. Security, human contact.

18

The *Forrest* took us in tow. It was dusk and the island darkened as we approached, as if hiding from a stranger's eyes. The mountain peaks were surrounded by cloud which aimed great banks at us. It seemed too surreal, but as we got closer to the land, I found that the clouds were accompanied by enormous katabatic winds. These winds were sometimes of storm strength and could back and veer without warning. The shores were littered with the wrecked backbones of old sailing ships.

I had found sailing into the treeless Hebrides some years earlier an extraordinary experience. This was similar, no trees, very little green, just the burnt shades of a Scottish moor. Yet here we were, the other side of the world away.

It was dark by the time we reached the inner natural harbour. A small township lay before the bow, fairy lights in hell. Kelp clutched at the keel and I realised I would need to be extremely careful if I had to leave unaccompanied. The kelp was so thick, it could easily hold a sailing vessel. The atmosphere of this strange place made me feel uncomfortable, yet there was no singular cause I could find. *Forrest* went alongside a jetty built upon the skeleton of a Cape Horner, and Captain Fantastic was made fast alongside. I had accepted the disappointment of making harbour; I could not go on without the steering working properly. Yet the tremendous relief I experienced on landfalls before was different this time. Something held me in check.

I was introduced to the men of the *Forrest* and the captain, who I eventually got to know quite well. The man who controlled the port in this colonial outpost was Harbour Master Les Halliday.

"You're more than welcome to come home for a bath," Les said. Les reminded me of an American film star. He was one of the best-looking men in Port Stanley, yet he seemed shy or suspicious. I couldn't decide which.

"Well, I guess I smell a bit too much for a home; perhaps I should get a shower at a hotel first."

"No, Peggy's expecting you," he said, "and there's plenty of hot water."

We were below, while Les checked the yacht's papers. There was a commotion on deck, which turned out to be a welcoming party from the radio-telephone station. Brian Summers, Susie and some of the people I had spoken to. These younger members of the community were very friendly. Brian was a stocky fellow with a red moustache that became sideburns part way along. Susie was slim and assured. The girls had an attractive country look about them. Les told them to stay above, but I said, Come on down. After all, I had known them for some days and they had been helpful and understanding. As we walked from the boat, another radio operator arrived. An attractive dark-haired girl who would have looked perfectly at home in Roxburghshire. This was Chrissie. She grabbed my arms and kissed me. My first affection since those brushes with fate.

"I thought that was very nice of her," I said as we drove to the Hallidays. I had suggested we walk, but Les said we would drive. It was just round the corner, but I was to learn that few islanders walked anywhere.

"Of course they'd been drinking," Les said. I looked to see if his expression were disapproving, but it was too dark in the Anglia van. "Did they invite you to the party?"

"Yes," I said. "I would have been great there, not having washed for ages. But it was nice of them."

"You could have gone. You didn't need to feel you were under any obligation to come home."

"I appreciate your offer, Les. I need a bath and it's good of you to be so hospitable."

Les seemed happier at this. "Peggy hasn't cooked a meal for you because we didn't know when you would arrive. But she'll probably make you an omelette."

Their home was similar to New Zealand houses in design. Wooden, practical and clean. But here the heat was intense, a feature of Falkland houses. The peat fires burn non-stop, keeping the houses like ovens. Yet, surprisingly, the locals wore bulky jerseys indoors and coats outside. They seemed to disregard the present weather and always dress for the worst. I was led to the bathroom, while the Hallidays and Peggy's father, a man with enormous almond-shaped eyes, sat quietly in the living room. It was a good bath and afterwards I enjoyed the omelette, which was a dark yellow because the eggs were free-range. She baked her own bread and that was delicious. They apologised for there not being room for me to stay in the house, but they would be pleased to see me for a meal again.

Les drove me back to the dampness of the yacht. He wouldn't hear of me walking the short distance to the jetty. I hoped there might be some sign of the party, but Stanley was silent.

"How long do you think you'll be here?" Les asked, as I climbed out into the cold air.

"Two days, possibly three," I said confidently. "It's absolutely vital I get back to sea as soon as possible. There's an awful long way to go, and I've lost a week in trying to make the Falklands."

"Will you do the work yourself?"

"Wish I could, Les. Some I will be able to do, but the steering needs an engineer. But Susie has found a man for me; she says he'll be at the jetty first thing."

The sleeping bag was still damp but, despite the strange feeling here, it was good to be back with people and to be clean again. Pentax had agreed to me staying in a hotel, and I would check in first thing tomorrow. I went to sleep wondering if Merran might find a way of flying here.

Rain was falling in the morning. It rained almost every day I was there. No sign of the engineer. I booked into the "best hotel" which was an adequate one-star hostel with an enormous tariff. I was soon to discover how expensive accommodation is in Stanley. I contacted Susie to find the missing engineer. She gave me his telephone number, but there was no reply. Now it was lunchtime and Les arrived to take me home for Falkland mutton. The conversation was more animated.

Les helped me try to trace the engineer. We visited various houses he was said to be working on, but we couldn't find him. Before long I was to discover that this was not an idiosyncrasy of his alone. Stanley people have a way of disappearing.

I began dismantling the self-steering system, but my main worry was the steering. I knew it would take two full days. Brian called to say he would take me out for a drink that night, which was encouraging.

I was surprised to find that many people didn't know the schooner was there. As the township sits on a hillside overlooking the harbour, you'd have to walk round with your eyes shut not to see what was happening at the jetties. It was another characteristic I was to learn about these islanders. They were as uninterested about what went on in the world as they were about foreigners in town. But, like all small communities, they revelled in gossip and within two days I knew who was into what and who was available. I learned, too, that many new settlers in the Islands were what the Americans call survivalists. They believed that civilisation would be destroyed in a nuclear holocaust, so they had taken themselves as far away from the likely bomb target as possible.

I didn't care much for the bar itself, but the beer was British and cheap, and it was good to be in company. Brian and I were chatting about cameras, when a thick-set man fell against me. He'd put a fair amount away. It was the missing engineer. He was suddenly anxious to know the problem and seemed concerned that I had so little time. He pointed to a surly customer nearby who he said was his partner. They would begin first thing in the morning. I never saw him again.

The next day, I continued with the self-steering and began drying out some of the gear.

Marje McPhee was a Celtic bundle of energy who ran a home laundry. When I took mounds of clothing to her for washing, including the sleeping bag, she said she would be happy to do any sewing I needed. So I gave her some of the torn polar wear. I feared it would be a long and expensive task, but Marje refused payment. She liked the idea behind the project and wanted this to be a donation. I thought of Marje kindly whenever I wore the gear afterwards, and when I think of a friendly Falkland face, hers is the one I see. In my search for an engineer, I received offers from people who would help on the boat, so when I telephoned Pentax to report on progress, I suggested that they host a small party for these volunteers. Pentax agreed and said a cheque would be on its way.

No money appeared so I had to swap hotels. It turned out to be not much cheaper. The next day, a strike hit the waterfront of Stanley and my "volunteers" disappeared. I now had most of the repairs finished, but the steering was still untouched.

I was in despair. My short time in Stanley was already more than a week old. I had no money and it soon became well known that the yachtsman was impoverished. Then the Falkland Islands Company announced that they had the cheque.

"It came a few days ago," the disobliging cashier told me.

I paid the first hotel off and checked on the price for a party at the second hotel for my prospective volunteers, who would turn up when the strike ended. His Excellency Rex Hunt, his wife and people who had helped, or promised to, were present. It was a great success, with the informal Governor giving an equally informal recitation.

Next day, I received the bill. I had apparently misread the

estimate. I sent off an embarrassed signal to my bank, not wishing to tap Pentax, and another long "broke" period began.

The most pleasant of the Islands' protectors was Captain Barker of the *Endurance* with whom I had a couple of lunches at Government House. He was busily writing a novel during his voyages back and forth to the ice, and was concerned about *Endurance*'s planned withdrawal from the Antarctic after that year's tour. It was a fear shared by most of the xenophobic Stanleyites.

I couldn't believe that Argentina would move against the Islands. They had so little to offer. People talked of undiscovered oil, but no one was able to say that any had been found. The hills produce mutton and wool, but the Islands are so inaccessible that it is cheaper to let more than twenty thousand carcases rot each year than to transport the food to meat-hungry Europe. Wild life could certainly attract tourists, but Argentina has it far more abundantly at Tierra del Fuego. I felt Argentina would only tackle the Islands if they thought Britain was finished there.

The strike ended, but it was days before I could get the promised volunteer help to the boat. Then began a long slow repair. The *Endurance* called into the harbour and Captain Barker loaned me his shipwright to try to complete the work. *Endurance* divers looked under the schooner to try to solve the riddle of the noisy keel, but they did not find anything.

Part of the main gearbox was stripped and taken to an engineering shop to await attention. I sat on the stern looking despondently at Mr Rowley, cheering myself up by watching some steamer ducks in action. They cannot fly, but use their wings for paddling when they want to move quickly, and are continually fighting. What high living the people of Stanley lacked was more than made up for by the exquisite wild life which visited the schooner. Seals, penguins, many varieties of fish. And Evi.

Evi was a journalist who had come to the Falkland Islands to get stories for a national magazine in Argentina. She stood beside the yacht asking for an interview.

Her English wasn't too good so when we had had some coffee, I invited her to my hotel for dinner in order to continue the laborious interview. Afterwards we went to the schooner where she said how beautiful the stars were, sitting on the doghouse roof studying them, and sighing Juliet fashion. At first I thought she was kidding, but later I learned that this was the proper conduct for a first night out in Argentina. Evi went home, I went to bed and wondered if, in becoming too modern, we were losing a lot of the romance of life.

The interview resumed next day on board. The after lines had been slipped to let *Forrest* out, and I was trying to get the stern mooring warp to land. Evi said she would walk across the amidships warp with it.

"No, you can't do that. The boat will give with the pressure on the rope and you will fall in."

"No fall in," she stormed. "Me Argentinian. We can do things like that."

Evi had misunderstood me when I described my Henri-Lloyd jacket to her. I said it floated and she took it to be some sort of wetsuit. Now she wore the trousers and jacket and found the diving goggles I used to protect my eyes from hail in fronts.

I tried to discourage her, but she walked out on the warp, the stern rope in her hands. Of course, Captain Fantastic leaned with the weight and, with schoolgirl shrieks, Evi plunged into the frozen water. She laughed and thought it was great fun. Les Halliday arrived in time to help her up the jetty. I was learning about the Argies, as the locals called them. They were spoiled kids who never grew up. They boasted like children and made silly mistakes like children. I couldn't understand why the Stanley residents hated them so violently and feared them. But despite all the bravado, Evi had guts and a good sense of fun.

"Few girls I knew in London would have dared that circus act. I like you, Evi."

"Excuse me?"

Brian Summers, from the radio station, invited me out with his girl friend Judy for a Saturday drive. We motored towards the airport, then swung off across rough terrain, following tracks that were scarcely discernible. A cold front was crossing the island and we could see its vicious edge towards the sea, which stretched away blue-grey for ever. The mountain peaks were clear and beyond lay the areas that were marked impassable on the charts. They were filled with stone-runs, virtual rivers of rocks. The view from high over the town was incredible. A barren desolate island, an unfriendly sea and an equally hostile interior. An old barque lay decomposing before us, and beyond was the town, which looked like the hydro-electric temporary towns I had known so well as a child in New Zealand. I wondered what could bring Brian and Judy to think of this God-forsaken place as home.

That evening I was invited to a dinner party, and it could have been a similar gathering in Croydon or middle-class Glasgow. Again I noticed that people asked less about the voyage here than anywhere else I had been; I got the feeling that they wanted to know as little as possible about anywhere else. This was their lot; it was bloody tough, but they didn't want to know about anything different.

Next day Evi cabled her editor, requesting another week in the Islands. He had every right to expect a pretty juicy story, I said, but I did not discover what she wrote. Evi helped me pass the time. We walked together on the hills around Stanley. Her magazine had not forwarded any expenses and she had picked on the one man in the town who was penniless. The weekend was almost here, so I did the rounds of likely places for my expected cheque. The Falkland Company. No. The post office, cable and wireless. No, no cheques have arrived. We moved out of hotel number two.

They say when poverty slips in the window, love goes out the door, but Evi stayed and shared the roughness. We had our meals out of ship's stores. But what was palatable at sea was not so tasty in port. To add insult to injury, the boat had been virtually arrested until the hotel bill was paid. Hurt, furious and frustrated, I complained in no uncertain terms to the Hunts next day, when I was invited to Government House for lunch.

By the time lunch was over a telex had arrived to say the cheque was at the island treasury.

I was grateful for their help. The hotel bill was paid and Les returned in a friendly spirit. He found me in the cellar forcing the remaining pieces of the steering together. By good fortune, rather than skill, the steering was in working order.

Evi and I hitched a Land-Rover ride to the airport and walked down through the tussock to the beach, a pale-blue sea and the green of thick kelp which protected the island from the swell. A massive elephant seal bathed near us as we ate tuna fish and Ryvita and duelled with insects for the wine. We found a large flock of penguins and Evi whooped and rushed through the birds terrifying them in her passion.

We had a last meal together. As usual the hotel dining room was full of Argentinians, this time flight crews from the once a week international jet.

Later that night I said, "I can't go to the airport with you, Evi. I'm terrible at farewells."

"No, you don't come. You stay there. May God bless you on the voyage. Just think, I go to shop to get cigarettes. I come back soon. Just think that is the way it is."

She blew kisses. She called I see you soon as she walked up into the gale and off the boat and out of my life.

It was my last day in town. Last-minute shopping, arranging a tow out, a trip to the library to check on a passage in Vito Dumas' book. I looked through the library list, but learned Naomi James' book, which had spoken warmly of the Falklanders, was not kept. The only copy I saw on the Islands was at the Hallidays – a gift from Naomi. It was a foul night again, with the rigging singing the treacherous song of the Shrieking Fifties. At dawn, Les arrived with freshly baked bread from Peggy, and Mavis Hunt stood in the rain with vegetables from Government House garden. The rest of Stanley slept.

In November 1755, William Clayton RN called the Falklands "that barren, dreary, boggy, rocky spot" and I couldn't agree more; but memorable, albeit contrasting.

The island was getting smaller. So many incongruous aspects to the Stanley people. They hated the Argies, and believed (rightly as it was to turn out) that they would be overrun one day. Yet there was no seaward watch maintained. In fact, all they had that looked out from Stanley was the lighthouse behind us, presently manned round the clock, but about to be made automatic.

When Argentinian tourists arrived, small groups of Stanley people picketed the shore-boats; with placards and abuse they told the Argies to piss off. You would imagine therefore that they would look to their protectors, the small band of hapless Royal Marines, as heroes. Yet a regular trial of young manhood was to pick on a soldier and attempt to beat him up. While I was there, a local youth chose a sailor on one of the British Antarctic Survey ships. He had to be thrown out by the steward.

The commanding officer of the Royal Marines couldn't have been more pleasant. He took me to the garrison, which was situated as far from the town as could be imagined, and I was surprised to see how short of material they were. I thought they were poorly equipped for a foreign-based military group with a Dad's Army quartermaster's store. We had lunch in his mess and all the food came from tins. It seems there was no budget for them to buy local produce.

I was very pleased to be heading back to the relative calm of the Southern Ocean.

19

Ahead my long, long racetrack. I'm going to go round the world the second time and I don't give a damn whatever happens. There's a big sea running off the entrance and the water is already coming over the side of the boat; just like old times, eh, Captain Fantastic? It's grey out here and the wind is strong. Then it's raining and the weather is very cold. Into warmer clothes; I'm taking some sail down and feeling very ill. Soon I'm forced to drop the mainsail. But by late in the day the wind is right down and we're almost becalmed. A big gibbous moon comes out and says welcome back to the outdoors.

Cook-up some chips and Peggy's eggs, fresh from the farm; very tasty, papas fritas, inspired by Evi, who's missed today. The wind comes back at thirty knots, abaft the beam. This is what we want, this is what it's all about. God, it's really good to be back at sea again.

I'd like to stay on this latitude but the wind comes round again and forces us south, the way things were in the other part of the Southern Ocean. The noise in the keel returned yesterday but went again. The *Endurance* divers who couldn't find anything in Stanley probably thought the noise was in my head.

Brian Summers comes on the radio-telephone from the Falklands with the weather forecast; he says it's going to back to the sou' west. That'll be chilly, but it should help us return to 50°. We're making good progress upwind at seven to eight knots, but all the leaks have opened up again. And, of course, the worst one over my berth. I've got a towel soaking up the drips at present.

My sun sight seems a bit shaky. I took two this morning but they did not work out. Fortunately, I found the mistake in the first and that came good. It's been a hazy sun. I guess I'm going to have to get used to it that way. For something to eat I had some of Mavis Hunt's lettuce from the Government House garden; it was really thought-ful, that. Peggy Halliday's bread makes great toast, even though my stomach and appetite have been absent without leave. There're some amazing flocks of prions in this part of the sea; these ones are white-bellied. The wind is at Gale 8 and it's bashing us from ahead. The seas are pounding right up near the crosstrees as we crash through. It stays as a gale for a while and then, overnight, it just drops away and there's nothing.

I wonder where we are? Well south of where I expect, I suppose. I thought Chrissie might come on Falkland Radio today, but they tell me she's gone. It was a nice kiss. A new voice this time, Tina. She gives us a moderate forecast, which is better than bad. Yesterday it was prions, and today skuas everywhere and some mollymawks and butterfly petrels; I say hello to them and renew our acquaintance. It's good to see friends about.

We came across a group of skuas in conference today, a couple were arguing in a circle around a clump of seaweed; seems a long time since I've heard those sounds. It's a week since we left Port Stanley and I seem to be a bit lost; I've been trying to get some sights for a couple of days, but fog comes down and blocks the sun and the horizon. I've also had a headache for several days. I wonder if it's because of the worry over not knowing where I am. We're well in the ice limit, I know that, but there's not much I can do. The wind resents us going north of east so I just push on and hope for the best.

I don't have to worry about looking out for icebergs now, I'm doing very well to see even the foremast much of the time. So tonight, with the barometer rising, I think to hell with the fog and to hell with the westerly gale, and we have a good party on board, including some cabbage from His Excellency's garden. I was thinking about Evi and Merran a great deal. I was looking forward to a telegram from Merran. I felt sure I could depend on her. But I've heard nothing. There's nothing on the amateur bands yet, either. It leaves me feeling very alone and in considerable doubt about the next long, long leg, the gear, the boat, the leaks, winter navigation; if the truth's known, it leaves me sick with worry. A voice would make all the difference. It's odd that earlier on, before the Horn, I was thinking of dispensing with most of the ham calls. I'd really hate it to happen.

A cable from Merran, that's what I need now. It's not much to ask and it can only happen in the next couple of days or so. After that, we'll be out of Falkland Radio contact.

The barometer drops eight millibars. Looking at the routing chart, at least we're clear of the area marked "extreme limit of pack ice". It seemed more than likely we'd come across some bergy bits in that area but I tried to put it out of my mind. I've been studying the parts on the boat which I think are being affected by severe wear, stuff that we weren't able to fix in the Falklands, but which I hoped would survive. Now I am very concerned about the deterioration. The boat is not really making enough speed; I don't quite understand why, but then there's the size of the seas here, which are incredible, even when the wind isn't blowing much.

Looking up to the top of the foremast, I happen to notice the crosstrees have been heavily pitted by the leeward running backstay. When I let it off, I have to carry it forward all the way along the edge of the boat and then rush back to the cockpit. Until I get it tightened, the thing bangs against the crosstrees. I thought they were strong enough to take it, but obviously they're not; it's amazing how bad the denting is. It looks like a series of teeth from down here. If the crosstrees go, the mast will come down.

Ironically, these running backstays were installed in Australia to make sure the mast stayed put. It all adds up to suicide, to carry on, but hopefully the picture will be clearer after a few more longitudes. But, oh, the water we're taking in the saloon. This is high summer – what on earth will it be like in June? After all the hours spent on Mr Rowley, he is complaining bitterly about the voyage and I have to keep reefing-down because when the speed builds, he cannot hold on. The control lines are blackened where they go through the after wheel. I have to keep altering the position. I'm not going to be able to maintain any good speed at all at this rate. The seas appear too big and the winds are so unruly that they play havoc with the wind-vane. It's crazy. At 40° the road is too long around the world, yet at 50°, where we could just manage distance-wise, the conditions are too violent for the equipment. Our course of action is going to be dictated long before the Greenwich meridian. It is such a blow.

Another night of thick fog. I track the *Bransfield* down at long last, but I get a short reply from them; they don't have any advice to give me about the presence of icebergs. I had gathered from the British Antarctic Survey in Cambridge that they would be able to help. I speak to some people on Signey Island, but they don't know the positions of any icebergs either. Try the frequency again tomorrow, they say. Some ship might be around and have them plotted. I think to myself, a lot can happen in twenty-four hours. I fear we're going to have to make a sharp northerly heading if the Antarctic Survey crowd are not going to help.

Bransfield came on the air tonight and were most helpful. They don't track icebergs, apparently, but they did happen to know the position of four very large ones. I look at the chart and find we must have passed by – or between – them yesterday. How incredible to have been so close to disaster and not know about it due to the thick fog. Had conditions been different, they would have made some fabulous photographs.

The wind is in the east again and it's raining. We're heeling over, but at least we're beating towards the north a little. The barometer is down one millibar. If the predictions are true, we're going to see a mighty fall of pressure. It will mean another storm. On the ham sked, John McKendrick comes up from Buenos Aires.

"Where the hell have you been?" he says.

How I need to hear that. It is so good to be able to speak to a friend. He says I've been using the wrong frequency for this sked and the NZ stations have been waiting for me further along the band. Even the weather seems to have picked up the improved mood; the barometer is staying high.

Valentine's Day and I feel well. A beautiful night of stars and a big moon. I've been expecting the worst and it's the quietest night for a very long time. Maybe it isn't always good to be getting weather forecasts. The size of the stars seems unbelievable; so much bigger and very few whose names I can recall.

The barometer is going up. Insomnia . . . I've been to sleep for an hour or two but then I couldn't return. Perhaps it's the excitement of having high pressure. It's a gorgeous sky. There're some light high clouds about but the moon's up centre with Venus nearby. I think Jupiter and Saturn are to the north west of her, and there's Mars. Mercury is low to the south. It's quite incredible to see such a show of planets and so unexpected. How I enjoy this; this is my sailing weather, not the other weeks of no night sky, days of fog and horror seas. That's not my idea of fun at all. And so strange to see Venus as a morning planet now. When we start seeing night skies again, God willing, it will be lonelier without Venus there. Sixty feet of dark whale passes by; he's going our way, but he doesn't stop to talk. He's probably working out his meridian. The fog returns and it's been raining. I speak with Ian White who is a pilot on the Falklands and Percy who lives in South America. Both say there's been concern about not being able to make contact – and Percy said Merran had been trying to reach me, too, which is very good to hear. I report that I'll make a decision on my course after reaching the Greenwich meridian.

Falkland Radio came on with some weather, which is encouraging but bears little relationship to the present. I try to get the operator, Stuart, to find out if there's an approaching front, but he can't hear me. Then he says there's a telegram: "I am waiting because I love you. Wish we were together, Merran." So there, a reply at last and that's very good.

The inside steering position broke today but I found the fault quickly; I'm getting to know that system so well. Surprisingly enough, the water temperature is up, at 11°C. That and Merran's wire makes it a great day. It's eleven hundred miles to the Greenwich meridian. Sometimes I'm absolutely sure I'll peel off for home then and at others I don't see how I can. It's ten weeks, possibly eleven, round to New Zealand again. That'll be the beginning of May, which is awfully late in the year, weatherwise. We've done 181 miles in the last twenty-three hours which is good, but for each day with these favourable runs there is one of being hove-to. Soon the weather can be expected to deteriorate as the winter moves into the Southern Hemisphere.

There are three major problems at present. The skeg is showing long rust patches to starboard; presumably corrosion found in Perth is worsening. The crosstrees are damaged and continue to be hit when the backstays are moved about; and now we are approaching warmer waters the toredo worm is likely to attack the hull, through the Stewart Island scars. I'll try to get some opinions from Bill Lowe. It's my last day of wearing the red oilskins. Tomorrow it's the yellow ones, to mark the beginning of my second circumnavigation. It's such a glorious day. I bring my cup of cappuccino with honey up into the sunshine to admire the birds. We have just come across a flock of silver prions; very attractive but as impatient as their western cousins. A royal albatross passes over. There's still quite a sea running and it throws me across the cockpit. The ignominy of cappuccino over head, scarf and, of course, the red oilies on their last day out. The news today reported that South Africa lost a frigate. South west of Cape Town, with thirteen guys missing.

I've been trying for so long to get good "human interest" shots of albatross. One bold fellow this morning was ideal. He dropped into the water right beside me three times. The light wasn't so good but I got the Pentax out ready and he came near, but did not stop. On one of the previous swims, he scratched his neck with a foot, the second time he was ruffling his feathers with his beak and wore a look of wide-eyed dopiness. I stayed with the camera for ages, then it started to rain. I'll get a great shot one day, but after all this time, I'm still waiting and trying.

The navigation's been a headache again; it always is when I can't find out what's wrong. I have been unable to relate the morning and afternoon sights, but eventually I found the trouble. I was using the wrong day's declination on the noon sight. We're certainly making progress, but we are still well within the iceberg limit. You can feel the conditions are improving, with a gradual rise towards the sunshine. Maybe it's imagination, but we've had steadily better weather since Tuesday's gale. These albatrosses look happier, too. A large wandering albatross went past this morning and I yelled, "Hello," as I often do, and the monster ground his beak as if his dentures were loose.

It's not been a terribly happy day for me because I've got to make the right decision. It's bound to disappoint someone no matter what I do, but it may be better to let someone down than to destroy Captain Fantastic.

Tonight I get a message via the hams from Pentax: "Very pleased with progress. Wishing you to continue on the second trip."

I've been looking over at the skeg and I see the rust is getting much worse. She's going to have to come out of the water to have that repaired. If I go on to Australia I'll have to winter over there which won't get me home till the summer of 1983. Well, that would upset my plans for the 1984 Single-handed Trans-Atlantic Race. At present I don't see any alternative to stopping at Cape Town. I could chance going on, but if the likely happened, people could be risking their lives looking for me. And I don't think there's any doubt that to lose the yacht in these latitudes is to lose me, through exposure or drowning. It's equal odds which. By the time we reach South Africa, we'll have gone further than any other solo circumnavigator except Moitessier. The sponsors ought to be pleased with that.

It's been a good day except for Mr Rowley. I've been adjusting him to make him take a greater speed, but he won't. I had a change of clothes. Smelling a bit sweeter at the moment, thanks to Marje and all her washing and mending. A seal appeared today which is quite incredible because we are hundreds of miles from anywhere. Tonight I slept without clothes on as it is a bit warmer. How relaxing that is. The water is up 1°C.

A message from Pentax, via the hams. "The sponsors will be contacting Jack Huke concerning various problems in order to seek advice from experts in the UK also. They telexed Fremantle to advise Bill Lowe you are trying to contact him via amateur radio and they will try to put Bill in the picture as to your problems." The planets bright at night, then the clouds come back and it's fog again.

Mr Rowley breaking down and Derek taking over. Then repairing the self-steering gear. We use gales to increase the mileage with

172

me steering all day and all night; 200 miles a day, 198 miles, 200 miles a day. The water temperature is 12.5°C, yet two days ago it was 14°C, so it seems we cross and recross the sub-tropical convergence line which twists about in this part of the ocean. The boat dries out and I mostly sleep with my clothes off now and the sleeping bag unzipped. I am not sleeping well, mainly due I think to lack of exercise. I have been feeling terribly randy over the last couple of days, perhaps because a landfall is in the offing. Perhaps from the relief of almost definitely deciding to accept one-and-a-bit-times-around circumnavigation. The fog goes, comes back again; this could be our farewell from the Southern Ocean. A reminder of life down here in case we return with too romantic a view of how things are in these wasteland latitudes.

How I hunger for the sun, how I need to get these clothes off. My legs keep coming up in strange acne-like growths. They want to feel the air, fresh and warm again. A bit of boat lightening, odd useless bits go to Davy Jones. If we're definitely saying goodbye to these latitudes, much more will follow. Decisions. We need a decision about what's to happen. According to my position, we're about 1°W by 42°S. I set a decision at 0° and that gives us a breathing space till tomorrow. I seem to be guided north. Would the boat survive the winter here? I doubt it. Still lots of desires, mixed wishes, to carry on; not to carry on. Good to say we did it, true; foolhardy to proceed. The boat's strong enough but the equipment isn't. If we perished it wouldn't help the sport, the sponsors, loved ones. No, it's not just because of me. I can't help but watch the deterioration of the ship and the equipment. Still, wait; no decision until tomorrow. I listen to the sound of the water on the hull, a constant companion since June. Enjoy the birds, the eerie beauty of the fog lifting ahead and closing behind as we pass. Decide tomorrow. A ten-minute jog in the doghouse, the third day in a row we've kept up the exercise.

Today is decision day. Water is back to 14°C which means we must at last be out of the iceberg limit. Bravo! Made my first link with the South African net this morning and spoke to the controller, Davina; sounds very nice indeed. To celebrate decision day, we had two quarter-bottles of Moët and I even baked a jacket potato. A black night and the phosphorescence is brilliant silver outside. Several dolphins racing behind the boat, some swinging wildly underneath, carving through the flaring stream from the keel. I can't see them, only their wakes. I do hope they're dolphins and not playful but not-so-agile whales. It's a fitful sleep and I dream I'm in

England and staying with Merran and some friends at a country hotel. We have different rooms. Merran explains it's because this is such a short break from my journey – she cannot adjust so quickly. Her make-up is thick and completely masks her lips as though a deliberate attempt were made to hide them away. I understand in the dream that this is the new craze.

Then reality hits me as a storm smashes the self-steering and raises huge seas. We keep up the number two yankee and make some excellent dashes. The rising wind and growing sea upset the self-steering completely, throwing us off course so the jib snatches and cracks loudly. I take over steering at about 7 am, planning to give in at 9 am, but we are making good timing with the speed hovering at nine knots, so I stay till lunchtime. I try to sleep, but Derek makes such a noise I only get about three-quarters of an hour. Derek and I alternate during the afternoon. The barometer starts to drop again, heavy black clouds appear and the wind increases to fifty-five knots. Mr Rowley is taking dreadful punishment in the mountains that rush upon us. I was pooped and got quite wet in the morning. I get the water-paddle out of the sea and tie it clear. The wind shrieks after dark, and the violent motion keeps Derek correcting all the time. It is a dreadful waste of power and the strain on him must be bad. The storm helps me decide. Mr Rowley won't take another winter. Seas wash right over us, roaring into the hollow aft of the weather bow wave and smashing into the beam, catapulting on to the deck. Angry phosphorescence and sheer might as these monsters threaten to tear off the hatches and stanchions. I worry about the skeg; how can it stand this battering, and I notice that the steering is starting to stiffen again.

Word from Bill today on the radio. He is concerned about the skeg and the crosstrees. So it's to Cape Town after all. I was very relieved to hear it as I'd already decided that there was no option.

I turn to medium wave and find a South African station. We must be getting close. It's March and the water has risen to 20°C. This is our old sailing ground, back in the wintertime. It's incredible to think that it has taken this long to get round the world and a quarter more. What a huge globe this is.

It's very dark and the wind is strong. I try to get some sleep but the increasing gale makes it impossible. I spot a ship to leeward, and turn on the lights. Then I get one of the greatest scares of the voyage. I see flares to seaward, possibly twenty-five yards off. White, so it isn't distress, but at the same time I think, My God, it's a ship upon us. Then the roar of a Nimrod or similar bomber as it thunders over at mast height. It is the most terrifying noise over the top of the gale. I don't know if it is some naval manoeuvre or me being identified; a very nervous face at the doghouse door. The loom of a light over the waves. The Agulhas current; you can smell it, just like the Waikato River. Phosphorescence incredible and quite frightening at times. I identify the light and bear off towards Cape Town. It's blowing Force 9 but it's bound to drop soon. I try to remember when I last slept; it is a long time ago.

I call port control. They have not heard of *Spirit of Pentax*, but nothing matters now as we are almost at Cape Town. Through the edge of the dawn I see Table Mountain and the extraordinary range of mountains running to the south; it is fabulous and I am elated. I have not been able to work out times yet, but I know this has been a world speed record run. We should be in port and tied up within two hours.

Then the storm hits us

20

Katabatic winds of fifty knots sweep down from Table Mountain, tearing the tops from waves, pushing Captain Fantastic over to the gunwales. We're beside Sea Point, only a couple of hundred yards off. I can see people going to work, bright clothes, traffic lights. A beautiful crisp morning, except for these horrendous winds.

We begin a beat to the harbour entrance. Every inch of the schooner is groaning under the strength of the wind, lee-ho, and on the other tack. The fierceness of these gusts is unbelievable. We battle for a quarter of an hour, half an hour. But we are going to destroy the rigging for sure.

I call up port control and say there is no chance of us making the harbour entrance in fifty knots on the nose. I hope that when the sun heats the land, the katabatic winds will change; that's the law of nature. But a friendly ham warns me, "Not always at Cape Town. Sometimes they can keep up for, well, quite a while."

I raise the storm jib on the staysail and edge slowly away; waiting. The sky is incredibly blue. The sea sparkles, white and gold gannets chase after a school of dolphins.

Phone Lilian and hear that my London business interest has folded: now I am liable for a small fortune. The port captain, via Cape Town Radio, wants to know my estimated time of arrival; they are concerned that I might be out in the shipping lanes during the night. What a bloody laugh. I can't get in until the wind goes down or leaves the east.

We smash our way over the sea for hours, but we cannot make it. Not today. Not the next day. Nor the next. Twice we try to make the harbour but are knocked down by sixty-knot gusts. Soon we are two hundred miles away from Cape Town and to think that I had been able to see the traffic lights. It must be the worst black south easterly ever.

"Wild is the wind," sings David Bowie on the radio; irony. Wild is reality; there's nothing for me at home now. I suppose they'll sell my flat to pay for what I owe. I like the song, though.

Port captain offers me a tow in if I can make the breakwater. But I can't. Back to sea again, slowly, slowly; disappointment, frustration, depression gather in my wake.

Log 1713 hours: Land-ho! To port, seven to ten miles off. Sun going down, big moon rising. But not much visibility, seems very indistinct. Amplitude of sun is 275° and should be 288°, showing a compass error of no less than 13°.

Log 1840 hours: It's Dassen Island. Cape Town here we come. There's been a fire on Table Mountain and visibility is down to three miles. I stay at the wheel in the calm to five knots conditions. Thank God I can still make a boat go in very light airs. Twenty hours later, *Kusvag* turns up and tows us in.

Our warp is thrown to a slim man in a pith helmet and safari suit. He takes the rope and some seamen wandering past help him.

"My name's Joe; we've spoken on the radio."

Joe Rabinowitz, who turns out to be a city councillor, yachting correspondent and prominent sailor, becomes a firm friend and helper.

A Royal Cape Yacht Club launch comes over and tows Captain Fantastic into the club marina. Newspaper people arrive. Can we photograph you here, would you stand by the wheel? Where was it the whale dived under the boat? What was the worst moment, how many days did you go without sleep before you arrived? What do you really think of South Africa? A telex from Pentax waiting in the clubhouse. "Pentax UK will not pay your expenses in South Africa." My message to them: "Then arrange for someone else to get the boat home." There's evidently been some change of policy and personnel in London.

Captain Fantastic sits outside the clubhouse waiting for a decision. I sit on the boat waiting, but the Pentax distributors are concerned. Clive Myles, their general manager in South Africa, takes me out to lunch and gives me an envelope. "We have a calamity fund and we'd like you to have this. Not everybody's the same in the world and we don't want you to get the wrong impression of South Africa."

The sun stays hot and the cruising yachtsmen look after me. Australians Lou and Ricki become the closest and they help me to clean out the schooner. We assess essential repairs needed and get a price. It is less than a thousand pounds, cheap for a boat of Captain Fantastic's size. A week has passed and still no decision from Pentax. Ah, well, I tell Lou, it couldn't happen in a nicer place.

Yet another week, but no word from the sponsors. The excitement of being on land has lost its edge. Winter is approaching and the schooner will have to go soon if she is to leave at all. Clive Myles sends another telex to London.

I heard on the maritime net one morning that David Scott Cowper was getting close to South Africa and planned to call into Cape Town for repairs. When he got near, I called the weather office for the latest met news and relayed it on. I was surprised when I met him. He was taller than I had imagined and on land seemed to adopt eccentricity as a façade.

We had a lot to talk about; I wanted to know how he had fared round Stewart Island and Tasmania. But people were busy on his boat. I couldn't think why. It was in perfect shape, not a drop of water in the bilges, everything spotless and all gear properly stowed. It made a brothel of Captain Fantastic. When David came along to talk, he and a friend with him were openly critical of my schooner, my gear, the general condition and the sheer lack of comfort. He was close to being right, but she had taken me round the globe one and a quarter times. Who wants to hear so much criticism of a temporary extension of oneself? Love me, love my boat, I thought, and left them to their bitching.

Commodore Kingon of the South African Navy invited me to meet a prominent yachtsman who had just arrived in town, but it was all hush-hush. We went to the Cruising Association of South Africa's headquarters and there was Robin Knox-Johnston. He was much bigger than I'd imagined; I seemed to be only chest height on him. It was hard to believe this quietly spoken fellow could have been the first to sail a yacht round the world non-stop: he seemed more of a public relations type, except the flared trousers suggested a man of the sea who flings upraised fingers to fashion.

Robin was in town to announce a single-handed round the world race. Was I interested in taking part? I said I would be, God willing I made England again. The next day Robin was at the Royal Cape Yacht Club to announce the race to the press, and he, David Scott Cowper and I were photographed together. Appearing in a newspaper photograph with a navigator I greatly admired, and being told that I was being officially invited as guest entrant in an international race, made me feel that my efforts had at last been recognised.

A telex finally arrived from Pentax instructing me to attempt a Cape Town to England solo speed run: in return the repairs would be paid for. Lou and Ricki oversaw the work, which was nearly finished when I heard on the radio that the Argentinians had invaded the Falklands. My thoughts went out to the Hunts, to Marje McPhee and the people at the radio-telephone station; a smaller voice wondered nastily if Stanley had managed to get the visitors' price lists up in time, in the shops and restaurants, before the Argies took over.

As I got ready to sail, so did the British fleet. The amount of sympathy and support for Britain in South Africa surprised me.

I'll miss you, South Africa. I was mesmerised by your bad press image before I arrived, but then you stole a large part of my heart when I wasn't looking. Out in Table Bay now, my good Cape friends disembark one by one. Then it is just me and Captain Fantastic.

Becalmed. Flat sea and a huge breathing swell. No power for the transmitters, no moving air for the sails. I'd stripped her out for this record attempt back to England. Hull cleaned off, skeg welded up, eaten-away parts of the rudder rebuilt. Ready for a flying trip, but no wind. It was three days, then four. Tacking inches at a time till I'm almost on the beach north of St Helena Bay. I'm in this close to catch any light air stimulated by the join of land and sea. Then a squall black and treacherous, moving fast, catching Captain Fantastic; I try to tack but she won't come round. Wear ship, wear ship, for God's sake, and we spin through the first of the surf breakers and clear the broken water. God's awake and watching us. Easing away from the land; bloody dangerous without an echo-sounder. Out through a pack of sleeping seals, which bark and whimper in fright as we sneak through. One sounds like a startled dog. A lighthouse disappears quietly in the night. No booze for this leg. Too great a risk of me falling overboard after a lone party, as I expect to be moving quickly now that I am racing against the clock.

A fortnight out of Cape Town and Mr Rowley has left us for ever. All that work repairing him, and he has broken a stainless steel jaw that holds the wooden paddle. I try to get a shorter arm to work and devote hours to him. But the paddle won't stay down, and eventually I have to admit he's gone for good. God was wise to stop me going back to the Southern Ocean. Now it's just me and Derek, like it was going down to the Roaring Forties. Except we have much less electricity this time. The batteries were flat after Cape Town and the Aquair is broken, the first time after thirty thousand miles. There's not enough moving air for the wind generator. But somehow the batteries give out enough to receive calls from Merran. But I have to say goodbye to the hams. Not enough power for them, nor David Scott Cowper, a fortnight ahead.

Twelve hours at the wheel, fifteen, ten, fourteen. Then the wind dies in the south-east trades. It's not supposed to go calm, but it does. It's a curse to me, but in the Falklands the world has gone crazy. Young men die on the frozen hills, and in the bleak freezing sea. Imagine trying to get out of a sinking battleship. My neighbours' kids leaving school can't get work, but more than £20 million of ship can sink to teach spoilt children a lesson. Keep off the land we don't want, and the poor old squaddie on both sides listens in to Queen's new record in the Top Twenty. Conveniently it's in English and Spanish. The BBC World Service has dug out a score of old Lord Haw-Haws from its cracked woodwork. How can you explain the madness to yourself when your own lot is so bewildering?

We're entering the doldrums. Don Maclean on the stereo. I keep playing "The Grave". Again and again. "And deep in the trench he waited for hours as he held his rifle and prayed not to die."

Moitessier decided against returning to Europe. He went on to Tahiti, to a lifestyle he respected. But I'm too urbanised. I have to go to Britain. The welcome home is as important to this type of voyage as passing the Horn. Captain Fantastic and I have gone through rough times, we've thought we were finished, but we are still here and now we are going for the climax.

We're out of the trades. The horse latitudes, a fitful wind. A good dinner, but no wine. Bed early. Derek at the helm. Struggling out for a leak. God, it's chilly. Get the old Henri jacket on first. Up on the side deck. Go to the shrouds. Lean through and let the pressure ease. A shake, turning back. Miss the shroud handhold, foot slipping on wet deck; off balance, the shrouds are above. Stanchion stabbing my back. God, I'm going. Over. Blackness. Awake now, hands grabbing in panic. My God, grab something. But only water. There's only water to grab. Stinging at my waist, gasping as it reaches the chest; over my head, swallowing, breathing, vile-tasting water. Going down. It's a long way down to Davy Jones. And it hurts, it hurts like hell and I'm choking to death and nobody bloody well cares. Phosphorescence streaming from mouth and nose, past stinging eyes; hands and arms waving useless like a baby. It's black, black, yet I'm in a capsule of silver. Fighting for air; it's just water inside and water outside. This must be home; we're made of water. I've got to breathe. In sub-aqua they say the loss of oxygen stops the muscles from working the lungs. You black out and die. Please let me black out, the pain is bloody awful.

I was ten then. I think I was ten, and the Dutch girl from over the street said come swimming and we went to the place where a tarsealed road went into the lake. It used to be a river, but now it was full and the lake was pushing a torrent past the generator house in exchange for electricity. And I climbed on her back because I couldn't swim and pushed myself into her and wished I were older. Hands round her neck near those big loving tits. She waded out and it was good and she smelled right. We'll just go to that little island. Then she leans forward and kicks off. A sudden panic grips me, and I pull on my arms. Garotting her. She squeals and goes under. The water is over us both. The pain in my chest, holding with every bit of strength to the struggling, fighting figure. Let go or you'll drown, but I can't let go; I can only squeeze tighter. There's a monster looking at me. It's her, head twisted round, eyes standing out in the dusk of the lake, struggling, pushing, scratching. Then a kick, a woman's foot in my child's groin. I wake up alone on the tarsealed road which goes into the lake, warming in the sun. My chest hurts.

I cannot explain what is happening. I am not part of the thing struggling there. It has surfaced. Yellow oilskin arms flaying the water for a handhold. Reaching the Aquair rope, which snatches at fingers like some poisonous snake. It has some fingers in a tourniquet. The pressure may rip them off. The figure splashing, yelling, screaming; it's got hold of the propellor. It is untying the rope from the propellor, with one hand. The other held by the snake. I can see all from here. The schooner, the sails scarcely filling, aerofoiled upwind, the squeak of the auto-pilot correcting, the wake, the figure splashing silver. It is shouting. I cannot tell if the words are profanities or prayers. The propellor is free. He has undone it and is trying to get the snake from his fingers. It's off, the tourniquet is off. Then the rope slips from his grasp and is a foot away, two feet away, is chasing after the boat and the figure is left there floating in the yellow oilskin.

I don't want to die. I know I want to live. And now I am somewhere in the sea and I cannot find my boat. God, let me live and I won't take it all for granted again. The pain in my chest. The dawn. I've been watching the weirdest object in the sky and it's just the dawn lighting up. The water is absolutely still. I'm floating here and I can see my feet. They look funny and very white. Bad for sharks that. A loud crash. Behind me. I turn round. The rope. My God, the rope, and beyond. I daren't look. But it is, it's the bloody boat. God, it's the boat. Becalmed, becalmed again. A hundred yards off. All sails set, and slamming in the stillness. Swim, swim for all you're worth. Go on, pull on the bloody rope. Got hold of the strut and now I'm on the rudder. But no energy left. Can't make the counter. Go on, keep trying. I swing round the backstay. I'm on the counter, in the cockpit, the doghouse, on the berth. Into the sleeping bag. The pain right through me, but worst of all in my chest. Pull down the lids, God, I've had enough.

Life is all we've got. Mortgages, cars, money, fame, it's all nothing. It's all ego, and life is the one thing we've got that is worthwhile. Life and the ability to make new life through love which is life itself. Now I know. It's muddled in my brain, yet it is so clear really. Life is all.

We've found the westerly winds. Captain Fantastic screaming along, white water either side of the hull, the speedo reading ten knots. She loves it. The sea of the North Atlantic is quite flat. Broken cloud. This is what it's all about. Another 200 miles a day, 195, 198, 200. We're near the continental shelf, pop music from Radio Luxembourg, then it's Radio One. Soon the double boom of Concorde. A tiny bird tries to make the boat, but it is hours before it finds the courage to land safely on the boom, exhausted. We know about clutching at straws, too, little bird. It is dusk. Something falls from his beak and later I find it with a torch. It is a moth, one of those big window-bangers, which is almost a quarter of the size of the bird. We're two hundred miles from any land. Brought your lunch with you; that's thoughtful. Next day, both are dead. I keep the bodies to get them identified and later bury the house martin under a bush in Plymouth. They are dead, I am alive. That is what is important.

We pass a dead whale in the foggy English Channel; so beautiful in life, so meaningless in death. I am so glad to be alive.

Fog, thick, but I think I know where we are. I can feel a population nearby. Soon I'll be back in civilisation. Dawn chorus, wind in tall green trees, grass and wild flowers. People. I'll be able to go to Boots in the morning, to become urban man. I'll smile at the assistant and pick up a deodorant from the choice of exactly 117 types. Yes, I'll be back in the world.

GLOSSARY

Auto-pilot: electronic device for steering a boat on a
    predetermined compass course. It gains its electricity from a
    generator driven by a small windmill on back of boat.

Blooper: pole-less, large, spinnaker.

Boom: metal or wooden pole extending horizontally from the
    mast along the bottom of the sail.

Broach: when the wind blows the boat right over on its side, so
    much so that the rudder comes out of the water and the boat is
    uncontrollable.

Foredeck: area of deck in front of the mast.

Golly wobbler: square sail which goes between the two masts.

Gybe: when the mainsail boom crosses from one side of the boat
    to the other as the wind changes.

Halyard: rope used to raise or lower sails.

Jackstay: lifeline running round boat.

Jib: triangular sail set forward of the mast.

Jumar clamp: mountaineering device which clamps on to rope to
    support a climber's weight when subjected to downward
    forces but which can be slid up the rope as a method of
    climbing it.

Lazarette: very end compartment of boat.

Pitchpole: when a huge wave comes up from behind, causing
    boat to somersault.

Pooped: wave from behind dumps itself in cockpit.

Reef: reduce area of sail exposed to wind in heavy weather by
    rolling or tying canvas up round boom.

Self-steering gear: wind-driven device for holding the boat on a
    course determined by the wind. Consisting of a water paddle
    in the water connected to a wind-vane up above. It is the effect
    of the wind on the vane which makes the paddle move, which
    exerts lateral pressure on the rudder and so steers the boat,
    while the yachtsman works or sleeps.

Sheets: ropes for controlling the trim of the sails.

Sheave: enclosed pulley wheel in which rope runs.
Skeg: downward-projecting rudder support and protector.
Sole: floor.
Stays: stainless-steel wire supports for the mast.

THANKS

Many friends and helpers get my sincere thanks, in addition to those who appear in the story. This list is incomplete, unfortunately, and my apologies to those unintentionally left out. There is no order of priority.

Britain: The late Sir Francis Chichester for inspiration. Pentax (UK) Ltd and in particular Gerry Dingley, the MD, and Doris Sawyer, who was always kindness itself. Brighton marina and the people who were kind to me, including Lionel Lacey-Johnson, managing director John Perkins, Freddie and harbour control staff, and the good lookers in the main building. Chris English of Brighton, the first journalist to get hold of the story of my voyage. Browns restaurant of Brighton and the ladies. Anne Graham, who cleaned up our accounts and did a thousand other jobs, and Keith "Ginger" Feakes of Stockwell Tools. C. H. Fowler for the excellent tool-kit. The amazing Adamsons of Portchester. Roy and Bill Teale of Trelade Ltd for work on the rudder. Malcolm and Janet Cannell of Bowdeck. Pat Powell of Sheen Batteries. The Beecham Group, South London Press, Australian Dried Fruit Board. My good friend Gavin Howe. Joan Newman of "Meermin" for yards of letter typing. Timex. The Smith engineering family at Newhaven. Barbican beer. Spenser Drummond of Petersfield. The late Jack "on a clear day you can see what you're up against" Brown, for initial help in getting it all going. My late aunt Esme Andrews, who brought home to me the plight of loneliness in the elderly. Don Henderson of Helly-Hansen. Edith Harding at Henri-Lloyds. Boots for vitamins and help. Pains-Wessex Schermuly for the super waterproofed distress flares. Scandinavian Suppliers (London) Ltd for Bran Crispbread which helped save my teeth. Captain Dudley Norman for advice. Donald Bird, Allan Jackson, Celtic Julie and Betty of the Mayflower marina. Commander Lloyd Foster and the Royal Western Yacht Club and Yvonne and Margaret and staff. Sally Shirley, Joan Pell, for giving up so much, and my generous good friend Marcus Westerby at Moët and Chandon. The Ryvita Co Ltd, Goldenlay Eggs, the Scottish Milk Marketing Board and their delicious Long Life Milk. Chris Jarvis and Executive Cameras staff. Linda Williams, her parents and grandmother. Stuart Quarrie and the National Sailing Centre people. Chris and Ruth Waddington. David Curry at Plymouth Museum for identifying the unlucky house martin and white-line dark moth. Eddie Ball and Barclays Bank at Lewisham High Street for staying friends. Argentine Naval Commission for advice about weather conditions at Cape Horn. Thomas Reed Publications for my favourite nautical almanac and ocean navigator logbooks. Also to David Jolly and David Busby for ham radio help. To my good navigator friend, Bruce Henly. And Hugh Merryweather for his brilliant wind and water generators.

Australia: C. R. Kennedy and Co Ltd and staff, including John Gummer, photos, and Karen Renfrey. Skipper and crew of *Genevieve*. Rod Edwards VK6 AOK, Arthur VK6 ART, and scores of hams whose call-signs I lost when the boat started to fill. Fremantle Sailing Club, including John Masarra, Jock Dunning and staff. Ivan and Mike of "Paragon Smash". Gene Lawles, Eric Skogles, Les Weston, Chris Piper. Ian Hutton for Ever Ready torches and batteries. Hanimex for recording tape, and my mate Jeffers Hugo for recording them. Vince Callet for half-baked bread. The long-suffering folk of Channels 2, 7 and 9 and a special thanks from my ego for Libby Stone and Valerie Davies. Albert Lowe and Vickers Haskins. To the hard-pressed scribes of the Fourth Estate, including Jody Robb, Moira O'Brien-Malone, Janet Wainwright and Debbie Bishop. Julian Clifford of the Bureau of Meteorology and his staff. Sarah and Rolly Tasker and the tall Siska crewman who looked after Captain Fantastic. And Stirling Adjusters Pty Ltd staff for tolerance and help.

New Zealand: Those great cobbers at Ravensbourne Boating Club, particularly Bryant Palmer and Ike and Colin Amos. And to Lou Vorgers, my long-time friend Graham McNeil, John Braun, Keith Henderson and the Otago Harbour Board. Lance Dickson at Progress Plastics, Keith and Mike at Bosun's Locker. Constable Bill Carr, Vern Haig, the New Zealand Apple and Pear Marketing Board and the Milk Marketing Board for tasty Zapp! The Seamen's Mission, those gallant sheilas and staff of the *Otago Daily Times* and Tony Benny and the patient souls at Dunedin TV. W. Gregg and Co for the best coffee of the voyage. Phil Henry and staff of 4ZB. Bernard Teague. Nigel Nicolson for remembering. The "other" pop station in Dunedin for the most extraordinary and flattering remarks. My folks for helping us tear their house to pieces.

Falklands: Captain Christopher Elliott of BAS, Kevin "Birdman of Malvinas" Standring for a tape of sea shanties he sang for me. The helpful VP8 hams, the McPhees, the staff at Government House, Captain and men of the *Forrest*, and the electronic wizards at Cable and Wireless.

Cape Town: Hampo Systems Pty Ltd and staff, including Tony Lewis and Anne "with an E" Steward. Konrad Erickson for being a good mate and timing the departure from Cape Town on behalf of the Slocum Society. Commodore Roy Kingon and the South African Navy meteorological service under Benjamin Sciocatti. George Nothnagel ZS1 QK and his team at Cape Town Radio, Captain Pim Zandee of Safmarine and skippers and men of *Kuswag* I and IV. Super Joan Fry and Dinkie and the Royal Cape Yacht Club for help and tolerance. Mark Lory. Ian and Ingrid of *Ocean*. Alistair Campbell of the Durban Maritime Net. And so much to Julie, *my liefling*.

Also: VP8 QG Deirdre, PY1 ZAK Peter, LU5 XE Percy, G8 OS Ernie, G4 FRN Bill, G3 OUA Dave, WA1 EZY Richard, ZS1 CZ Ali, G4 FPO Rudi, G3 TJY David